CLEP® HUMAN GROWTH AND DEVELOPMENT

Patricia Heindel, Ph.D.

And the Editors of
Research & Education Association

Research & Education Association
Visit our website at: www.rea.com

Research & Education Association
61 Ethel Road West
Piscataway, New Jersey 08854
E-mail: info@rea.com

CLEP® Human Growth and Development with Online Practice Exams

Published 2015
Copyright © 2014 by Research & Education Association, Inc.
Prior editions copyright © 2008, 2007, 2004, 2003, 2001, 2000,
1998, 1996 by Research & Education Association, Inc. All rights
reserved. No part of this book may be reproduced in any form
without permission of the publisher.

Printed in the United States of America

Library of Congress Control Number: 2013954117

ISBN-13: 978-0-7386-1179-2
ISBN-10: 0-7386-1179-4

Cover image © istockphoto.com/Eraxion

REA® is a registered trademark of
Research & Education Association, Inc.

CONTENTS

About the Editor

Patricia C. Heindel, Ph.D., is professor of psychology and area chairperson, Human and Social Development, at the College of Saint Elizabeth in Morristown, New Jersey. She has been teaching in higher education for more than 25 years. She received her bachelor's degree in psychology from Rowan University and her Ph.D. in psychology from Rutgers University. Her professional research focuses particularly on the development of perception and memory. Dr. Heindel teaches undergraduate courses in research methods, developmental psychology, cognitive psychology, and sensation and perception, as well as graduate courses in counseling research.

About Research & Education Association

Founded in 1959, Research & Education Association (REA) is dedicated to publishing the finest and most effective educational materials—including study guides and test preps—for students in middle school, high school, college, graduate school, and beyond.

Today, REA's wide-ranging catalog is a leading resource for teachers, students, and professionals. Visit *www.rea.com* to see a complete listing of all our titles.

Acknowledgments

We would like to thank Pam Weston, Publisher, for setting the quality standards for production integrity and managing the publication to completion; John Paul Cording, Vice President, Technology, for coordinating the design and development of the online REA Study Center; Larry B. Kling, Vice President, Editorial, for his supervision of revisions and overall direction; Diane Goldschmidt and Michael Reynolds, Managing Editors, for coordinating development of this edition; Transcend Creative Services for typesetting this edition; and Christine Saul for designing our cover.

▼
CHAPTER 1

Passing the CLEP Human Growth and Development Exam

Chapter 1

Passing the CLEP Human Growth and Development Exam

Congratulations! You're joining the millions of people who have discovered the value and educational advantage offered by the College Board's College-Level Examination Program, or CLEP. This test prep focuses on what you need to know to succeed on the CLEP Human Growth and Development exam, and will help you earn the college credit you deserve while reducing your tuition costs.

GETTING STARTED

There are many different ways to prepare for a CLEP exam. What's best for you depends on how much time you have to study and how comfortable you are with the subject matter. To score your highest, you need a system that can be customized to fit you: your schedule, your learning style, and your current level of knowledge.

This book, and the online tools that come with it, allow you to create a personalized study plan through three simple steps: assessment of your knowledge, targeted review of exam content, and reinforcement in the areas where you need the most help.

Let's get started and see how this system works.

Test Yourself and Get Feedback	Assess your strengths and weaknesses. The score report from your online diagnostic exam gives you a fast way to pinpoint what you already know and where you need to spend more time studying.
Review with the Book	Armed with your diagnostic score report, review the parts of the book where you're weak and study the answer explanations for the test questions you answered incorrectly.
Ensure You're Ready for Test Day	After you've finished reviewing with the book, take our full-length practice tests. Review your score reports and re-study any topics you missed. We give you two full-length practice tests to ensure you're confident and ready for test day.

THE REA STUDY CENTER

The best way to personalize your study plan is to get feedback on what you know and what you don't know. At the online REA Study Center, you can access two types of assessment: a diagnostic exam and full-length practice exams. Each of these tools provides true-to-format questions and delivers a detailed score report that follows the topics set by the College Board.

Diagnostic Exam

Before you begin your review with the book, take the online diagnostic exam. Use your score report to help evaluate your overall understanding of the subject, so you can focus your study on the topics where you need the most review.

Full-Length Practice Exams

Our full-length practice tests give you the most complete picture of your strengths and weaknesses. After you've finished reviewing with the book, test what you've learned by taking the first of the two online practice exams. Review your score report, then go back and study any topics you missed. Take the second practice test to ensure you have mastered the material and are ready for test day.

If you're studying and don't have Internet access, you can take the printed tests in the book. These are the same practice tests offered at the REA Study Center, but without the added benefits of timed testing conditions and diagnostic score reports. Because the actual exam is Internet-based, we recommend you take at least one practice test online to simulate test-day conditions.

AN OVERVIEW OF THE EXAM

The CLEP Human Growth and Development exam consists of approximately 90 multiple-choice questions, each with five possible answer choices, to be answered in 90 minutes.

The exam covers the material one would find in a one-semester college-introductory level course in developmental psychology or human development. The exam stresses understanding the major theories and research related to physical, cognitive, and social development of humans from infancy through adulthood.

The approximate breakdown of topics is as follows:

10%	Theoretical perspectives
5%	Research strategies and methodology
10%	Biological development throughout the life span
7%	Perceptual development throughout the life span
12%	Cognitive development throughout the life span
8%	Language development
4%	Intelligence throughout the life span
10%	Social development throughout the life span
8%	Family, home, and society throughout the life span
8%	Personality and emotion
8%	Learning
5%	Schooling, work, and interventions
5%	Atypical development

ALL ABOUT THE CLEP PROGRAM

What is the CLEP?

CLEP is the most widely accepted credit-by-examination program in North America. The CLEP program's 33 exams span five subject areas. The exams assess the material commonly required in an introductory-level college course. Examinees can earn from three to twelve credits at more than 2,900 colleges and universities in the U.S. and Canada. For a complete list of the CLEP subject examinations offered, visit the College Board website: *www.collegeboard.org/clep*.

Who takes CLEP exams?

CLEP exams are typically taken by people who have acquired knowledge outside the classroom and who wish to bypass certain college courses and earn college credit. The CLEP program is designed to reward examinees for learning—no matter where or how that knowledge was acquired.

Although most CLEP examinees are adults returning to college, many graduating high school seniors, enrolled college students, military personnel, veterans, and international students take CLEP exams to earn college credit or to demonstrate their ability to perform at the college level. There are no prerequisites, such as age or educational status, for taking CLEP examinations. However, because policies on granting credits vary among colleges, you should contact the particular institution from which you wish to receive CLEP credit.

How is my CLEP score determined?

Your CLEP score is based on two calculations. First, your CLEP raw score is figured; this is just the total number of test items you answer correctly. After the test is administered, your raw score is converted to a scaled score through a process called *equating*. Equating adjusts for minor variations in difficulty across test forms and among test items, and ensures that your score accurately represents your performance on the exam regardless of when or where you take it, or on how well others perform on the same test form.

Your scaled score is the number your college will use to determine if you've performed well enough to earn college credit. Scaled scores for the CLEP exams are delivered on a 20–80 scale. Institutions can set their own scores for granting college credit, but a good passing estimate (based on recommendations from the American Council on Education) is generally a scaled score of 50, which usually requires getting roughly 66% of the questions correct.

For more information on scoring, contact the institution where you wish to be awarded the credit.

Who administers the exam?

CLEP exams are developed by the College Board, administered by Educational Testing Service (ETS), and involve the assistance of educators from throughout the United States. The test development process is designed and implemented to ensure that the content and difficulty level of the test are appropriate.

When and where is the exam given?

CLEP exams are administered year-round at more than 1,200 test centers in the United States and can be arranged for candidates abroad on request. To find the test center nearest you and to register for the exam, contact the CLEP Program:

CLEP Services
P.O. Box 6600
Princeton, NJ 08541-6600
Phone: (800) 257-9558 (8 A.M. to 6 P.M. ET)
Fax: (610) 628-3726
Website: *www.collegeboard.org/clep*

The new CLEP iBT exams

To improve the testing experience for both institutions and test-takers, the College Board's CLEP Program has transitioned its 33 exams from the eCBT platform to an Internet-based testing (iBT) platform. All CLEP test-takers may now register for exams and manage their personal account information through the "My Account" feature on the CLEP website. This new feature simplifies the registration process and automatically downloads all pertinent information about the test session, making for a more streamlined check-in.

OPTIONS FOR MILITARY PERSONNEL AND VETERANS

CLEP exams are available free of charge to eligible military personnel and eligible civilian employees. All the CLEP exams are available at test centers on college campuses and military bases. Contact your Educational Services Officer or Navy College Education Specialist for more information. Visit the DANTES or College Board websites for details about CLEP opportunities for military personnel.

Eligible U.S. veterans can claim reimbursement for CLEP exams and administration fees pursuant to provisions of the Veterans Benefits Improvement Act of 2004. For details on eligibility and submitting a claim for reimbursement, visit the U.S. Department of Veterans Affairs website at *www.gibill.va.gov.*

CLEP can be used in conjunction with the Post-9/11 GI Bill, which applies to veterans returning from the Iraq and Afghanistan theaters of operation. Because the GI Bill provides tuition for up to 36 months, earning college credits with CLEP exams expedites academic progress and degree completion within the funded timeframe.

SSD ACCOMMODATIONS FOR CANDIDATES WITH DISABILITIES

Many test candidates qualify for extra time to take the CLEP exams, but you must make these arrangements in advance. For information, contact:

College Board Services for Students with Disabilities (SSD)
P.O. Box 8060
Mt. Vernon, Illinois 62864-0060
Phone: (609) 771-7137 (Monday through Friday, 8 A.M. to 6 P.M. ET)
TTY: (609) 882-4118
Fax: (866) 360-0114
Website: *http://student.collegeboard.org/services-for-students-with-disabilities*
E-mail: ssd@info.collegeboard.org

6-WEEK STUDY PLAN

Although our study plan is designed to be used in the six weeks before your exam, it can be condensed to three weeks by combining each two-week period into one.

Be sure to set aside enough time—at least two hours each day—to study. The more time you spend studying, the more prepared and relaxed you will feel on the day of the exam.

Week	Activity
1	Take the Diagnostic Exam at the online REA Study Center. Your score report will identify topics where you need the most review.
2—4	Study the review, focusing on the topics you missed (or were unsure of) on the Diagnostic Exam.
5	Take Practice Test 1 at the REA Study Center. Review your score report and re-study any topics you missed.
6	Take Practice Test 2 at the REA Study Center to see how much your score has improved. If you still get a few questions wrong, go back to the review and study the topics you missed.

TEST-TAKING TIPS

Know the format of the test. Familiarize yourself with the CLEP computer screen beforehand by logging on to the College Board website. Waiting until test day to see what it looks like in the pretest tutorial risks injecting needless anxiety into your testing experience. Also, familiarizing yourself with the directions and format of the exam will save you valuable time on the day of the actual test.

Read all the questions—completely. Make sure you understand each question before looking for the right answer. Reread the question if it doesn't make sense.

Read all of the answers to a question. Just because you think you found the correct response right away, do not assume that it's the best answer. The last answer choice might be the correct answer.

Work quickly and steadily. You will have 90 minutes to answer 90 questions, so work quickly and steadily. Taking our timed practice tests online will help you learn how to budget your time.

Use the process of elimination. Stumped by a question? Don't make a random guess. Eliminate as many of the answer choices as possible. By eliminating just two answer choices, you give yourself a better chance of getting the item correct, since there will only be three choices left from which to make your guess. Remember, your score is based only on the number of questions you answer correctly.

Don't waste time! Don't spend too much time on any one question. Your time is limited so pacing yourself is very important. Work on the easier questions first. Skip the difficult questions and go back to them if you have the time.

Look for clues to answers in other questions. If you skip a question you don't know the answer to, you might find a clue to the answer elsewhere on the test.

Be sure that your answer registers before you go to the next item. Look at the screen to see that your mouse-click causes the pointer to darken the proper oval. If your answer doesn't register, you won't get credit for that question.

THE DAY OF THE EXAM

On test day, you should wake up early (after a good night's rest, of course) and have breakfast. Dress comfortably, so you are not distracted by being too hot or too cold while taking the test. (Note that "hoodies" are not allowed.) Arrive at the test center early. This will allow you to collect your thoughts and relax before the test, and it will also spare you the anxiety that comes with being late.

Before you leave for the test center, make sure you have your admission form and another form of identification, which must contain a recent photograph, your name, and signature (i.e., driver's license, student identification card, or current alien registration card). You may wear a watch. However, you may not wear one that makes noise, because it may disturb the other test-takers. No cell phones, dictionaries, textbooks, notebooks, briefcases, or packages will be permitted, and drinking, smoking, and eating are prohibited.

Good luck on the CLEP Human Growth and Development exam!

CHAPTER 2

Theories of Development

Chapter 2

Theories of Development

There are several theories that have been offered by psychologists to describe and explain human development. Before examining these theories, it is helpful to understand some of the basic issues on which they agree and disagree.

CONTROVERSIAL ISSUES REGARDING DEVELOPMENT

Nature versus nurture

The **nature versus nurture controversy** is an old argument in philosophy and psychology. The question posed in this debate is whether our development is influenced more by the experiences we have (the nurture position) or by the genetic endowment we inherit from our biological parents (the nature position). According to the nurture side, at birth the human mind is like a blank slate, or **tabula rasa**, that experience writes upon. It is argued that we are shaped by the nurturing, care and environmental influences that impact us. According to the nature view, development is an unfolding process guided by preprogrammed, genetic information. Development is seen as a predictable, predetermined unfolding of inherited traits and abilities. Theories of human development tend to emphasize one or the other of these influences on development, but most theorists agree that it is implausible for nature or nurture to be the sole influence on our growth and development. Both nature and nurture interact from conception forward. The goal of research in development today is to understand the relative influence of each factor in the development of particular traits or abilities like intelligence or personality. In other words, what proportion of mature level of intelligence is the product of experience and what proportion is controlled by genes?

Patterns of development

Theories differ in how they describe development. Discontinuity or **stage theories** argue that development progresses through a series of stages. Each stage is seen as involving a specific task. Once the task is accomplished, the child moves on to the next stage. The developing person is seen as not changing quantitatively, but qualitatively. **Continuity theories**, on the other hand, suggest development is best described as a steady growth process. Developmental change is described as occurring in small steps or increments. Skills and behavior improve but do not change qualitatively. The older child, for example, can remember more information compared to a younger child, but does not go about remembering the information in a qualitatively different way.

Child development versus life span perspective

Some theories of development argue that development is complete at the end of childhood. Sigmund **Freud** and Jean **Piaget** are examples of theorists who argued development was complete once one reached adolescence. However, life span theories of development argue that growth and change continue to occur throughout the entire life span. Erik **Erikson** is a theorist who took a **life span perspective**.

Universality versus context-specific development

Some developmentalists search for universals of development. These theorists underscore the similarities in development across cultures and historical time periods. Other developmentalists instead emphasize the role that cultural contexts play in the course of development. Jean Piaget is an example of the former approach. He argued that all children progress through the same stages of cognitive development in the same order and at the same approximate age. Hence, for Piaget there was a **universality** of cognitive development.

Urie **Bronfenbrenner** represents the alternative view. Bronfenbrenner has created an ecological systems theory of development that describes various contexts in which development takes place and how the reciprocal relationships between the child and the people in these sociocultural contexts affect the child's development. Psychologists who argue for **context-specific** development point out that there are differences in development between people from **collectivist cultures** and those who are from **individualistic cultures**. A collectivist culture places greater value on the common good than individual achievement. An individualistic culture values individual achievement and the pursuit of individual goals.

THEORETICAL PERSPECTIVES

Cognitive-developmental theory

Until his death in 1980, Jean Piaget was a predominant figure in the field of cognitive psychology. It is safe to postulate that perhaps no other single individual has had greater influence on educational practices than Piaget. Basically, his **cognitive-developmental theory** is based on the notion that cognitive abilities (or one's ability to think) are developed as individuals mature physiologically and have opportunities to interact with their environment. Piaget described these interactions as the equilibration of **accommodation** and **assimilation** cycles or processes. In other words, when individuals (who, according to Piaget, are innately endowed with certain cognitive predispositions and capabilities) encounter a new or novel stimulus, they are brought into a state of **disequilibrium**.

That is a way of saying that they are thrown off balance; they do not know or understand what is new or unfamiliar. However, through the complementary processes of accommodation (adjusting prior knowledge gained through former experiences and interactions) and assimilation (fitting together the new information with what has been previously known or understood), individuals come to know or understand that which is new. Once again, individuals are returned to a state of equilibrium where they remain until the next encounter with an unfamiliar stimulus. For Piaget, this is how learners learn. Piaget's position is called **constructivism** because he argued children construct schema, organized patterns of thought or action, based on the experiences they have actively exploring the environment.

Piaget also predicted that certain behaviors and ways of thinking characterize individuals at different ages. For this reason, his theory is considered a stage theory. Stage theories share the common tenet that certain characteristics will occur in predictable sequences and at certain times in the life of the individual.

According to Piaget, there are four stages of cognitive development, beginning with the sensorimotor stage, describing individuals from birth to around the age of two. The second stage, preoperational (describing cognitive behavior between the ages of two and seven), is characterized by egocentrism, rigidity of thought, semilogical reasoning, and limited social cognition. Some cognitive psychologists have observed that this stage seems to describe how individuals think more in terms of what they can't do than what they can do. This stage describes the way children in preschool and kindergarten go about problem solving. Many children in the primary grades may also be at this stage in their cognitive development.

The remaining stages of Piaget's theory, however, may be most important for elementary and secondary school teachers since they describe cognitive development during the times that most students are in school. The third stage, concrete operations, is the beginning of operational thinking and describes the thinking of children between the ages of seven and eleven. Learners at this age begin to decenter. They are able to take into consideration viewpoints other than their own. They can perform transformations, meaning that they can understand reversibility, inversion, reciprocity, and conservation. They can group items into categories. They can make inferences about reality and engage in inductive reasoning; they increase their quantitative skills; and they can manipulate symbols if they are given concrete examples with which to work. This stage of cognitive development is the threshold to higher-level learning for students.

Finally, formal operations is the last stage of cognitive development and opens wide the door for higher-ordered, critical thinking. This stage describes the way of thinking for learners between the ages of eleven and fifteen, and for Piaget, constitutes the ultimate stage of cognitive development (thus, also describing adult thinking). Learners at this stage of cognitive development can engage in logical, abstract, and hypothetical thought; they can use the scientific method, meaning they can formulate hypotheses, isolate influences, and identify cause-and-effect relationships. They can plan and anticipate verbal cues. They can engage in both deductive and inductive reasoning, and they can operate on verbal statements exclusive of concrete experiences or examples. These cognitive abilities characterize the highest levels of thought.

Lawrence **Kohlberg** extended Piaget's model of cognitive development to the study of the development of moral reasoning. His stage model of moral reasoning is discussed at length in Chapter 9, Social Development Throughout the Life Span.

A newer approach to studying cognitive development is the **information processing approach**. This theoretical perspective uses the computer as a metaphor for the human mind and studies how the human mind processes information. Information processing theorists describe changes in information processing capacity and speed that are associated with age. This approach is discussed in greater depth in Chapter 6, Cognitive Development Throughout the Life Span.

Learning theory

Learning theory or the **behaviorist perspective** describes developmental change as the product of learning. These theorists fall more heavily on the nurture side of the nature-nurture debate and are continuity theorists. Learning is defined as changes in observable behavior. In 1913, an American psychologist named John Watson founded a school of psychology called Behaviorism (or Behavioral Psychology) from which the learning theory of development comes. Important figures in this theoretical perspective include Ivan **Pavlov**, John Watson, B.F. Skinner, and Albert Bandura.

Learning theory suggests that behavior is controlled by stimuli in the environment. For Pavlov, a Russian physiologist who lived from 1849 to 1936, learning takes place when reflexive behavior comes under the control of a novel stimulus in the environment. He called this process **classical conditioning**. A reflex is an unlearned behavior that is present at birth and occurs without conscious control or volition. Pavlov called the components of a reflex the **unconditioned stimulus** (UCS), which is the stimulus that automatically elicits a motor response without training or conditioning, and the **unconditioned response** (UCR), the untrained motor response. An inborn reflex is the result of a UCS-UCR connection. Pavlov accidentally discovered classical conditioning while studying the salivary reflex in dogs. The salivary gland automatically stimulates secretion of salivary juices when food is placed on the tongue. Pavlov discovered that dogs in his laboratory would salivate to stimuli that regularly accompanied the food stimulus. A stimulus that is consistently paired with the UCS is called the **conditioned stimulus** (CS). After several pairings of a UCS with a CS, for example the food and a bell, the CS alone elicits the reflexive response. The motor response is now called the **conditioned response** (CR). Pavlov believed classical conditioning was the result of an associative bond forming between the UCS and the CS.

Pavlov also demonstrated **generalization**, **discrimination**, and **extinction** in his laboratory. Generalization is observed when a conditioned response is elicited by stimuli similar to the original CS. Pavlov demonstrated that the strength of the response is determined by the degree of similarity between the original CS and the test stimuli. Discrimination is the opposite of generalization. This is the process of conditioning a response to occur only after a specific stimulus is presented. Extinction is the unlearning of a CR. Pavlov found that the CR will disappear after repeated trials where the CS is presented without the UCS. After conditioning the dog's salivary response to a bell, repeatedly presenting the bell without food eventually causes the salivary response to the bell to be extinguished.

John Watson extended the work of Pavlov by studying classical conditioning of emotional responses in children. Watson believed that at birth we have a small number of emotional responses in our behavioral repertoire. These are love, anger, and fear. He argued that through experience we learn to associate new environmental stimuli with these reflexive emotional responses. Watson tested his theory in a classic experiment with an infant named Little Albert. In 1920, Watson and his assistant, Rosalie Raynor, attempted to condition the fear response in Albert. They conducted several experiments with Albert where they simultaneously presented a neutral stimulus, a rat, for example, with a fear-producing UCS, a loud noise. They reported being somewhat successful at conditioning Little Albert to show a fear response when presented with the rat alone. However, the conditioned response was not consistently determined and they found little evidence for generalization. One of Watson's students, Mary Cover Jones, later successfully extinguished a phobia in a child using the techniques of classical conditioning. The work of Watson, Raynor, and Jones served as the foundation for the classical conditioning theory of phobias or irrational fears.

Another American psychologist, B.F. **Skinner** (1904–1990), developed a learning theory called **operant conditioning** (or instrumental conditioning). Skinner also believed that learning is controlled by stimuli in the environment but added that behavior is shaped by the rewarding or punishing consequences that follow it. He called the process of rewarding a behavior **reinforcement**. He argued that these two processes, reinforcement and **punishment**, control the **shaping** of behavior. If a behavior is followed by reinforcement, the probability that the behavior will be repeated under the same stimulus conditions in the future increases. If a behavior is followed by punishment, the probability of that behavior being repeated under the same stimulus conditions in the future decreases. Skinner further distinguished between positive and negative reinforcement. A **positive reinforcement** is a reward or rewarding condition that is experienced after a behavioral response. Since it is a form of reinforcement, it works to increase the probability that the response will be repeated under the same stimulus conditions in the future. **Negative reinforcement** is when a noxious or unpleasant condition is removed when the behavioral response is emitted. If you are trying to shape a child's behavior by increasing the frequency that the child emits the goal behavior, you could use either type of reinforcement. Applying positive reinforcement would be giving the child a bag of candy after the child makes his or her bed. Applying negative reinforcement would be making the child stay in his or her room until he or she makes the bed. The important assumption being made in this example is that the candy is rewarding to the child and staying in the bedroom is unpleasant.

Social-cognitive theory

Albert **Bandura** created a major shift in thinking about learning in the late 1960s with a social-cognitive theory of learning (also called **social learning theory**). He introduced the idea that changes in behavior are acquired not only through the processes of conditioning, but also through **observational learning**. Modeling is observing the behavior of a model and then later imitating that behavior. Bandura observed that people can emit a new behavior in its complete form after simply watching someone else perform that behavior. In short, we can learn by observation. Bandura went on to study the factors that control modeling, including what influences one's choice of a model and the underlying cognitive processes required for modeling, such as self-efficacy beliefs. Self-efficacy is the subjective judgment a person makes that he or she will be successful in the attempt to imitate a model. Although individuals are more in control of their own behavior in this theoretical perspective, reinforcement and punishment still play a role in learning. Bandura used the term **vicarious reinforcement** for the affect that seeing a model being reinforced has in observational learning. If the model is observed being reinforced, it is more likely a child will imitate that model.

Psychodynamic theory

Psychodynamic theories (also called psychoanalytic theories) of personality descended from Sigmund Freud and his theory of personality. For most psychodynamic theorists, personality is mainly **unconscious**. That is, it is beyond our awareness. In order to understand someone's personality, the symbolic meanings of behavior and deep inner workings of the mind must be investigated. Early experiences with parents shape personalities, according to psychodynamic theorists.

Freud's Theory

Sigmund Freud (1856–1939) was a medical doctor from Vienna, Austria, who specialized in neurology. His psychodynamic approach to personality developed as a result of his work with adult patients who had psychiatric and emotional problems.

Freud's theory emphasized three main points:

(1) Childhood experiences determine adult personality.

(2) Unconscious mental processes influence everyday behavior.

(3) Conflict causes most human behavior.

According to Freud, each adult personality consists of an id, an ego, and a superego.

Freud's Personality Components

Personality component	When it develops	How it functions
Id	at birth	pleasure principle; unconscious instincts; irrational; seeks instant gratification; contains the libido
Ego	around six months	reality principle; mediates id and reality; executive branch
Superego	around six years	morality principle; personal conscience; personal ideals

According to Freud, the id is unconscious and has no contact with reality. It works according to the pleasure principle—the id always seeks pleasure and avoids pain. The id contains the **libido** or sexual energy.

The ego evolves from the id and deals with the demands of reality. It is called the executive branch of personality because it makes rational decisions. The reality principle describes how the ego tries to bring individual id demands within the norms of society. The ego, however, cannot determine if something is right or wrong.

The superego is capable of determining if something is right or wrong because it is our conscience. The superego does not consider reality, only rules about moral behavior.

According to Freud, behavior is the outcome of an ongoing series of conflicts among the id, ego, and superego. Conflicts dealing with sexual and aggressive impulses are likely to have far-reaching consequences because social norms dictate that these impulses be routinely frustrated.

Freud considered personality to be like an iceberg—most of our personality exists below the level of awareness just as most of an iceberg is hidden beneath the surface of the water. Freud referred to the hidden part of our personality as the unconscious. Through a process he called **repression**, unwanted thoughts are pushed down into the unconscious. Even though Freud felt that many thoughts, memories, and desires were unconscious, they nonetheless influence our behavior. The conscious part of our personality consists of whatever we are aware of at any particular point in time.

The preconscious, according to Freud, contains material that is just below the surface of awareness but can be easily retrieved. An example of preconscious awareness would be your mother's birthdate. You were not thinking of your mother's birthdate but can if you need or want to.

Defense mechanisms are unconscious methods used by the ego to distort reality and thereby protect us from anxiety. Anxiety can result from the irrational pleasure demands of the id or from the superego causing guilty feelings about a real or imagined transgression.

Common defense mechanisms are:

Rationalization   Creating false but plausible excuses to justify unacceptable behavior.

Example: Reducing guilt for cheating on your taxes by rationalizing "everyone does it."

Repression   Pushing unacceptable id impulses out of awareness and back into the unconscious. Sometimes called "motivated forgetting."

Example: Having no memory of an unpleasant experience.

Reaction Formation   Behaving exactly the opposite of one's true feelings.

Example: A mother who feels resentment toward a child may be overly cautious and protective.

Regression   Reversion to immature patterns of behavior.

Example: Temper tantrums.

Projection   Attributing one's own thoughts, feelings, motives, or shortcomings to others.

Example: A wife who constantly suspects her husband of having an affair because unconsciously she has thought of having an affair.

Displacement   Shifting unacceptable feelings from their original source to a safer, substitute target.

Example: You are mad at your boss, but you do not yell at your boss; instead you become angry with a family member when you return home.

Sublimation   A useful, socially acceptable course of behavior replaces a socially unacceptable or distasteful impulse.

Example: A person who feels aggression due to a lack of control plays an aggressive game of basketball with friends every other day.

Intellectualization   By dealing with a stressful situation in an intellectual and unemotional manner, a person detaches him- or herself from the stress.

Example: A person who has lost a family member due to an illness will speak of the medical terminology of the illness, but will not discuss the emotional aspects of the illness.

Denial   Denying that a very unpleasant thing has happened.

Example: A person with severe stomach pains, possibly an ulcer, refuses to see a doctor because he or she feels it is only indigestion.

Stages of Psychosexual Development

Freud believed that we go through five stages of psychosexual development in forming our personalities. Each stage represents a different erogenous zone or part of the body where pleasure originates.

Freud's Psychosexual Stages

Stage	Age	Erogenous Zone	Description
Oral	0–1 year	Mouth	Stimulation of mouth produces pleasure; infant enjoys sucking, biting, chewing. Weaning is major task or conflict.
Anal	1–3 years	Anus	Toilet training is major task. Expelling and retaining feces produces pleasure.
Phallic	3–6 years	Genitals	Self-stimulation of genitals produces pleasure. Oedipal (for boys) and Electra (for girls) complexes occur—children have erotic desires for opposite-sex parent as well as feelings of fear and hostility for same-sex parent. Successful resolution of this conflict results in identification with same-sex parent.
Latency	6–12 years	None	Sexual feelings are repressed. Social contacts beyond immediate family are expanded. Focus shifts to school and same-sex friendships.
Genital	Puberty onward	Genitals	Establishing intimate, sexual relations with others is main focus.

According to Freud, children experience conflicts between urges in their erogenous zones and societal rules. Fixation can result when these urges are either frustrated or overindulged in any one erogenous zone. Fixation results in one's personality becoming permanently locked in the conflict surrounding that erogenous zone.

Freud felt that the first three psychosexual stages were the most important for personality development. Examples of possible personality traits resulting from fixations in the first three psychosexual stages are presented here.

Stage	Examples of traits related to fixation
Oral	Obsessive eating
	Smoking
	Drinking
	Sarcasm
	Overly demanding
	Aggressiveness
Anal	Extreme messiness
	Overly orderly
	Overly concerned about punctuality
	Fear of dirt
	Love of bathroom humor
	Anxiety about sexual activities
	Overly giving
	Rebelliousness
Phallic	Excessive masturbation
	Flirts frequently
	Excessively modest
	Excessively timid
	Overly proud
	Promiscuity

Erikson's psychosocial stages of development

Another psychodynamic theory of personality development was offered by Erik Erikson. Erikson was trained as a psychoanalytic or Freudian theorist. Erikson's theory, however, is very different from Freud's. For instance, Erikson believed that personality continues to develop over the entire life span (not just through childhood). Also, Erikson did not stress unconscious motives or desires. However, like Freud, Erikson did feel that events that occur early in development can leave a permanent mark on one's later social-emotional development.

Like Freud, Erikson offered a stage theory but called it a psychosocial, as opposed to psychosexual, theory of human development. While Freud described development as the resolution of conflicts arising between the instinctual drives of the id and social expectations for our behavior, Erikson argued that the developing individual is faced with social emotional tasks that progressively enable the individual to function in the social world. At each stage in development, the ego either develops a strength that enables success in this endeavor, or a weakness that makes the process of adapting socially more and more difficult. For each of eight stages, he identified a developmental task described in terms of two polarities. The polarities are pairs of potential positive and negative resolutions to each stage's psychosocial crisis. Psychosocial crises arise at each stage as a product of the interaction between development and the changing social context. The goal for each of the eight stages of development is to resolve the crisis at hand in a positive way and hence add the ego strength associated with that stage to the ego. He is also one of the few theorists to discuss development throughout the life span.

A description of Erikson's eight stages of psychosocial development follows. Each stage represents a specific task or dilemma that must be resolved with some degree of success for further development.

CHILDHOOD	
Trust versus Mistrust (Birth–1 year)	Infant's needs must be met by responsive, sensitive caretakers. If this occurs, a basic sense of trust and optimism develops. If not, mistrust and fear of the future results.
Autonomy versus Shame and Doubt (1–3 years)	Children begin to express self-control by climbing, exploring, touching, and toilet training. Parents can foster a sense of autonomy by encouraging children to try new things. If restrained or punished too harshly, shame and doubt can develop.
Initiative versus Guilt (3–6 years)	Children are asked to assume more responsibility. Through play, children learn to plan, undertake, and carry out a task. Parents can encourage initiative by giving children the freedom to play, to use their imagination, etc. Children who are criticized or discouraged from taking the initiative learn to feel guilty.
Industry versus Inferiority (6–11 years)	In elementary school, children learn skills that are valued by society. Success or failure while learning these skills can have lasting effects on a child's feelings of adequacy.

ADOLESCENCE	
Identity versus Role Confusion	The development of identity involves finding out who we are, what we value, and where we are headed in life. In their search for identity, adolescents experiment with different roles. If we establish an integrated image of ourselves as a unique person, then we establish a sense of identity. If not, role confusion results and can be expressed through anger and resentment.
YOUNG ADULTHOOD	
Intimacy versus Isolation	At this time we are concerned with establishing intimate, long-term relationships with others. If we have successfully resolved the identity crisis, then we can be warm and open with others. If we are unsure of our identity or if we have developed an unhealthy identity, then we may avoid others or keep them at an emotional distance.
ADULTHOOD	
Generativity versus Stagnation	This stage centers around a concern for the next generation. Successful development shows adults sharing their life-acquired wisdom and caring for the growth of the community. Complacency in this stage leads to stagnation and potentially to depression and loneliness.
LATE ADULTHOOD	
Ego Integrity versus Despair	If a person looking back on his or her life can believe that it has been meaningful and relatively successful, then a sense of integrity develops. If all that is seen are wasted opportunities and meaninglessness, then the person will be disgusted. Despair will follow disgust if the person feels it is too late to change.

Sociocultural theory

The **sociocultural theory** of development argues that there is a bidirectional relationship between the child and the sociocultural environment, such that a child influences the people and the environments he or she interacts with, as much as those people and environments influence the child's development. This is known as **reciprocal determinism**. Lev **Vygotsky** and Urie Bronfenbrenner are two theorists who emphasize the influence of sociocultural contexts on development. Vygotsky offered a sociocultural theory of cognitive development and Bronfenbrenner developed an **ecological systems theory** of development also called the bioecological approach.

Lev Vygotsky was a Russian psychologist who created an alternative cognitive developmental theory to Piaget's approach. Vygotsky was critical of Piaget because he believed Piaget had not taken the social influences on cognition into consideration. A child interacts with peers and adults, not just objects in the environment. Vygotsky believed a great deal of cognitive growth comes from these social interactions. He observed that societies had particular, culturally specific ways of understanding the world. These understandings therefore must be transmitted through the members of the culture. The transmission of ideas is done through cooperative dialogue among peers and especially between children and adults. Older children and adults provide what Vygotsky called scaffolding. Scaffolding is cognitive support provided to a younger thinker by a more advanced thinker. In this theory, the zone of proximal development is the range of performance on a particular task a child is capable of doing. The lowest level of performance appears when the child is working alone. The upper limit of performance appears when the child is working with a more skilled other. Cognitive development is therefore socially mediated in Vygotsky's view. Vygotsky also studied the role of language in cognition.

Urie Bronfenbrenner's bioecological approach describes development as taking place within the context of several systems. He studied how the psychological and biological changes within a developing child influence his or her environment and, in turn, how various environmental systems influence the child's developmental outcomes. According to Bronfenbrenner, a child's development is affected by several contexts or systems including the microsystem (the immediate environmental contexts the child experiences directly, like the family), the mesosystem (the interrelationships between events of different microsystems), the exosystem (the contexts that significant others in the child's life directly experience but the child does not), and the macrosystem (the larger cultural context in which all of the other systems exist). In this way, experiences a child has at home (microsystem) may affect his or her performance in school and vice versa. The interaction of these two microsystems occurs in the mesosystem. The exosystem is a social context that indirectly influences the child's development, such as a parent's work, and the macrosystem is the cultural context in which all the other systems are embedded and which affects interactions in those systems.

Evolutionary theory

Ethology and evolutionary psychology are theoretical perspectives on development that grew out of Charles **Darwin's theory of evolution**. The main characteristics of Darwin's theory were:

(1) there are never enough resources in the environment for all members of a species to survive, so there is a constant struggle for existence among members of a species;

(2) there are variations in traits and abilities among members of a species that are the product of chance combinations of inherited traits from their ancestors;

(3) some chance variations in traits better enable members of a species to adapt and survive in the environment in which they live; and

(4) those members who do survive, reproduce, passing on the chance variations they inherited into the gene pool.

Therefore, through this process called **natural selection**, species' traits evolve very gradually over time. Chance variations that do not increase chances of survival evolve out of the species' gene pool. Those chance variations that do increase survival are passed down to offspring. Darwin also argued that there is continuity between species and that humans evolved from related animal species.

Both ethology and evolutionary psychology see human development within the framework of Darwin's theory of evolution. Both attempt to identify the historical roots of human traits and behaviors in evolution and to understand their adaptive value, i.e., how they contribute to survival. Ethologists conduct comparative studies of humans and other animal species like the chimpanzee. An important finding of ethologists is that there are **critical periods** in development. A critical period is a narrow frame of time within which a behavior must develop or it will never appear. An example of a behavior that has a critical period for development is imprinting in ducklings, i.e., following a mother duck. Ducklings will imprint when they are a few days old if they are exposed to their mother, but will never imprint if this exposure does not take place during a critical window of time. When applying this phenomenon to humans, psychologists prefer the term **sensitive period** to critical period. There may be a window of time that is the most conducive for the development of a human behavior or skill, like language, but humans can still acquire such behavior to some degree beyond this time.

Evolutionary psychologists focus on discovering the adaptive, survival value of specific animal and human behaviors. Evolutionary psychologists view human development over the life span as recapitulating the evolution of our species. Traits and behaviors in the newborn, for example, are viewed as residuals of the behavior of our oldest ancestors. Konrad Lorenz and John Bowlby are among the more influential theorists within this perspective. Both Bowlby and Lorenz studied the mother-infant relationship in animals. Their work is discussed in more detail in Chapter 9, Social Development Throughout the Life Span.

CHAPTER 3

Research Strategies and Methodology

Chapter 3

Research Strategies and Methodology

Psychological research is based on the scientific method. The scientific method consists of

(1) defining a research problem;

(2) proposing a hypothesis and making predictions;

(3) designing and conducting a research study;

(4) analyzing the data; and

(5) communicating the results and building theories of behavior.

A **sample** is a subset of a **population** selected to participate in the study. All of the participants in a research study make up the sample. A population includes all members of a class or set from which a smaller sample may be drawn and about whom the researcher wants to draw conclusions. A **random sample** is one in which every member of the population being studied has an equal chance of being picked for inclusion in the study. A biased sample occurs when every member of a population does not have an equal chance of being chosen. Researchers are better able to generalize their findings to the population of interest if a random sample is used.

THE EXPERIMENT

Psychologists use experiments to determine cause-and-effect relationships. An **experiment** requires that the researcher systematically manipulate and control one or more variables and then observe how the research subjects or participants respond to this manipulation. The variable that is manipulated is called the **independent variable**. The response that is measured after the **manipulation** of the independent variable is known as the **dependent variable**.

An experiment consists of at least two groups of participants. The experimental group is the group that is exposed to the manipulation of the independent variable. Some experiments have more than one experimental group, meaning there are several manipulations of the independent variable. The control group of an experiment is not exposed to the independent variable. The responses of participants in the control group are compared to the responses of participants in the experimental group(s) in order to determine if the independent variable(s) had any effect on the dependent variable.

Participants usually are assigned to groups in an experiment based on random assignment, which ensures that each participant had an equal chance of being assigned to any one of the groups. Random assignment helps guarantee that the groups were similar to one another with respect to important characteristics before the manipulation of the independent variable. When participants are not randomly assigned to groups, the study is referred to as a quasi-experiment. A study is called a **field experiment** if it is conducted in the participants' natural setting rather than a laboratory. This is the preferred method when a researcher is concerned that the artificiality of the laboratory setting might affect the experimental outcome.

Subject bias occurs when research participants' behavior changes because they know they are being studied or because of their expectations. A placebo is an inactive substance given in the place of a drug in psychological research. A placebo effect occurs when a participant believes they are experiencing a change due to an administered drug that is really a placebo. Observer or researcher bias occurs when the expectations of the researcher influence what is recorded or measured. To control both subject and observer biases, a double-blind technique is used. In the double-blind technique, neither the participants nor the researcher who is measuring the dependent variable know who is assigned to which group in an experiment. A single-subject experiment involves the participation of only one subject. The independent variable is systematically changed over time, and the subject's behavior at one time is compared with the same subject's behavior at another time. In this case, time is used as the control.

NONEXPERIMENTAL METHODS

Nonexperimental methods of research do not include the systematic manipulation of variables by the researcher and thus cannot be used to discuss cause-and-effect relationships.

Correlational research involves measuring two (or more) variables in order to determine if they are related. If the value of one variable increases in value as the other also increases in value, this is known as a positive correlation. A negative correlation occurs when there is an inverse relationship between the variables measured; as the value of one increases, the value of the other decreases. A **correlation coefficient** is a number that represents the strength of the relationship between the variables measured. A correlation coefficient can range in value from 0 to 1. A correlation coefficient of 0 indicates no relationship between the variables measured. A correlation coefficient of 1 indicates a perfect relationship between the two variables: You can predict one variable perfectly by knowing the value of the other. Therefore, the closer a correlation coefficient is to 1, the stronger the relationship between the variables measured, and the closer a correlation coefficient is to 0, the weaker the relationship. Even if a strong correlational relationship is found, however, cause-and-effect conclusions *cannot* be made because there is no systematic manipulation by the researcher.

Descriptive or observational research methods are used to obtain accurate records of behavior without manipulating or controlling any variables. **Naturalistic observation** is a descriptive research study that occurs in a natural setting that has not been manipulated by the researcher. The researcher systematically observes and records what occurs in an unobtrusive manner. This is done so that the behavior of the participants being tested is not altered. Interobserver reliability is the amount of agreement between two (or more) observers who simultaneously observe the same event.

A **case study** is a descriptive research method that is an in-depth study of a single subject. It can include interviews, observations, and test results.

Survey research is another descriptive method that requires the researcher to ask a group of people about behaviors, thoughts, or opinions. Data is collected through questionnaires or interviews. The **interview** has the advantage over a questionnaire in that the interviewer can see the reactions of the person being interviewed and may also be able to ask follow-up questions. The disadvantage is that a person being interviewed face-to-face with an interviewer may not provide complete and/or truthful information. Responding to questions in a way that is perceived to be more acceptable to the interviewer is called social desirability.

DEVELOPMENTAL RESEARCH METHODS

All of the research methods already discussed are employed by developmental psychologists. In addition to those, there are three research methodologies particularly well-suited for answering research questions about development. These are the cross-sectional, longitudinal, and sequential research designs.

Cross-Sectional Research Design

The **cross-sectional research design** is used to examine differences between different-aged subjects at one point in time. The researcher recruits two or more samples of participants of differing ages and measures them on the variable of interest. For example, a research interested in age differences in short-term memory capacity could administer the same memory test to thirty 10-year-olds and thirty 50-year-olds. One weakness of this design is that if the younger group performs better than the older group on the memory test, the group difference could be due to either differences in age or because they are from two different **birth cohorts** (generations). The researcher cannot conclude that memory capacity declines with age. However, the strength of this approach is that it is a quick and easy way to collect information on how different age groups differ at one point in time.

Longitudinal Research Design

The **longitudinal research design** measures changes on a variable of interest in the same group of participants at several points in their lives. For example, a developmental psychologist interested in the development of memory capacity could recruit 30 participants who are 10 years old and measure them at Time 1 and again at Time 2 when they are 20 years old, and again at Time 3 when they are 30 years old. A strength of this approach is differences in performance can be interpreted as indicating changes that occur with age. One weakness is that it is time consuming and expensive to carry out. In addition, subject mortality (subject drop out) is a problem with this design. Findings may be biased if subject drop out has occurred. The participants who complete the study may differ in significant ways from those participants who have dropped out. The participants who complete the memory study described above may be healthier or have better memory ability compared to those who dropped out.

Sequential Research Design

The **sequential research design** was created recently by Schaie to examine developmental changes in intelligence in adulthood. Schaie was concerned that there are significant differences in intelligence between birth cohorts or generations. He designed this methodology, which combines the cross-sectional and longitudinal designs, to examine cohort differences. At Time 1 in a sequential design, two or more different-aged groups of participants are tested. At Time 2 (10 years later) these participants return to be tested again and a new group is added that has participants the same age at Time 2 as the youngest group was at Time 1. At Time 3 (after another 10 years), all participants return to be tested again and replacement groups are added again, and so on. After data collection at Time 3, the same group of participants can be compared across the three testing times (longitudinal comparisons), groups who differed in age at Time 1 can be compared, as well as the groups who differed in age at Time 2, and the different age groups at Time 3 (cross-sectional comparisons). Finally, the same-aged participants who were tested at Time 1, 2, and 3 can be compared. This last comparison assesses birth cohort differences. In other words, how did the performance of 10-year-olds who were 10 in the year 2000 compare with the performance of 10-year-olds who were 10 in the year 2010? Researchers have been able to quantify **birth cohort effects** using this design.

COMPARING RESEARCH METHODS

Method	Strengths	Weaknesses
Experiment	Can make cause-and-effect relationships. Researcher has control.	Sampling errors. Often hard to generalize to the real world.
Correlation	Can study real-world behavior. Can determine relationships.	Cannot determine cause-and-effect.
Naturalistic Observation	Can gather information in its usual setting as it naturally occurs.	Cannot determine cause-and-effect. Observer bias possible.
Case Study	Intensive information can be gathered about individuals.	Cannot determine cause-and-effect. Expensive and time consuming. May not be able to generalize information gathered to others. Biased sample possible.
Survey	Large amounts of information can be gathered from many people in a relatively short period of time.	Cannot determine cause-and-effect. Biased sample possible. Response bias possible. Survey questions might not be reliable or valid.
Cross-sectional	Data show differences between different-aged people at one point in time. Relatively quick and inexpensive.	Cannot show changes that occur with age. Findings may be subject to birth cohort effects.

Method	Strengths	Weaknesses
Longitudinal	Data show how a sample of people change as they age.	Time-consuming and expensive. May not be able to generalize the findings to other birth cohorts. May have the problem of subject drop-out.
Sequential	Has the strengths of both the cross-sectional and longitudinal methods and can also measure birth cohort effects.	Time-consuming and expensive. May have the problem of subject drop-out.

CHAPTER 4

Biological Development Throughout the Life Span

Chapter 4

Biological Development Throughout the Life Span

Psychologists studying development make a distinction between developmental changes that are the result of learning versus changes due to **maturation**. Maturation is a term used to describe a genetically programmed biological plan of development that is relatively independent of experience. Changes in the three areas of development—biological development, cognitive development, and psychosocial development—differ in the degree to which they are controlled by experience versus maturation. Biological development is an area controlled substantially by maturation but still affected to some degree by environmental influences.

GENES AND HEREDITY

Evolutionary psychologists study species' heredity, that is, the traits and behaviors that are common in all humans. For example, all healthy neonates (newborns) are born equipped with the same set of motor reflexes. Psychologists also study individual inheritance to understand individual differences in traits and abilities. Both types of inheritance are controlled by information carried in the thousands of **genes** on the 46 **chromosomes** found in the nucleus of each cell in the human body.

Chromosomes are arranged in pairs. Twenty-two of these pairs are called **autosomes** and carry genetic material that controls all of our characteristics with the exception of biological sex. These 22 pairs of chromosomes are the same in males and females. The two chromosomes of the 23rd pair are called the **sex chromosomes**. In normal females, the sex chromosome pair is XX and normal males inherit an XY pair. Biological parents pass on one set of 23 chromosomes in each **sperm** cell or **ovum**. The mother can only pass on an X sex chromosome since she has an XX pair, but the father can pass on either an X or a Y chromosome in each sperm cell. The biological father's sperm cell therefore determines the sex of the offspring.

When the sperm cell of the biological father penetrates and fertilizes an ovum (egg cell) from the biological mother, conception occurs, and the new cell that is formed is called a **zygote**. This process of fertilization normally takes place in the fallopian tube of the mother, and the zygote then travels down the tube to the uterus and embeds in the uterine wall. The zygote contains the 23 pairs of chromosomes that control its maturation. The zygote will develop into a female unless there is a Y sex chromosome present. A gene on the Y chromosome causes the fertilized cell to differentiate into a male.

Dominance/Recessiveness Principle of Inheritance

Some of the genes controlling our characteristics are dominant while others are recessive. A dominant gene is the stronger, more powerful of the two types. A recessive gene will not be able to exert any influence on a characteristic if it is paired with a dominant gene. Pairs of genes can be dominant gene-dominant gene, dominant gene-recessive gene, or recessive gene-recessive gene pairs. A trait carried on a dominant gene is called a dominant trait, and a trait that is carried on a recessive gene is called a recessive trait. A trait carried on a dominant gene will always be expressed regardless of what type of gene it is paired with. A recessive trait can only be expressed as a characteristic of the individual if the individual inherited a recessive-recessive gene pair. Someone who inherits a dominant gene-recessive gene pair is called a carrier. Carriers can pass on a dominant gene or a recessive gene to their offspring. **Genotype** is the term used to describe all of the traits carried in a person's genetic material, including recessive traits, but the characteristics that are actually expressed are referred to as an individual's **phenotype**.

The dominance/recessiveness principle becomes very important when studying genetic diseases. Some diseases are inherited because the program for the disease is carried in a gene or set of genes. There are genetic diseases carried by dominant genes and diseases carried by recessive genes. Genetic testing can be done in couples considering having children to determine if either person is a carrier of a genetic disease. **Genetic counseling** is available to help couples make decisions about childbearing given their chances of passing on genetic diseases to their offspring.

Genetic Diseases and Abnormalities

Some developmental abnormalities have a genetic basis, but there are several different mechanisms of inheritance that produce normal traits as well as these abnormalities. Single gene-pair inheritance is when an individual inherits a gene pair that controls a trait or causes a disease. (Remember that single gene-pair inheritance follows the dominance-recessiveness principle.) Sickle-cell disease, cystic fibrosis, phenylketonuria (PKU), Huntington's disease, and

Tay-Sachs disease are all caused by single gene-pair inheritance. All of these are recessive traits, except for Huntington's disease which is carried on a dominant gene.

Sex-linked inheritance is when a trait or disease like color blindness or hemophilia is carried by a gene on the sex chromosomes. Color blindness is carried on a recessive gene on the X chromosome and is therefore called a **sex-linked recessive trait**. A male who inherits this recessive gene will be color blind because it is impossible for him to also have a dominant gene on a second X chromosome to repress the recessive trait. Females who are color blind have a recessive-recessive gene pair. Hemophilia is also carried the same way as color blindness. There are also **sex-linked dominant traits**. These genetic diseases are discussed at greater length in Chapter 14, Atypical Development. Although we have discussed only single gene-pair and sex-linked inheritance in this section, most of our traits are in fact controlled by polygenetic inheritance. Polygenetic inheritance is when multiple genes work together to produce a trait.

Abnormalities can also be caused by chromosomal abnormalities and genetic mutations. A genetic mutation is a change to the structure of inherited genetic material that occurs spontaneously or is the result of environmental toxins. Chromosomal abnormalities occur if a child has inherited too few, too many, or abnormal chromosomes. Down syndrome, or trisomy 21, is caused by having three rather than two chromosomes at the 21st chromosome position. Turner syndrome occurs when a female is born with only one X chromosome (X0). Klinefelter's syndrome occurs when a male is born with an extra X chromosome (XXY). These syndromes are discussed at greater length in Chapter 14, Atypical Development.

HORMONAL INFLUENCES ON DEVELOPMENT

The **endocrine system** is the system of the body responsible for managing hormone levels in the blood stream. It consists of a number of glands. The **pituitary gland** is called the master gland because it causes other glands to secrete hormones. The pituitary gland is controlled by the hypothalamus of the brain. It also secretes **growth hormone** (GH) which stimulates physical growth and development. Without the hormone GH, children do not grow taller than four feet. Hormones secreted from the pituitary gland stimulate the adolescent growth spurt. The thyroid gland also controls physical growth and development and development of the nervous system. It secretes the hormone thyroxin. Without adequate levels of thyroxin, infants become mentally retarded. Early treatment is effective and children who develop a thyroxin deficiency after brain maturation is completed have stunted physical growth but no intellectual disability (formerly mental retardation).

Males and females have differing levels of sex hormones in the body. Sex hormones called **androgens** control the development of sex organs as well as secondary sex characteristics. At conception, the fertilized egg cell has either of two sex chromosome pairs: XX or XY. During the 7th and 8th week of fetal development, a gene on the Y chromosome triggers the development of male reproductive organs. This process begins with the development of the testes. The testes secrete the male hormone **testosterone** which stimulates the development of male reproductive organs in the fetus and inhibits the development of the female reproductive organs. In the third month of prenatal development, the penis and scrotum appear in the male and female genitalia are present in the female. In females, the ovaries are the endocrine glands that control sexual maturation. Ovaries produce **estrogen** and **progesterone**.

There is a relationship between stress and hormone secretions in the body. Under stressful conditions, the body secretes stress hormones that control our body's flight or fight response. **Adrenalin** and cortisol are some of these stress hormones. Evolutionary theory suggests this hormonal system was quite adaptive in our species' past. The body is quickly prepared for flight or fight due to the actions of cortisol on several biological systems of the body. Blood flow shifts from the core of the body to the extremities. There is a decrease in blood pressure and an increase in heart rate. All of these autonomic reactions get the body ready for action. Unfortunately, the body responds the same way to stress as it does to a real physical threat. Researchers suggest the long-term effect of high cortisol levels in the blood is reduced immune response.

During pregnancy, stress is debilitative because it draws blood flow away from the fetus and to the muscles of the mother. This deprives the fetus of oxygen. Adrenalin and cortisol also can pass through the semi-permeable placenta and cause an increase in fetal heart rate. This can cause stunted prenatal growth, low birth weight, and birth complications. Studies suggest that infants born to mothers who were stressed during pregnancy have a heightened reactivity to stress in their own life and a reduced physiological ability to manage stressful conditions. Furthermore, studies have shown that emotional stress during pregnancy predicts anxiety, aggression, anger, and over activity among school-aged children. These effects appear after controlling for things like smoking during pregnancy, low birth weight, postnatal maternal anxiety, and low socioeconomic class.

PRENATAL DEVELOPMENT

Prenatal development refers to the period of development from conception to birth and is divided into three stages or trimesters. The **first trimester**, or germinal period, lasts for the first 13 weeks of pregnancy. The **second**

trimester, or period of the **embryo**, lasts from the 14th to the 27th week, and the **third trimester**, or period of the **fetus**, lasts from the 28th week until birth. The average pregnancy lasts 270 days or 40 weeks.

After conception, the zygote repeatedly divides as it travels down the fallopian tube to the uterus where it becomes attached to the uterine wall. If a mother is carrying multiples (twins, triplets, etc.), it is due to one of several possibilities. There are two types of twin pairs, **monozygotic** (identical twins) and **dizygotic** (fraternal twins). Monozygotic twins occur when the fertilized ovum divides abnormally creating two developing zygotes. Both zygotes embed into the uterine wall and develop separately. Monozygotic twins have identical genetic endowments. Monozygotic twins are frequently studied by psychologists interested in the nature versus nurture controversy since they share the same genes but have different environmental influences. This research will be discussed in greater detail in Chapter 8, Intelligence Throughout the Life Span. Dizygotic twins are the result of two ova being fertilized by two different sperm cells at the same time. Triplets or larger sets of multiple births are produced this same way. Fertility drugs meant to stimulate the release of ova during ovulation often cause multiple births.

There are reproductive technologies available to help infertile couples conceive. **Artificial insemination** involves injecting sperm from the father into the uterus of his partner. **In vitro fertilization** is when a sperm cell fertilizes an ovum outside the mother's body and then the fertilized egg is implanted in the uterus. These techniques can be done using the couples' reproductive cells or donor cells.

Stages of Prenatal Development

The three stages of prenatal development are outlined below.

Germinal   The first two weeks after conception. The zygote is a microscopic mass of multiplying cells. It travels down the fallopian tube and implants itself on the wall of the uterus. The **placenta** (provides nourishment and allows wastes to pass out to the mother) begins to form. The **umbilical cord** carries nourishment from and waste to the placenta. Thin membranes keep fetal and maternal bloodstreams separate.

Embryo   Second to eighth week after conception. The embryo is only about one inch long by the end of this stage. Most vital organs and bodily systems begin to form. Major birth defects are often due to problems that occur during this stage. The amniotic sac, a fluid-filled sac that surrounds the embryo, protects and provides a constant temperature for the embryo.

Fetus   From two months after conception until birth. Muscles and bones form. Vital organs continue to grow and begin to function. During the last three months, the brain develops rapidly.

An outline of *what* develops *when* during the prenatal period is as follows:

Approximate prenatal week	Development
2nd week	Implantation on uterine wall.
3rd–4th week	Heart begins to pump.
4th week	Digestive system begins to form. Eyes begin to form.
5th week	Ears begin to form.
6th week	Arms and legs first begin to appear.
7th–8th week	Male sex organs form. Fingers form.
8th week	Bones begin to form. Legs and arms move. Toes form.
10th–11th week	Female sex organs form.
12th week	Fetus weighs about one ounce. Fetal movement can occur. Fingerprints form.
20th week	Mother feels movement. Reflexes—sucking, swallowing, and hiccuping appear. Nails, sweat glands, and soft hair developing.
27th week	Fetus weighs about two pounds.
38th week	Fetus weighs about seven pounds.
40th week	Full-term baby born.

Prenatal development is most successful if the mother has good prenatal medical care, good nutrition, is between the ages of 16 and 35, and does not expose the developing fetus to the harmful affects of **teratogens**. Teratogens are any agents that may cross the placental barrier from mother to embryo/fetus causing abnormalities. Possible teratogens include maternal diseases, diet, drug use (including alcohol and nicotine), exposure to X-rays, and other environmental influences. For instance, fetal alcohol syndrome (resulting in a short nose, thin upper lip, widely spaced eyes, small head, and intellectual disability) can occur as a result of alcohol consumption during pregnancy. This syndrome and other prenatal abnormalities caused by teratogens are discussed in greater depth in Chapter 14, Atypical Development. Maternal stress over an extended period of time can also cause fetal damage. Stress causes the release of the hormone adrenalin, which passes through the placenta barrier and enters the bloodstream of the fetus. Adrenalin increases the motor activity of the fetus and increases fetal heart rate. If this occurs over an extended period of time it can cause stunted prenatal growth, low birth weight, or birth complications.

What abnormalities occur from teratogens depend on the timing of exposure, what is developing prenatally, as well as what the harmful agent is. The fetus is generally not affected by a teratogen if exposure occurs during the first or third trimester. Because so many vital organs and body parts are developing during the embryo stage or second trimester, harmful agents are especially dangerous during this prenatal period. This is often referred to as a critical period in prenatal development. A critical period is any time during development that some developmental process must occur or it never will. For example, if something interferes with legs developing or forming prenatally, they will not develop or be formed later.

There are several prenatal tests available to screen for abnormalities in prenatal development. While an ultrasound can be used to detect the number of fetuses in the uterus and may detect some visible defects, better assessment techniques include **amniocentesis** and **chorionic villus sampling**. Amniocentesis involves testing fetal cells in amniotic fluid removed from the amniotic sac in the uterus for indicators of genetic abnormalities. The disadvantage of this technique is that it cannot be done until the 16th week of pregnancy. Chorionic villus sampling (CVS) can be done as early as the sixth week of pregnancy. In CVS, tiny hair cells of a membrane surrounding the fetus (called the chorion) are extracted via a small tube inserted into the vagina. The hair cells contain genetic material from the fetus.

BIOLOGICAL DEVELOPMENT IN THE NEWBORN/INFANT

The Birth Process

The birth process is a several-stage process including labor, delivery of the fetus, and delivery of the placenta. Conditions during the birthing process can be harmful to the neonate. Anoxia is a condition caused by reduced oxygen flow to the fetus during birth. Oxygen deprivation can be due to a build-up of mucous in the throat of the baby or a crimp in the umbilical cord. The harm to the baby from anoxia depends on the degree and length of time of the oxygen deprivation. Medications taken by the mother to reduce pain during labor and delivery generally slow down the birth process and also increase the risk of harm to the fetus. The **Apgar scale** was developed as a quick way to assess the overall condition of the **neonate** immediately after birth and again five minutes after the birth.

Normal delivery is a vaginal delivery in which the baby is pushed through the vaginal canal by the mother. **Caesarian section** is an alternative birthing method in which the fetus is surgically removed from the uterus of the mother. Many couples prepare for the birth of a child using the **Lamaze** or prepared childbirth method. This method teaches a pregnant woman and her partner how to use breathing and other relaxation techniques to reduce the experience of the pain of labor and delivery.

Early Brain and Nervous System Development

The nervous system is made up of the brain and the spinal cord (the central nervous system) and the neural circuitry of the peripheral nervous system. The complex circuitry of the nervous system contains billions of single cells, called neurons, which form connections or synapses with other neurons. The human brain has a great deal of plasticity, meaning these neural circuits change over time as a result of stimulation. New circuits are formed and unused or faulty circuits are lost through a process called pruning. For the first two years after birth, there is a brain growth spurt involving both the production of neurons and neural circuits, as well as this pruning. The brain is the most developed part of the body at birth but still has to develop further. It is 75 percent of adult weight at age two and 90 percent of its adult weight by the age of five.

There are two hemispheres of the cerebral cortex of the human brain. In adults, each hemisphere is somewhat specialized to do different tasks. In most people, the left hemisphere controls the right side of the body and the right hemisphere controls the left side. The left hemisphere generally controls language processing, while the right hemisphere controls spatial processing, although this is an oversimplification. The specialization of the hemispheres is called brain **lateralization**. Newborns show brain lateralization. For instance, most newborns show a preference for grasping objects with their right hand rather than their left. However, lateralization strengthens with age. The presence of handedness in newborns has led some people to suggest that handedness is genetically controlled.

Motor Development

A number of reflexes (involuntary responses to stimuli) can be elicited in newborn infants. All healthy newborns exhibit them and many of these reflexes will disappear with age. For example, healthy newborn infants will blink when a light shines in their eyes and will suck on an object placed in their mouth. These reflexes do not disappear with time. But other reflexes, such as the **Moro** (extension of arms when an infant feels a loss of support), **Babinski** (spreading the toes when the bottom of the foot is stimulated), **grasping** (squeezing any object placed in the hand), and rooting (turning toward an object brushing the cheek and sucking) reflexes will disappear over the course of the first year of life. Evolutionary psychologists consider these newborn reflexes to be remnants of behaviors that were adaptive during earlier times in our species' evolution but no longer contribute to survival. Clearly, the **sucking reflex** and the eye blink reflex, that protects the eye from injury, have survival value.

The **proximodistal principle** of development describes the center-outward direction of motor development. For instance, children gain control of their torso before their extremities (e.g., they can sit independently before they can stand). The **cephalocaudal principle** describes the head-to-foot direction of motor development. That is, children tend to gain control over the upper portions of their bodies before the lower part (e.g., they can reach and grasp before they can walk). Children generally master **gross motor skills**, such as standing, before **fine motor skills**. Gross motor skills require the coordination of large parts of the body, while fine motor skills involve small, coordinated movements of the hands, fingers, or toes. Infants show a fairly well-developed fine motor skill of manipulating objects with their fingers by about 9 to 12 months of age.

The developmental norms or average age of achievement for gross motor development are as follows:

Age	Behavior
1 month	While prone (on stomach), can lift head.
2 months	While prone, can hold chest up. Can roll from side to back.
3 months	Can roll over. Will reach for objects.
6–7 months	Sits without support. Stands holding on to objects.
8–10 months	Crawls.
8–12 months	Pulls self up to stand.
11–12 months	"Cruises"—walks by holding on to objects.
12–18 months	Walks alone.

Physical Growth

The average newborn is 20 inches long and weighs between 7 and 7½ pounds. Infants reach about half of their adult height by the age of two. Obviously this indicates that infancy is a period of rapid physical growth called a **growth spurt**. An illustration of the interactive affects of nature and nurture is that while a child's mature physical size is preprogrammed in his or her genotype, a child may not reach that size. Environmental influences like poor nutrition or hormonal abnormalities can stunt the physical growth of the child. There is also a syndrome called failure to thrive that affects an infant's physical growth which is discussed at greater length in Chapter 14, Atypical Development.

BIOLOGICAL DEVELOPMENT IN THE CHILD

Brain and Nervous System Development

During childhood, and throughout the rest of life, the neural circuitry of the brain continues to change and develop. In childhood, brain lateralization becomes stronger as parts of the cortex take over different functions, and a process called myelination that was begun at birth continues. Myelination is the coating of the part of a neuron called the axon with fatty material. Myelination speeds up the transmission of neural messages. This may be what is responsible for the increased reaction time in older compared to younger children.

Motor Development and Physical Growth

Develop of motor skills is slow but steady during childhood compared to the spurts of development in infancy. The muscles of the body get stronger and parts of the body are closer to adults in relative size and proportion. Fine motor and gross motor coordination continues to improve during this period and reaction time speeds up.

BIOLOGICAL DEVELOPMENT IN THE ADOLESCENT

Brain and Nervous System Development

The part of the cerebral cortex called the prefrontal cortex matures during adolescence. This area of the cortex is responsible for higher order thinking and processing of complex information. The maturation of this area may be responsible for the improved focused-attention capacity in the adolescent compared to the younger child. Myelination continues during adolescence and into adulthood. The full weight of the brain is achieved by the age of 16.

Physical Growth

There is a rapid period of growth in adolescence. The adolescent growth spurt in males is triggered by the testes secreting large amounts of testosterone and other male sex hormones. The increase in androgen levels in the blood causes a rapid growth spurt and growth of male sex organs. GH and thyroxin are also secreted in larger quantities and stimulate body size increases and skeletal maturity. In females, the ovaries secrete an increased amount of estrogen which in turn triggers the production of GH and leads to the female adolescent growth spurt. The hormone secretions during the growth spurt stimulate the development of the breasts, pubic hair, uterus, and vagina. They also trigger an increase in fat storage. Estrogen and progesterone also control the menstrual cycle in females. The adrenal glands, which produce adrenalin, also contribute to bone and muscle growth and physical maturation in females. Females reach their full height by around the age of 16, four years or so ahead of males.

Along with the adolescent growth spurt is **puberty**, achieving full sexual maturity. Females generally are thought to have reached puberty at **menarche** (the first menstrual cycle) although some girls may not be able to reproduce for several years after menarche. The average age of menarche is 12½ years but can range from ages 11 to 15. At about age 13, boys will experience their first ejaculation which marks puberty for them. However, ejaculation does not necessarily mean sperm are viable enough to reproduce.

The timing of the adolescent growth spurt has been shown to have psychosocial affects on adolescents. Early maturing boys and late maturing girls tend to have the best psychosocial outcomes, whereas late maturing boys and early maturing girls fair worse. Early maturing boys may benefit from being larger and appearing older than their late maturing counterparts. Early maturing girls, on the other hand, may face challenges from having an early menarche and/or because other people may treat them as if they were more mature and expect them to act as if they were older.

There is a growing concern in our country about the rising rates of **obesity** in children and adolescents. Obesity is defined as weighing 20 percent more than the average for people of similar age, height, body type, and sex. Obesity correlates with increased risk of cardiovascular disease, high blood pressure, diabetes, and liver and kidney problems. Adolescents have a greater risk of obesity than children because their metabolism rates start to decline. This risk continues to climb in adulthood as metabolism continues to slow down.

BIOLOGICAL DEVELOPMENT IN THE ADULT
Brain and Nervous System Development

The brain continues to show plasticity and develops/prunes neural circuits throughout adulthood. However, along with this growth there are declines that are the result of normal or biological aging. It is important not to confuse the effects of biological aging with the effects of diseases that occur with greater frequency in old age. Normal changes in the brain include a slowing of the transmission of neural messages, decreased blood flow to the brain, loss of neurons, loss of brain weight, and decreased amount of neurotransmitters—the chemicals that form connections between neurons at the synapses. Hence, there is a slowing of neural processing associated with normal aging and a loss of brain mass, but new neural circuits can continue to be formed to replace those lost.

Physical Growth

The body reaches full adult size at the end of adolescence. Most of the physical functions of the body are at peak levels of performance in early adulthood and then begin a slow, but steady, decline. Researchers studying aging generally agree that there is an inevitable process of **biological aging** that eventually would cause death even in the absence of disease. Evidence for this view is that there appears to be a maximum length of life for humans. There is no record of anyone living beyond 110 years or so. Maximum length of life is different from **life expectancy**. Life expectancy is the average length of life expected for members of a particular birth cohort. Researchers disagree on the nature and cause of biological aging. One theory, the wear and tear theory, suggests the human body, like a machine, eventually wears out from normal use. However, continued physical activity in adulthood has been shown to correlate with both physical as well as mental health.

Other researchers argue that biological aging is in part due to the gradual failure of the endocrine system. The gradual decrease in GH that occurs with age is associated with loss of muscle and bone mass, an increase in body fat, thinning of the skin, and a decrease in cardiovascular functioning. Diet and physical exercise have been found to partially mitigate these effects. A decrease in secretions from the thymus is also correlated with age. Secretions from the thymus help in the body's immune response. Stress hormones discussed earlier also decrease the body's immune response.

Hormones also control the **climacteric** or menopause in females. The climacteric is the cessation of a female's reproductive capacity. The climacteric typically spans a 10-year period and usually begins in a woman's early fifties.

A drop in estrogen levels in the body triggers the climacteric. Lowered levels of estrogen in the body cause changes in the female's sex organs. Organs shrink and genitals react more slowly to stimulation. The vagina secretes fewer lubricants during arousal. The body also loses the protections afforded by estrogen. Estrogen helps protect against plaque build-up on the walls of arteries and helps maintain good bone mass density. Lowered levels of estrogen are also associated with mood fluctuations, hot flashes, and night sweats. Hormone therapies have been developed to combat these side effects of menopause. Hormone treatments include estrogen replacement therapy (ERT), which is normally used only with women who have had hysterectomies, or hormone replacement theory (HRT) in which both estrogen and progesterone are given. There is ongoing controversy about the risks associated with ERT and HRT. If administered late in menopause, HRT may increase the patient's risk for developing Alzheimer's disease but, if started earlier, may actually reduce this risk. ERT has been shown in some studies to increase the risk of breast cancer and blood clots.

The male climacteric is caused by decreasing amounts of testosterone, but it is a more gradual, less obvious process compared to the female climacteric. Some men may never lose their reproductive capacity. It is difficult to determine if changes in sexual activity or a male's sexual arousal is due to hormone levels or other factors.

There is a gradual loss of bone density associated with aging. This loss of bone mass is due to decreased levels of calcium and GH in the body. Loss of bone density can lead to a bone disease called **osteoporosis** in which bones are very brittle and may spontaneously fracture. Post-menopausal women have a higher risk for osteoporosis. Physical activity and calcium supplements have been found to help prevent this bone disease.

▼

CHAPTER 5

Perceptual Development Throughout the Life Span

Chapter 5

Perceptual Development Throughout the Life Span

Sensation is the process of registering stimulation and transmitting that information to cortical brain centers. Perception is the process of assigning meaning to the sensation. The five sensory perceptual systems, although not fully developed, are all functional at birth. Furthermore, perception researchers have discovered that neonates have preferences for what they look at, taste, or hear. These neonate preferences and perceptual abilities have been studied using very creative experimental procedures since a newborn cannot simply tell us what they see. Many of these experiments take advantage of the fact that newborns show a simple form of learning called habituation. Habituation is decreasing attention to a familiar stimulus. When newborns are shown a new picture they look at it and scan it. However, over time they look away. When this picture is presented side by side with a new one, newborns look longer at the new picture. Habituation, therefore, lets the infant tell us that a stimulus is familiar or old. Young infants can also be trained using Skinner's operant conditioning techniques. An infant can learn to respond a certain way (for example, look left when a certain tone is presented) to receive a reinforcement. In this way, a researcher can study an infant's ability to discriminate different sounds.

As the newborn receives sensory stimulation, his or her perceptual abilities improve and the neural circuits in the brain centers that control each sensory perceptual function are strengthened. Sensory deprivation research with animals indicates that there are sensitive periods for receiving sensory stimulation. Some chimpanzees raised in the dark have permanently impaired vision due to the degeneration of the optic nerve—the nerve that transmits visual information to the cortical vision center. However, if the deprivation lasts no longer than seven months, the damage is reversible. Human infants born blind due to cataracts (clouding on the lens of the eye) sometimes do not fully recover normal visual acuity.

It is important to note that while the perceptual development in each modality will be discussed separately, perception is really intermodal, that is, the result of coordination and communication among the sensory perceptual systems. When we are looking at a scene, we also experience sounds and smells.

In turn, the sensory perceptual experiences we have are associated in memory. For example, we associate a particular face with a particular voice. Meltzer and Borton reported evidence of intermodal perception in one-month-old infants. Infants in the study looked longer at a picture of a smooth nipple if they had previously sucked on, but could not see, a smooth nipple. Other infants in the study showed the same pattern with a bumpy nipple.

PERCEPTUAL FUNCTIONING IN THE NEWBORN/INFANT

Vision

Vision is accomplished after light waves enter the opening of the eye (the pupil) and are reflected by the lens onto the retina in the back of the eye. Visual receptor cells in the retina transmit signals to the vision center in the occipital lobe of the cortex. An image forms on the retina that will vary in size depending on the distance and size of the visual object, but the retina does not see. Rod and cone cells of the retina are designed to respond to light energy and begin a process of transforming light information into neural impulses. Sensitivity to a perceptual stimulus is measured by the **absolute threshold**. The absolute threshold is the minimal intensity of a stimulus an observer can detect. The newborn's absolute threshold for vision and hearing is higher than a normal adult's, but rapidly decreases. Young infants do not hear very soft whispers that adults with normal hearing can.

At birth, neonates can see although their **visual acuity** is poor. Visual acuity is the ability to see fine gratings or details in a visual stimulus. Perfect acuity is quantified as 20/20. Newborn visual acuity ranges from about 20/400 to 20/800. What this means is a newborn can see something as clearly at 20 feet as a person with normal vision could see clearly at 600 to 800 feet. Newborn infants can see objects clearly that are about nine inches away. The poor acuity in newborns is because the muscles that control the lens, the part of the eye that has to reflect light onto the retina, are weak. Visual acuity improves rapidly over the first four months of life. Newborns are also capable of **tracking** a moving object, although their tracking movements are not very smooth or coordinated. They track by moving the entire head rather than just the eyes.

By the time infants can crawl, they indicate that they have **depth perception** by refusing to crawl across the deep side of a **visual cliff**. Depth perception involves the interpretation of visual cues in order to determine how far away objects are. There is currently a debate as to whether depth perception is an inborn ability or a learned response as a result of experience (nature versus nurture).

Gibson and Walk (1960) developed an apparatus they called the visual cliff that is used to measure depth perception in infants and toddlers. The visual cliff consists of an elevated glass platform divided into two sections. One section has a surface that is textured with a checkerboard pattern of tile, while the other has a clear glass surface with a checkerboard pattern several feet below it so it looks like the floor drops off. Gibson and Walk hypothesized that if infants can perceive depth, they should remain on the "shallow" side of the platform and avoid the "cliff" side, even if coaxed to come across by parents. When they tested infants from 6 to 14 months of age, Gibson and Walk found that infants would crawl or walk to their mothers when the mothers were on the "shallow" side of the platform, but would refuse to cross the "deep" side, even with their mothers' encouragements to cross. The results of this and other visual cliff studies still do not prove that depth perception is innate because, before infants can be tested, they must be able to crawl and may have already learned to avoid drop-offs.

Another important characteristic of visual perception is the **perceptual constancy**, or stability, of the shape, size, brightness, and color of objects in our visual fields. We are able to recognize the same objects at a variety of angles, at various distances, and even under different colored lighting because of perceptual constancies. The four perceptual constancies are as follows:

Size Constancy—Objects we are familiar with seem to appear the same size despite changes in the distance between us and the objects.

Shape Constancy—Objects appear to be the same shape despite changes in their orientation toward the viewer.

Brightness or Lightness Constancy—Objects appear to stay the same brightness despite changes in the amount of light falling on them.

Color Constancy—The hue of an object appears to stay the same despite changes in background lighting.

Newborns have been shown to have size constancy. In a clever experiment, newborns were shown to habituate to a particular-sized cube even though the cube was presented at different distances from the newborn. After habituation, the newborns preferred to look at a different sized cube even when it projected the same sized image on the retina as the training cube.

Studies of color perception using the habituation paradigm report that very young infants see color and have a mature ability to perceive color by two to three months of age.

Newborns and infants also have visual preferences. They prefer to look at faces and other visual stimuli that have contour, contrast, complexity, and movement. Some two-day-old infants are even capable of discriminating their mother's face from a stranger's face. By three months of age almost all infants can. Six- and seven-month-old infants will show surprise when shown a face with jumbled parts.

Young infants show **selective looking**. They will scan the borders and edges of objects in a visual stimulus while older infants will scan inside the edges. This difference may be due to the fact that young infants are still learning to pick out objects in a scene which older infants can accomplish very quickly. The older infant has more time to scan inside the contours of an object for details.

Hearing

Infants can hear prior to birth. There are many sounds in the womb including the sound of their mother's voice. Shortly after birth, newborn infants are capable of discriminating between sounds of different duration, loudness, and pitch. Newborns also appear to prefer the sound of a human voice to other sounds and prefer to hear complex sounds over pure tones. Young infants will listen longer to the sound of a person speaking than non-speech sounds. At birth, infants will suck more on a nipple in order to hear their mother's voice compared to a stranger's voice, and to hear their native language as compared to a foreign language. By six months of age, infants can discriminate between any two basic sounds, called phonemes, used in all the world's languages. In fact, they can make discriminations between phonemes that older children and adults can no longer make. These findings have led many psycholinguists, psychologists who study language, to argue that humans are innately prepared to acquire a language.

Smell

The sense of smell is also well-developed in the newborn. The fetus is exposed to many odors as well as sounds in the womb. By six weeks of age, infants can smell the difference between their mother and a stranger. Four-day-old, breast-fed infants prefer the smell of their own mother's breast compared to that of an unfamiliar woman who is also breast feeding.

Taste

Infants' ability to discriminate tastes has been studied by observing changes in infants' facial expressions after different flavored liquids are placed on the tongue. Infants respond differently to the four basic tastes (sweet, sour, salty, and bitter), and they show a clear preference for sweet flavored liquids. There is even evidence that sugar water has a soothing affect on newborns, particularly if the infant is experiencing pain.

Touch, Temperature, and Pain

Infants are also very responsive to touch. Touch is one of the best developed senses at birth and the earliest sensory perceptual systems to develop prenatally. Some research has shown that female infants may be more sensitive to touch than males. Swaddling infants, that is wrapping them tightly in cloth, has a soothing affect on infants perhaps because of the stimulating affect swaddling has on this sense of touch. Gentle massaging has also been found to improve the development of premature infants. At birth, infants are also highly sensitive to pain and are sensitive to warm and cold temperatures.

PERCEPTUAL DEVELOPMENT IN CHILDHOOD AND ADOLESCENCE

Most perceptual development in childhood and adolescence is really a matter of the development of attention. As children age they acquire more control of perception. Attention is the process of focusing on particular aspects of the sensory world. Between four and ten years of age, visual search of a stimulus becomes more controlled and systematic. Attention spans increase from 18 minutes in two- to three-year-olds to more than an hour in six-year-olds. Learning to read requires these attentional capacities and is probably the most significant perceptual challenge for children.

PERCEPTUAL DEVELOPMENT IN ADULTHOOD

Absolute thresholds for sensory stimuli rise with age in adulthood. Adults gradually lose some sensitivity for sights, sounds, flavors, and odors. In addition, there is a slowing of the processing of sensory stimulation. For example, older adults may have trouble understanding rapid speech.

Vision

There are changes that occur to the eye associated with aging. The lens of the eye gradually loses flexibility and therefore cannot change its shape to reflect light as well as it did at an earlier age. The lens of the eye also can develop deposits called cataracts. Cataracts can be surgically removed but will lead to blindness if left uncorrected. Another condition called **glaucoma** appears more frequently in people over 50 years of age. Glaucoma is a build-up of pressure from excess fluid inside the eyeball. If left untreated, glaucoma causes blindness. Glaucoma can be detected early during routine eye examinations.

Together the changes to the eye in older adults cause adults to see more glare, have less sensitivity under dim lighting conditions, and have difficulty with near vision. The latter condition is called **presbyopia** and is present in most people after the mid- to late 40s. Presbyopia is corrected with lenses that help focus images from near objects onto the retina. Distance vision also shows a steady decline in old age after peaking in the 20s and staying steady in middle age.

Older adults perform more poorly on tests of selection attention and visual search compared with younger adults.

Hearing

Changes in hearing with age are caused by changes in the inner ear. The inner ear contains hair cells that are bent when vibrations of the eardrum cause fluid of the inner ear to move in a wave. Hair cells degenerate and are lost in increasing numbers with age. The loss of hearing associated with aging is called presbycusis and is first a loss of sensitivity to high frequency sounds. Later, after the age of 50, low frequency sounds are also more difficult to hear. There is approximately a 20 percent loss of hearing in people who are 45 to 54 and a 75 percent loss in people 75 years and older. Some hearing loss can be corrected with hearing aids or more sophisticated devices like cochlear implants. Understanding speech becomes more difficult for the older adult, particularly when there is background noise in the room.

Taste and Smell

Older adults have difficulty discriminating among salty, bitter, and acidic flavors. Sensitivity to sweetness, however, does not change. There is an increased absolute threshold for taste so food tastes blander to an older person. The same is true for detecting odor. The absolute threshold rises even more for odor than for taste. Among older subjects, females are better at detecting odors than males.

Touch, Temperature, and Pain

Sensitivity to temperature and body temperature regulation both decline in older adults. Absolute thresholds for touch and for pain do not change significantly. Older adults are no more or less sensitive to strong pain stimulation than younger adults.

CHAPTER 6

Cognitive Development Throughout the Life Span

Chapter 6

Cognitive Development Throughout the Life Span

ELEMENTS OF COGNITIVE DEVELOPMENT

Thinking is defined as the manipulation of mental representations. Cognition includes the mental activities involved in the acquisition, storage, retrieval, and use of knowledge. The most rapid cognitive development takes place during the first few years of life when the brain is growing rapidly. As the following discussion shows, however, cognitive development is best described as a life-long process.

Concepts

A basic element of thought is the concept. A concept is a label that represents a class or group of objects, people, or events that share common characteristics or qualities. We organize our thinking by using concepts, and concepts allow us to think about something new by relating it to a concept we already know.

Some concepts are well-defined, and each member of the concept has all of the defining properties; no nonmember does. An example would be registered voters—you either are or are not registered to vote. Other concepts are not so clearly defined but are encountered frequently in our everyday life. These natural concepts have no set of defining features but instead have characteristic features—members of this concept must have at least some of these characteristics. "Bird" is a natural concept. Birds range from chickens to sparrows to ostriches. Prototypes are objects or events that best represent a natural concept. A sparrow or robin would be considered a prototypical bird by many individuals. New concepts are easier to learn if they are organized around a prototype.

Reasoning

Reasoning involves processing information to reach a conclusion. It includes evaluating and generating arguments to reach a conclusion. Inductive reasoning involves reasoning from the specific to the general. For example, drawing conclusions about all members of a category or concept based on only some of the members is inductive reasoning. Deductive reasoning is reasoning from the general to the specific. Making a prediction based on a theory involves deductive reasoning. Logical reasoning involves using mental procedures that yield valid conclusions.

Problem Solving

Problem solving is the mental activity used when we want to reach a certain goal that is not readily available. Problem solving includes understanding the problem; planning a solution; carrying out the solution; and evaluating the results. Problem representation or the way you think about a problem can make it easier or harder to solve. We can represent problems visually, verbally, with symbols (e.g., mathematically), or concretely with objects.

THEORIES OF COGNITIVE DEVELOPMENT
Piaget's Stage Theory

Piaget believed cognitive development proceeded through four stages: the **sensorimotor intelligence** stage, which lasts from birth to approximately 18 months of age; the **preoperations** stage, which lasts from two to seven years of age; the stage of **concrete operations**, which covers the years seven to 12; and finally, the **formal operations** stage, which extends from 12 years on. Children's thinking becomes more logical as they progress through the stages with the end result being the capacity to think logically and to problem solve using abstract concepts. Through a process Piaget called **adaptation**, children construct cognitive **schema** to organize their experiences. Adaptation involves the complementary processes of assimilation and accommodation. When a child assimilates, he or she understands a new experience through the lens of an already existing scheme. An example would be a child seeing a pony and saying "dog." Accommodation involves changing an existing scheme to incorporate a new experience. Accommodation occurs, for example, when a child first experiences a beach ball after only playing with small balls. The child is thrown into a state Piaget called disequilibrium because his or her ball scheme does not fit this new object that Daddy calls a ball. The child's understanding of the size of objects that can be picked up and bounced develops as the result of accommodating to this new experience and the child returns to a state of equilibrium.

According to Piaget, the order in which children pass through the stages does not vary but the rate at which children pass through them can vary from child to child. Piaget argued that each stage of cognitive development represents a qualitatively different way of thinking. That is, children in each stage think differently from children in the other stages. Therefore, it is not just that children acquire more information as they grow older, but how they think actually changes with age.

Vygotsky's Sociocultural Theory

Lev Vygotsky disagreed with Piaget's explanation of cognitive development. He argued that children interact not only with objects in their environment but with people in a sociocultural context. He described how the interactions children have with more sophisticated thinkers helps their own thinking develop. **Guided participation** is his term for how older adults transmit the values and beliefs of the culture to children. Vygotsky used the term **zone of proximal development** to describe children's problem-solving ability with and without the aid of an older guide. Teachers and parents serve as scaffolds or guides for children working on a problem-solving task. Working alone, the child performs at the lowest level of his or her zone of proximal development. Working with a teacher or parent, a child can perform at the upper level of that range. Vygotsky observed that teachers and parents will adjust the amount of **scaffolding** they provide as the child shows more sophisticated problem-solving behaviors.

Vygotsky believed that language also played a role in thinking. Social speech, speech that involves talking with other people, leads to **private speech**, talking aloud to oneself, which eventually becomes **inner speech**. Three- and four-year-olds often talk aloud while engaged in an activity, but older children tend to use private speech when faced with a problem to solve. He suggested that preschool children talk aloud to themselves when engaged in a task because the language directs their thinking about the task at hand. Often children increase the use of private speech when they get stuck on a problem or with a task. Incorporated into the private speech of these children are solutions they remember from their earlier collaborations with adults. Private speech goes inward to become inner speech, silent verbal thought, in the elementary school years.

Information Processing Theory

A relatively new and popular approach to studying cognition comes from the information processing approach. Theorists in this approach use the computer as a metaphor for the human mind, which is viewed as an information processing machine. Studying how the mind processes information has led to new understandings about cognitive processes. In particular, memory has received a great deal of attention by information processing theorists. In their view, memory is information storage and involves the processes of registration, **encoding**, storage, and **retrieval**. Information processing theorists study cognitive development by examining changes to these and other processes that occur with age. They tend to argue that development is more continuous rather than discontinuous. Changes that occur with age frequently are described as capacity or speed improvements but not the emergence of qualitatively new processes.

Information processing theorists have identified several different memory systems and have constructed a flow chart showing the transfer of information from one system to another. The memory systems include **sensory memory**, **working memory** (also called **primary memory** or **short-term memory**), and **long-term memory** (also called **secondary memory**). Information that comes into a sensory perceptual system, registers automatically in sensory memory. The sensory register holds information for a very brief period of time, up to only a few seconds. Information that is not transferred from sensory memory to working memory is lost. The process that causes this transfer is attention.

Attention is a cognitive resource, cognitive energy if you will, that captures sensory perceptual information for further processing. Attention to information in sensory memory moves that information to working memory. Information can be held in working memory for slightly longer time periods compared to sensory memory or retained even longer through the process of **rehearsal**. An example of rehearsal is repeating the telephone number of a pizzeria to yourself while you walk to the telephone. If rehearsal stops, the information will be lost after 20 or 30 seconds unless it is further processed to be stored in long-term memory.

Working or short-term memory is also limited in the amount of information it can hold at one time. The average adult can hold between five to nine bits, or chunks, of information in short-term memory. George Miller proposed the magical number seven, plus or minus two, as the capacity of short-term memory. The capacity of short-term memory can be increased by using larger chunks of information or by what Miller referred to as chunking. Chunking involves organizing or grouping separate bits of information into larger units or chunks. For example, 5 8 1 2 7 8 6 3 could be chunked into 58 12 78 63. This transforms eight bits of information into four, thereby freeing up space in short-term memory.

Short-term memory is also called working memory because a great deal of information processing takes place in that system. It is where conscious thinking takes place. Whatever you are thinking about right now is in your short-term memory. In order for information to be stored (transferred) into long-term memory, it must be encoded. The better the encoding done in short- term memory, the better the chance the information can be later retrieved from long-term memory.

Long-term memory is the system that holds information for an extended period of time. Some information processing theorists suggest long-term memories are permanent and what we call forgetting is a failure of retrieval not loss of memory. However, there is a great deal of disagreement and several competing theories of forgetting have been offered. Unlike short-term memory, long-term memory appears to have unlimited storage capacity. Long-term memory is also a very organized system. Research has suggested that new memories are fit into a network of pre-existing, organized knowledge.

What we think of as remembering is the process of locating and retrieving information from long-term storage. Retrieval can be either **recall** or **recognition**. Recognition is remembering when the cue for retrieval is the information to be remembered. Selecting the correct response to a multiple-choice question is an example of recognition. Recall, a much more difficult retrieval process, involves remembering after being given a less helpful cue. Answering the question, "What did you eat for breakfast?" is an example of the recall process.

COGNITIVE DEVELOPMENT THROUGHOUT THE LIFE SPAN

Thinking

Birth to Two Years

According to Piaget's theory, newborns are equipped with sensory perceptual systems that enable them to interact with the environment. Young infants also explore their environment by sucking on objects, holding and manipulating objects, and visually tracking moving objects. Out of this sensorimotor activity, infants construct sensorimotor schema. A scheme is an organized pattern of action or thought. An example of a sensorimotor scheme is the grasping scheme. To successfully grasp an object, an infant must coordinate a sequence of actions. This sequence of action forms the grasping scheme. In the first two years of life children are in Piaget's sensorimotor stage of cognitive development. They construct motor schema and improve their ability to engage in co-ordinated action. A child in this stage develops skills in problem solving when the problem involves sensorimotor activities or goals. Another achievement of the sensorimotor stage is **object permanence**.

Piaget tested for object permanence by taking a toy and hiding it under a blanket in full view of the child and then observing the child's reaction. Infants who are four to eight months of age act as if an object that is no longer in their sight, no longer exists. They do not search for the hidden toy. Between eight and 12 months of age a child will search under the blanket for the toy. However, these children have not fully grasped object permanence. If you first hide the toy under a blanket and then move the toy to a hiding spot under the couch, children in this age range will first look under the blanket and then go to the couch. It is as if they retrace their actions because their own actions had something to do with making the toy reappear. According to Piaget, object permanence is not fully achieved until the end of the first stage.

The final achievements of the sensorimotor stage are **symbolic representation**, the ability to use one thing to stand for another, and **deferred imitation**. Symbolic representation is illustrated in the pretend play of children. Children can and will use a broom as a horse. Words are also examples of symbolic material. Deferred imitation is modeling someone else's behavior some time after observing the model. This requires the ability to create a mental representation of the behavior and later retrieve and use the representation. When a child engages in pretend play and shows deferred imitation, he or she has shifted into the second stage of preoperations. Piaget gave this stage the name preoperations because even though a child in this stage is capable of using mental schema (operations), these schema are not logical.

Two to Seven Years

The preoperations stage describes the way that children in preschool and kindergarten go about problem solving; also, many children in the primary grades may be at this stage in their cognitive development. The preoperational child lacks the logical concepts of **conservation, classification, seriation**, and **class inclusion** which develop in the next stage. Conservation is the understanding that the quantity of liquid, or number, or volume does not change unless you add or take some away. Conservation of liquid, for example, is the understanding that the quantity of liquid held in a tall, thin beaker does not change when it is poured into a short, wide beaker. Preoperational thinkers are fooled by the perceptual change in how the liquid looks and believe the quantity has changed (for example, more liquid in the short, wide beaker). Seriation is the ability to rank order objects on a dimension like height or length.

Classification is the ability to organize items into groups based on shared characteristics or features. If a toddler is given some red and blue triangles and red and blue circles and is asked to put together what goes together, they do not group them in a logical way. Rather than putting all the same shapes together or putting all the same colors together, their grouping is unsystematic.

Class inclusion is the ability to represent exemplars of categories in superordinate and subordinate levels. Toddlers have difficulty keeping multiple levels of a hierarchically organized system in mind at the same time. If you showed a toddler a collection of five green beads and three red beads and asked if there are more green beads than beads all together, the preoperational child will say there are more green beads.

Preoperational thought also has several other characteristic features. Children in this stage engage in **egocentric thinking**. They are unable to take the perspective of another person. Piaget first demonstrated egocentrism with his Three Mountain Task. A child is seated at Position A at a table. On the table are several mountains made of clay that are different sizes and that partially occlude each other. The child has the view of the mountains one would have from being at Position A, but that view is different from the view one would get if seated at Position B, which is to the right. The child is shown photographs taken from each of four seating positions, including A and B, and asked to pick the photograph that shows what a person sitting at Position B would see. Children in preoperations pick the photograph that shows the mountains from their own view.

Preoperational children do not reason logically about cause and effect. Piaget called this **transductive reasoning**. They may infer a causal relationship between events that simply co-occur or mistakenly identify an event as the cause, when in fact it has followed the effect. Preoperational children also engage in **animistic thinking** and project human abilities and traits onto inanimate objects. Their thinking lacks **reversibility,** that is, the ability to mentally rewind a thought.

Seven to Twelve Years

The next two stages, concrete operations and formal operations, describe cognitive development during the times that most students are in school. The third stage, concrete operations, is the beginning of operational thinking and describes the thinking of children between the ages of seven and eleven. Learners at this age begin to decenter. They are able to take into consideration viewpoints other than their own. They can perform transformations, meaning that they can understand reversibility, inversion, reciprocity, and conservation. They can group items into categories. They are capable of seriation. They can make inferences about reality and engage in inductive reasoning; they increase their quantitative skills, and they can manipulate symbols if they are given concrete examples with which to work.

Adolescence

Finally, formal operations is the last stage of cognitive development and opens wide the door for higher-ordered, critical thinking. This stage describes the way of thinking for learners between the ages of 11 and 15, and for Piaget, constitutes the ultimate stage of cognitive development (thus, also describing adult thinking). Not all people reach this stage according to Piaget. Learners at this stage of cognitive development can engage in logical, abstract, and hypothetical thought; they can use the scientific method, meaning they can formulate hypotheses, isolate influences, and identify cause-and-effect relationships. They can plan and anticipate verbal cues. They can engage in both deductive and inductive reasoning, and they can mentally operate on verbal statements that do not have concrete terms or examples. These cognitive abilities characterize the highest level of thought. The end goal of cognitive development for Piaget is **hypothetico-deductive reasoning** about abstract concepts.

Elkind pointed out that there is a new form of egocentrism that emerges in adolescence which he called adolescent egocentrism. This egocentrism takes two forms, the imaginary audience and personal fable. Unlike the egocentrism of childhood, which is caused by the young child's inability to take the perspective of the other, adolescents have a newfound ability to think about their own and other people's thoughts and this appears to cause a heightened concern about other people's thoughts. Imaginary audience comes from the belief that other people are focused on what you think is important. If a teenager has a pimple, he or she is very aware of it and believes other people will be too. Personal fable is believing that what you feel and experience is unique. The adolescent believes that no one else has ever been as sad, as happy, as in love, or as disappointed as he or she is.

Adulthood

Labouvie-Vief suggests that there is an additional form of thought after adolescence called post-formal operations. This way of thinking is characterized by the understanding that there is often more than one right answer to a problem. To the relativistic thinker, truth is understood as relative to the knower and problems are understood to have more than one possible solution. An absolute thinker thinks linearly and expects that there is one truth and that every problem has one correct solution.

Another capacity we tend to associate with adulthood and aging is **wisdom**. Wisdom is defined as insight into the practical problems of life. While we assume wisdom comes with age, research has shown that not all older adults are wise and that wisdom comes more from the quality and richness of lived experience than from chronological age.

Memory Development

Over the course of development, children use more and more sophisticated methods to remember, and their memory performance improves as a result.

Although young infants (before three months of age) demonstrate memory capability when they recognize and remember familiar people, smells, objects, etc., in their environment, the use of intentional strategies for remembering have not been documented until around two years of age. These early strategies for remembering include looking, pointing, and naming.

By early elementary school, children are using rehearsal as a method for remembering. Rehearsal is a generic term for a variety of memory strategies that involve repetition as a method for remembering (e.g., repeating the phone number over and over until you dial it or, writing your spelling words ten times each). While three- and four-year-olds will rarely use the strategy of rehearsal, 10 percent of five-year-olds, over 50 percent of seven-year-olds, and nearly 85 percent of 10-year-olds will.

Organization, or clustering, strategies develop by seven to nine years of age and involve the semantic grouping of materials into meaningful units (e.g., grouping spelling words by their prefix).

Elaborative strategies involve creating verbal or visual connections that add meaning to material and do not develop until adolescence or later. An example would be creating the phrase "Every good boy does fine" to remember that "e," "g," "b," "d," and "f" are the lines of the treble clef in music.

Metacognition or the executive function is the capacity to be aware of one's own cognitive processing. Metamemory is one's knowledge about memory, and it has been divided into person (everything we know about the memory abilities of ourselves and others), task (everything we know about memory tasks), and strategy (everything we know about techniques of learning and remembering) factors. As with strategy use, metamemory improves with age during childhood. At first, young children are unrealistic and make overly optimistic predictions about their memories (i.e., they believe they can remember everything!) and with age they become more realistic in their expectations. They also know more about possible strategies for remembering with age.

In sum, older children have a greater memory capacity, coming closer to the adult capacity of seven plus or minus two items. They are more aware of effective memory strategies and are more likely to use organization and elaboration over rehearsal. They also have more metamemory awareness. These improvements continue through adolescence.

Researchers studying memory processing in adulthood describe a general decline in cognitive capacity and in speed of processing. It is also possible that older adults do not perform as well on memory tests as younger adults because of anxiety about their performance, motivational factors, or because of the non-meaningful information that participants are typically asked to remember in a memory experiment. However, older adults are able to compensate for changes in memory ability because of their increasing knowledge base, and specialized knowledge for important tasks.

Problem Solving

Siegler has studied problem solving in children using what he has called a rule assessment approach. He observed problem solving in participants aged three to 20 years to determine what aspects of the problem they focused on and what rule they developed based on that information to solve the problem. Most three-year-olds will just guess at a solution but four- to five-year-olds will select information they deem to be important and form a rule using that information. The issue with their problem solving is that they fail to take all important information into account when forming the rule. By age 12, children are sophisticated in determining all of the information relevant to the problem and then forming a rule to apply in solving it.

Older adults often perform best on problem-solving tasks in domains in which they have a great deal of knowledge and experience. They solve problems more efficiently in their area of expertise than outside their expertise. They also outperform younger subjects on problem-solving tasks that involve everyday problems. As mentioned earlier, it may be that this build-up of domain-specific knowledge and experience in solving everyday problems compensates for the slowing down of cognitive processing that has been found in older adults.

Attention

Attention is the process of focusing on particular aspects of the sensory world. Infants, as we have seen, are quite capable of perceiving the world around them. Infants, however, have their attention captured by stimuli more than they are capable of controlling and directing their attention. An infant's looking is attracted by a novel stimulus rather than intentionally directed toward that stimulus. As a child develops, attention changes to become more selective and attention span lengthens. **Selective attention** is directing one's attention toward a particular aspect of the sensory field while at the same time ignoring other distracting stimuli. In Chapter 14, Atypical Development, disorders of attention are discussed in which selective attention does not develop normally.

Selective attention research has shown that the ability to guide one's attention begins around the age of two. During the school years this ability continues to improve but children still have difficulty ignoring distracting stimuli. Adolescents are much better at selective attention tasks and do very well on tasks that require divided attention, which is systematically switching attention between two on-going tasks. Older adults perform more poorly than younger adults on selective attention and divided attention tasks. The more distracters during the task, the worse older adults perform. Therefore, the ability to ignore irrelevant stimulus appears to decline with age.

Visual search experiments examine how participants search complex arrays for pre-identified targets by recording eye movements during the search. Older children's searches are more systematic than younger children. The eye movements of younger children appear to be randomly directed at different parts of the stimulus array. Between ages four and ten, visual search of a stimulus becomes more controlled and systematic. Adolescents continue to improve on visual search tasks. Older adults are slower on visual search tasks than younger adults and because of their declining ability to ignore irrelevant stimuli, they do worse as the number of distracters in the array increases or the similarity between the distracters and the target increases. However, older adults benefit from training on visual search tasks, so this decline does not appear to be irreversible. Some researchers report that on familiar and on less complex search tasks, older adults perform just as well as younger adults.

Attention spans increase from 18 minutes in two- to three-year-olds to more than an hour in six-year-olds. Learning to read requires these attentional capacities and is probably the most significant attentional-perceptual challenge for children. Throughout adolescence and adulthood attention span lengthens.

Play

Someone once said that play is the work of childhood. The time from two to five years has even been named the play years. Play serves a variety of functions in children's development. It reflects, as well as stimulates, cognitive development, and it helps children develop social interaction skills.

The child engages in several major categories of play: sensorimotor (or functional) play, **pretend play**, parallel play, associative play, or cooperative play. The type of play children are engaged in depends on the existence and degree of interaction among the players. Sensorimotor play is engaged in during infancy. It involves the manipulation of objects. This manipulation provides the child with pleasurable stimulation but also serves a cognitive purpose as described by Piaget. Sensorimotor play also consists of motor activities such as crawling, walking, running, or waving. Older infants and toddlers often engage in functional play like pushing a toy car back and forth for no obvious reason.

Pretend or imaginative play involves games of make-believe. According to Piaget this type of play requires the cognitive ability of symbolic representation. The child may imagine that he or she is someone or something else, that the activities he or she engages in are something other than what they really are, or possibly he or she imagines that the objects he or she is playing with are something different than what they appear to be. Daydreaming is a major form of imaginative play. Daydreaming, however, involves no physical activity as compared to the other types of play. It is pure imaginative thinking.

The last three types of play consist of sequential types. Each is named and described in terms of the existence of interaction among the players. The first type, parallel play, begins shortly after infancy. Here, children play side by side but do not interact. They might use the same play materials but any sharing is unintentional. Four- and five-year-olds gradually engage in more associative play than parallel play. Associative play is when children playing near each other interact and may intentionally share tools or toys during play, but their play does not have a common goal.

Between the ages of two and five, children begin to act out fantasies, pretending that they are various characters. When children find that they share knowledge of various characters or fantasies, they engage in cooperative play as they act out fantasies together. Any type of play that involves interaction and cooperation among the players is called cooperative. One special type of cooperative play is called sociodramatic play. This type requires that the child's imagination and perception be highly active and alert—quick to pick up cues from the other players. It is comparable to the improvisation of professional actors. Through sociodramatic play, the child learns how to behave in society. In addition, the groundwork is laid for interpersonal relationships.

In addition to teaching the child how to interact socially, play is also an influencing factor in cognition. Sutton-Smith (1967) considered play an activity in which the infant can work through new responses and operations and increase his or her range of responses. Sutton-Smith called play a mechanism for the "socialization of novelty." Children whose play is varied are given a chance to experience situations that increase their ability to respond appropriately to novel situations that may arise in the future. Children whose play is restricted are less able to respond in unfamiliar situations. Thus, play enlarges a child's repertoire of responses and thereby allows him or her to adjust quickly to new situations.

CULTURAL AND ENVIRONMENTAL INFLUENCES ON COGNITIVE DEVELOPMENT

There are cultural and environmental influences on cognitive development. Chapter 14, Atypical Development, discusses in more detail how influences in the prenatal environment and in childhood can disrupt the normal course of cognitive development. There are many factors, for example, that cause intellectual disability in children that stem from these environments. Furthermore, although the domains of development (biological, cognitive, psychosocial) are discussed separately, they in fact interact throughout life. Poor nutrition or poor social relationships, in turn, can have a negative impact on cognitive development.

Early childhood education programs can positively influence cognitive development. There are many different types of programs and many different approaches used in these programs, but research has shown that a wide range of such early education programs can have a positive effect on cognitive development. The key factors of programs that promote cognitive growth are having a staff that feels qualified to create an appropriate curriculum and to respond to the educational needs of children, taking a holistic approach when designing the curriculum so activities in different domains like music and reading are integrated, and having parents involved in the program.

The family environment can also affect cognitive development. Caldwell and Bradley have developed the **HOME** scale (Home Observation for Measurement of the Environment) to assess the amount of intellectual stimulation in the home environment. HOME measures things such as the amount of appropriate play materials, parental involvement with children, and the amount of intellectual stimulation (for example, the number of books in the home). Studies have shown that scores on the HOME scale positively correlate with later measures of intelligence. Adopted children show gains in IQ scores when they move from an impoverished household to a stimulating one. In fact, children who live in households with high HOME scores tend to show gains in IQ scores between one and three years of age, while the opposite is true of children from households with low HOME scores. These patterns hold for European-American and African-American households but not for Mexican-American households. More research is needed to explore these cultural differences regarding the home environment.

Developmental psychologists have investigated whether the pattern of cognitive development described by Piaget is universal, that is, found in all children. Michael Cole pioneered the study of cultural influences on cognitive development to test this universality. His study of the development of thinking in children from non-Western cultures showed children in those cultures took longer to achieve concrete operations and were unable to achieve formal operations. The explanation for this difference is that the achievement of concrete and formal operational thought correlates with formal schooling. Cultures that define intelligence as logical, hypothetico-deductive thought design schooling to foster the development of this type of reasoning. But not all cultures have formal schooling, nor do they define intelligence that way. Some cultures equate intelligence with good social skills and still others view slow and deliberate problem solving as more intelligent than being quick. This is the opposite of the Western view. Children from other cultures are also better able to show their capacity for logical thinking if the problems and the materials are familiar to them. It is clear that culture influences cognitive development.

CHAPTER 7
Language Development

Chapter 7

Language Development

MAJOR PROPERTIES OF SPOKEN LANGUAGE

Language and thinking are two abilities that make us uniquely human. A spoken language requires the use of signs and symbols within a grammar. Grammar determines how the various signs and symbols are arranged and is a set of rules for combining the symbols, or words, into sentences. Language also allows us to use the signs and symbols within our grammar to create novel constructions.

Some characteristics of spoken language include:

Phonemes—The smallest unit of sound that affects the meaning of speech. The English language consists of 53 phonemes. By changing the beginning phoneme, the word "hat" becomes "cat."

Morphemes—The smallest unit of language that has meaning. A word can be one morpheme but morphemes are also roots, stems, prefixes, and suffixes. When speaking of more than one bat, we add the morpheme "s."

Semantics—The study of meaning in language.

Syntax or Grammar—The set of rules that determine how words are combined to make phrases and sentences.

Phonetics—The study of how sounds are put together to make words.

Pragmatics—Includes the social aspects of language, including politeness, conversational interactions, and conversational rules.

Psycholinguistics—The study of the psychological mechanisms related to the acquisition and use of language.

Noam **Chomsky** distinguished between a sentence's surface structure (the words actually spoken) and its deep structure (its underlying meaning). Two sentences, therefore, could have different surface structures but similar deep structures. An example would be, "The dog bit the boy" and "The boy was bitten by the dog." The surface structure of a sentence could also have more than one deep structure (e.g., "Visiting relatives can be boring."). When we hear a spoken sentence, we do not retain the surface structure, but instead transform it into its deep structure. Chomsky referred to this theory as transformational grammar theory.

Speech perception is guided by both bottom-up and top-down perception. Bottom-up processing in perception depends on the information from the senses at the most basic level, with sensory information flowing from this low level upward to the higher, more cognitive levels. For instance, the phoneme "c" in the word "cat" is perceived, in part, because our ears gather precise information about the characteristics of this sound. Top-down processing emphasizes the kind of information stored at the highest level of perception and includes concepts, knowledge, and prior knowledge. We are so skilled at top-down processing, for example, that we sometimes believe that we hear a missing phoneme. Warren and Warren found that subjects reported they heard the word "heel" in the following sentence in which the * indicates a coughing sound: "It was found that the *eel was on the shoe." Subjects thought they heard the phoneme "h" even though the correct sound vibration never reached their ears. This is an example of top-down processing because prior knowledge and expectations influenced what subjects perceived they had heard.

LANGUAGE DEVELOPMENT

An outline of language development follows.

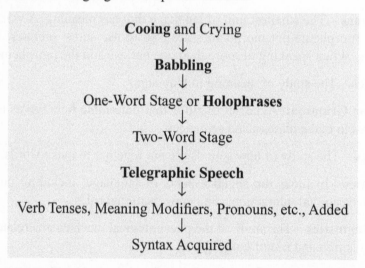

Cooing and Crying
↓
Babbling
↓
One-Word Stage or **Holophrases**
↓
Two-Word Stage
↓
Telegraphic Speech
↓
Verb Tenses, Meaning Modifiers, Pronouns, etc., Added
↓
Syntax Acquired

The first vocalizations that infants make include cooing and crying. At about four months of age, infants begin to babble. Their babblings are comprised of a repetition of syllables (e.g., "mamamama"). By six months of age, an infant is more likely to babble when an adult is talking to the infant. Babbling appears to be an innate ability because even deaf infants usually babble.

Infants usually begin to understand several individual words that caregivers are saying by five to eight months of age. A child's first words are ordinarily spoken between 10 and 12 months of age. This is referred to as the one-word stage because they can usually only use one word at a time. The first words that children use tend to be concrete nouns and verbs. Children often underextend and overextend the meanings of their first words. Underextension occurs when a child only uses a word in a specific context (e.g., only says "duck" when in the bathtub with a toy duck but never refers to this toy by name when outside the bathtub). **Semantic overextension** or overgeneralization occurs when a child uses a word to mean more than an adult speaker would. For instance, a child who calls *all* four-legged, furry animals (cats, dogs, etc.) "doggie" is overextending or overgeneralizing.

Some researchers have referred to children's one-word utterances as holophrases—that is, this one word could be interpreted to mean an entire phrase. For instance, a child points at an object and says "Cookie." This one-word could possibly mean, depending on context, "I want a cookie," "There is a cookie," or "Is that a cookie?"

Children from 18 to 20 months of age are in the two-word stage of language development because they are now making short, two-word sentences (e.g., "More milk," "Where ball?"). Their vocabulary is also expanding rapidly during this stage. They may learn several new words each day. Carey has suggested that this vocabulary growth spurt is explained by a process she called **fast mapping**. She argues that children assign a meaning to a word very rapidly after only a brief encounter during this phase of language development.

Telegraphic speech quickly follows the two-word stage and consists of sentences that do not contain any morphemes, conjunctions, prepositions, or any other function words. Telegraphic speech only contains the content words necessary to convey meaning, similar to a telegram (e.g., "Doggie kiss Jeff."). Children's first sentences follow the subject-verb-object sequence, and children often rely on this word order to make their meaning clear.

Eventually, children add verb endings, adjectives, auxiliary verbs, and morphemes to their utterances. Interestingly, initially children tend to use the correct verb tenses, even the exceptions (e.g., "went," "ran"). By age four or five, however, they are often using incorrect forms ("goed," "runned"). These errors called **overregularizations** seem to indicate that children are acquiring general rules about their language and for a period of time they overgeneralize these rules to the exceptions. Eventually children use the exceptions appropriately. By age five, children have acquired most of the syntax of their native language.

When speaking to infants and older language-learning children, older children and adults typically use motherese. Motherese is speech that contains short sentences that are often repeated. This speech tends to consist of concrete nouns and active verbs. Pronouns, adjectives, conjunctions, and past tenses are usually absent. The sentences are enunciated clearly, often in a high-pitched voice. Many researchers believe that motherese helps children learn language. However, recent research has shown that mothers typically use two techniques, **expansions** and **recasts**, that have a positive effect on childrens' language development. An expansion is when a mother repeats a child's verbalization after making it more complex. If a child says "Mommy up," mother might reply "Oh, you want me to pick you up." A recast is repeating a child's utterance after correcting grammatical mistakes. If a child says "He goed," mother might reply "Yes, he went home."

School-age children continue to improve their pronunciation of language and both school-age children and adolescents continue to increase their vocabulary. While there is a tremendous vocabulary spurt during the preschool period, school-age children and adolescents continue to increase their vocabulary by many words a day. Last, children show an improved understanding of the pragmatic rules of language as they age.

The understanding of word meanings expands in adulthood and older adults continue to have gains in vocabulary. While older adults may have more difficulty retrieving words, that may be due to a memory processing deficit, not a language deficit. Language skills are remarkably maintained through late adulthood.

THEORIES OF LANGUAGE DEVELOPMENT

An ongoing nature versus nurture debate has been whether language is basically an innate, biological process or a learned phenomenon. Many researchers hold the view of the **nativist theory** that children are somehow biologically programmed to learn language. According to Chomsky, a **language acquisition device** gives children an innate ability to process speech and to understand both the fundamental relationships among words and the regularities of speech. Researchers have also proposed a sensitive period for language learning during childhood. If exposed to language during this sensitive period, language learning will take place. After the sensitive period has passed, however, language learning will be much more difficult.

The **empiricist theory** of language development argues that humans are born with a mind that is a tabula rasa or blank slate and that all aspects of language are learned. B. F. Skinner and other **learning theorists** proposed that language learning takes place similar to other forms of learning. That is, parents selectively reinforce and shape babbling sounds into words. When parents speak to their children, children receive attention and often affection as well. Children then try to make these reinforcing word sounds themselves and try to imitate their parents because it is reinforcing to do so.

Comparing Theories of Language Development

A sensitive period for language development would support the nativist view. There is some evidence for a sensitive period from studies of feral children, abused children or children raised by animals, who were not exposed to language until after their discovery. These children can acquire some use of language but do not reach the level of language development found in the normal adult. The sensitive period for language is said to end at or around puberty.

Additional support for the nativist position comes from studies of infants' sound discrimination. Young infants have the capacity to discriminate all of the phonemes used in all of the world's languages, and they lose this ability over time as they are only exposed to the phonemes of their native language. Infants can also make all of the sounds used in all of the world's languages during the babbling phase. This ability also declines with age. Furthermore, the consistent pattern of errors in children's speech, like overregularization, supports the nativist view.

While it seems apparent that there is a good deal of evidence to support the nativist view of language acquisition, the learning theory is also helpful in explaining language development. Children's speech clearly undergoes a shaping process as their pronunciation of words improves. The learning mechanisms of imitation and reinforcement likely explain these changes.

There is also ample evidence that how parents talk to their children affects their language development, as well as socioeconomic status and gender differences in language use. Clearly both nature and nurture interact in language development.

Bilingualism

Bilingualism is having some degree of fluency in more than one language. Ten to fifteen percent of children in the United States are bilingual and many other countries of the world have significantly higher bilingualism rates. Some bilingual children, called balanced bilinguals, are equally fluent in both languages, but many others are not. Early research on the cognitive development and academic achievement of bilingual children in the United

States showed they had deficits compared to their monolingual peers. However, the earlier studies confounded socioeconomic conditions and the effects of prejudice with bilingualism. Recent work has shown that after controlling for these disadvantages, bilinguals, particularly, balanced bilinguals, have cognitive advantages over monolingual peers. They have better linguistic awareness and greater cognitive flexibility.

CHAPTER 8

Intelligence Throughout the Life Span

Chapter 8

Intelligence Throughout the Life Span

INTELLIGENCE TESTING

Because **intelligence** is a hypothetical construct, psychologists have disagreed on how to define it. Different intelligence tests, therefore, ask different questions and may measure different abilities.

Some definitions of intelligence include:

- The capacity to acquire and use knowledge.

- The total body of acquired knowledge.

- The ability to arrive at innovative solutions to problems.

- The ability to deal effectively with one's environment.

- Knowledge of one's culture.

- The ability to do well in school.

- The global capacity of the individual to act purposefully, to think rationally, and to deal effectively with the environment.

- Intelligence is what intelligence tests measure.

A major question related to intelligence has been "does intelligence consist of a single core factor or does it consist of many separate, unrelated abilities?" Responses to this include:

Charles Spearman   Concluded that cognitive abilities could be narrowed down to one critical g-factor, or general intelligence. (The s-factors represent specific knowledge needed to answer questions on a particular test.)

J. P. Guilford   Proposed that intelligence consists of 150 distinct abilities.

L. L. Thurstone   Used a statistical technique known as factor analysis to find seven independent primary mental abilities: numerical ability, reasoning, verbal fluency, spatial visualization, perceptual ability, memory, and verbal comprehension.

Raymond B. Cattell   Argued that a g-factor does exist, but cognitive ability consists of **fluid intelligence** (reasoning and problem solving) and **crystallized intelligence** (specific knowledge gained from applying fluid intelligence).

Robert Sternberg   Proposed a **triarchic theory of intelligence** that specifies three important parts of intelligence: componential intelligence (includes metacomponents, performance components, and knowledge-acquisition components), experiential intelligence (abilities to deal with novelty and to automatize processing), and contextual intelligence (practical intelligence and social intelligence).

Howard Gardner   Theory of **multiple intelligences** proposed seven different components of intelligence that include not only language ability, logical-mathematical thinking, and spatial thinking but also musical, bodily kinesthetic, interpersonal, and intrapersonal thinking.

History of Intelligence Testing

Early interest in intelligence testing dates back to the eugenics movement of Sir Frances Galton. Galton believed that it is possible to improve genetic characteristics (including intelligence) through breeding.

The first effective test of intelligence was devised in the early 1900s by French psychologist Alfred Binet. Binet was appointed by the French Ministry of Public Instruction to design an intelligence test that would identify children who needed to be removed from the regular classrooms so that they could receive special instruction.

Binet and his colleague Theodore Simon devised an intelligence test consisting of 30 subtests containing problems of increasing difficulty. The items on the test were designed to measure children's judgment, reasoning, and comprehension. This first test was published in 1905 and then was revised in 1908 and 1911.

The 1908 revision of the Binet and Simon scale introduced the notion of mental age. **Mental age** is a measure of a child's intellectual level that is independent of the child's chronological age (actual age).

Shortly after Binet's original work, Lewis M. Terman of Stanford University and his colleagues helped refine and standardize the test for American children. Their version came to be the Stanford-Binet Intelligence Scale, and its latest revision is still being used today. (A further discussion of this scale can be found later in this chapter.)

Terman and others (e.g., L. William Stern of Germany) developed the idea of the I.Q., or **intelligence quotient** (sometimes referred to as the ratio I.Q. score). To calculate I.Q., a child's mental age (MA) (as determined by how well he or she does on the test) is divided by his or her chronological age (CA) and multiplied by 100.

The major advantage of the I.Q. score over simple MA is that it gives an index of a child's I.Q. test performance relative to others of the same chronological age. The major problem with the ratio I.Q. score is that most people's mental development slows in their late teens. But as MA may remain fairly stable throughout adulthood, CA increases over time. Using CA as the divisor in the I.Q. formula, therefore, results in an individual's I.Q. score diminishing over time (even though MA has not changed).

David Wechsler corrected this problem with ratio I.Q. scores by devising the deviation I.Q. score. This deviation I.Q. score is calculated by converting the raw scores on each subtest of the test to standard scores normalized for each age group. These standard scores are then translated into deviation I.Q. scores. Wechsler reasoned that intelligence is normally distributed, or follows the bell-shaped curve—that is, the majority of people score at or around the mean, or average, score of 100 and progressively fewer people will achieve scores that spread out in either direction of the mean. A group of I.Q. scores can be portrayed as a normal, bell-shaped curve with an average score of 100 and a standard deviation (average deviation from the mean) that is the same (i.e., 15) at every age level.

The advantage of the deviation I.Q. is that the standing of an individual can be compared with the scores of others of the same age, and the intervals from age to age remain the same. Deviation I.Q. scores, therefore, indicate exactly where a test taker falls in the normal distribution of intelligence.

Terman adopted the deviation I.Q. as the scoring standard for the 1960 revision of the Stanford-Binet Intelligence Scale, although he chose a standard deviation of 16 rather than 15. Almost all other intelligence tests today use deviation I.Q. scores.

Current Intelligence Tests

The two most widely used versions of intelligence tests today are described next. These tests are individually administered, which means that they are given only by trained psychologists to one test taker at a time.

The first Stanford-Binet Intelligence Scale was published in 1916 by Lewis Terman and his colleagues. It was revised in 1937, 1960, and 1986 and remains one of the world's most widely used tests of intelligence (although there are criticisms of the scale). It can be used with individuals from age two through adulthood.

In its latest revision, Stanford-Binet Intelligence Scale: Fourth Edition, the term intelligence has been replaced by cognitive development. The terms intelligence, I.Q., and mental age are not used; instead, the term Standard Age Score (SAS) is used. The fourth edition measures four areas of cognitive development and a SAS can be calculated for each area as well as an overall composite score. The four areas measured are verbal reasoning, abstract/visual reasoning, quantitative reasoning, and short-term memory.

Because the Stanford-Binet initially appeared to be unsatisfactory for use with adults, in 1939 David Wechsler published a test designed exclusively for adults. This test has since been revised and is now known as the WAIS-R or Wechsler Adult Intelligence Scale, Revised.

Eventually, Wechsler published two scales for children and these are now known as:

WPPSI-R Wechsler Preschool and Primary Scale of Intelligence, Revised (for children 4 to 6 years of age)

WISC-III Wechsler Intelligence Scale for Children, third edition (for children 6 to 16 years of age)

The Wechsler scales were known for at least two major innovations when they were first developed. First, they were less dependent on verbal ability than the Stanford-Binet and included many items that required nonverbal reasoning. His tests allow the computation of three scores, a verbal I.Q. score, a performance I.Q. score, and an overall full scale I.Q. score. For example, subtests from the verbal and performance sections of the WAIS-R include:

Verbal Subtests	Performance Subtests
Information	Digit Symbol
Comprehension	Picture Completion
Arithmetic	Block Design
Similarities	Picture Arrangement
Digit Span	Object Assembly
Vocabulary	

Second, Wechsler developed the deviation I.Q. score based on the normal distribution of intelligence and abandoned the notion of intelligence quotient. Wechsler's scales of intelligence are still widely used and respected today.

The **Bayley Scales of Infant Intelligence** is a test designed to be used with infants aged 2 to 30 months. There are three scales on this test, including the motor scale, the mental scale, and the infant behavior record. The degree to which the infant has achieved developmental milestones, can coordinate goal-directed behavior, and can follow directions, are examples of what is measured on these scales. Infants receive a developmental quotient (DQ). Scores on the Bayley Scales do not predict later I.Q. very well. However, a low DQ score may be a sign of intellectual disability or neurological problems.

Intelligence tests, as with any other test, must have reliability and validity in order to be of good quality. Most intelligence tests used today (e.g., Stanford-Binet and Wechsler scales) demonstrate good reliability or consistency of scores. The validity of intelligence tests is the degree to which the tests measure what they are intended to measure. Validity is often assessed using criterion validity. This entails correlating test scores with another independent measure of intelligence. The validity of intelligence tests depends on the criterion being used. For example, they do a good job of predicting success in school. Although intelligence test scores correlate with occupational attainment, they do not predict performance within a given occupation.

Intelligence tests have been criticized as being biased. Children who have low socioeconomic status score on average lower than children from middle to upper socioeconomic classes. Some experts suggest that mainstream intelligence tests tap into experiences that people from the middle to upper status groups have rather than the experiences of people from low status backgrounds. This **test bias** has led to several recent attempts to create a **culture fair intelligence test**.

Intelligence test scores can and do change over time. For instance, infant and preschool scores are not good predictors of intelligence in later childhood, adolescence, or adulthood. It is not until late elementary school (e.g., after ages 8–10) that intelligence test scores begin to stabilize. It is also possible, however, to make substantial gains or losses in intelligence during adolescence and adulthood.

DETERMINANTS OF INTELLIGENCE

The nature versus nurture debate related to intelligence addresses whether heredity or environment determines one's intellectual skills. Heritability is an estimate of how much of a trait in a population is determined by genetic inheritance. **Twin studies** have become the most popular research tool to examine this issue.

Correlational studies with twins suggest that heredity influences the development of intelligence. For instance, the correlation of intelligence test scores for identical twins (who have identical genetic make-up) is higher than the correlation for fraternal twins. Even identical twins reared apart have more similar I.Q.s than fraternal twins reared together in the same household.

There is research evidence, however, to indicate that environment also exerts a strong influence on intelligence. Sandra Scarr and other researchers have shown that underprivileged children placed in homes that provide an enriching intellectual environment have shown moderate but consistent increases in intelligence. Children placed in various enrichment programs have also shown gains in I.Q. The I.Q.s of identical twins reared together in the same environment are more similar than those for identical twins reared apart.

The term reaction range has been applied to the nature vs. nurture debate of intelligence. Reaction range implies that genetics may limit or define a potential range of I.Q., but that environment can influence where along this range an individual's I.Q. score falls. For instance, children in an enriched environment should score near the top of their potential I.Q. range.

Racial and cultural differences in I.Q. are very small when compared to the range of genetic differences within each group. Research has suggested, for example, that the differences between mean intelligence test scores for black and white Americans may be due to differences in parental education, nutrition, health care, schools, and motivation for doing well on the test.

Many have argued that intelligence tests are culturally biased because they have been developed by white, middle-class psychologists. There is some research evidence to support this claim. Attempts have been made to produce language-free, culture-fair tests of intelligence. The Raven's Progressive Matrices is one such test.

INTELLIGENCE THROUGHOUT THE LIFE SPAN

Many children show considerable fluctuation in I.Q. scores through childhood. Children may show both gains and losses. Children who live in poverty or are being raised by parents with low I.Q.s show noticeable declines in I.Q. This has been explained by the cumulative deficit hypothesis that suggests the negative effects of living in a non-stimulating environment build up over time. On the other hand, some children show noticeable gains in I.Q. These tend to be children who are exposed to stimulating environments and have parents who foster their achievement. Some of these children also may have benefited from intervention programs like Head Start, which have been shown to produce improved I.Q. scores.

During adolescence I.Q. scores become much more stable and continue to be so through a good deal of adulthood. Research on intelligence in adulthood paints a very complex picture.

Early research on intelligence in adulthood was cross-sectional and longitudinal. Recall that both of these research methodologies have flaws. Both types of research reported declines in I.Q. with some suggesting the decline began as early as the forties and others reporting a decline beginning in the sixties or seventies. There was typical agreement that the steepest decline occurred in the eighties.

Schaie conducted a seminal sequential study of intelligence in adulthood which he began in 1956 and ended in 1984. Recall that this developmental research method is the strongest of the three and resolves the flaws of both cross-sectional and longitudinal designs. Furthermore, Schaie measured changes in fluid and crystallized intelligence. He found that fluid intelligence did show declines in adulthood and that this decline began earlier and was more steep than declines in crystallized intelligence. Crystallized intelligence remained the same or even improved and then started to decline somewhat after the '60s. Not all people showed declines. There were some who maintained the same levels of both fluid and crystallized intelligence into later life. Most important, Schaie found large birth cohort differences in the patterns of both fluid and crystallized intelligence in adulthood. Younger birth cohorts retained higher levels of intelligence into late adulthood than members of older birth cohorts.

What has been particularly challenging in the study of intellectual performance in older adults is controlling for the confounding factor of disease or health. Diseases like cardiovascular disease are correlated with steeper intellectual decline, and there also is a phenomenon that has been observed called **terminal drop**. Terminal drop is a rapid decline in intellectual performance shortly before death.

EMOTIONAL INTELLIGENCE

Daniel Goleman recently suggested another form of intelligence he calls **emotional intelligence**, or E.Q., defined as a person's ability to understand, and adapt to, emotion and emotional situations. People with high E.Q.'s have an exceptional ability to understand and deal with their own emotions and the emotions expressed by other people. His controversial prediction is that E.Q. is a better predictor of success in life than I.Q. It remains to be seen what the relationship is between E.Q. and intelligence.

CREATIVITY

Psychologists differentiate between intelligence and **creativity**. Creativity is the ability to produce something new and unique or that combines elements in new ways. Creative problem solving involves coming up with a solution that is both unusual and useful. Creative thinking usually involves **divergent thinking**, or thinking that produces many different correct answers to the same problem or question. Creating a sentence with the word "Springfield" would involve divergent thinking—there is no one specific correct response. A response to the question "What is the capital of Illinois?" would require **convergent thinking**—one correct answer is expected. Convergent thinking does not appear to be related to creativity. Although all creative thought is divergent, not all divergent thought is creative. Tests (e.g., Remote Associates Test) have been developed that measure creativity. Almost all of these tests require divergent thinking. In general, these tests of creativity have not been good at predicting who will be creative in real-life problem-solving situations. There is a modest correlation between creativity and intelligence. Highly creative people tend to have above-average intelligence, but not always. Furthermore, having a high I.Q. does not necessarily mean that someone is creative. Children who are creative tend to engage in more pretend or fantasy play and enjoy new experiences. But the factors that generally predict I.Q. in children, do not predict creativity. The development of creativity may be fostered by certain types of parenting, or the home environment, but clearly is not controlled by genetics. Identical twins do not have more similar creativity scores than fraternal twins or siblings.

Creativity seems to be a capacity that is maintained through later life. Even if creative production declines in older adults, or if they score lower on measures of creativity, the capacity to be creative is retained. Some creative people continue to produce great works until the end of their lives.

CHAPTER 9

Social Development Throughout the Life Span

CHAPTER 9

Social Development
Throughout the Life Span

Chapter 9

Social Development Throughout the Life Span

Social development refers to the development of behaviors and thoughts the child engages in when he or she interacts with others. The need for social affiliation or a desire to be with other people is strong. Evolutionary psychologists describe social affiliation as an example of a species behavior that evolved because of its survival value. Humans seek out the company of others especially when afraid. In a classic series of studies, Stanley Schachter manipulated the fear level of college women by leading them to believe they would receive electric shocks in a laboratory experiment. He then measured whether the women preferred to wait for the experiment to begin either alone or with others. The majority preferred to wait with others.

This chapter will cover topics in the study of children's social development such as interpersonal relationships and attachment, gender role development, moral development, and social cognition. The process through which children learn the values and acceptable behaviors of their society is called socialization. Key influences on children's socialization are the family, school, and the media. These influences are discussed in the next chapter.

SOCIAL COGNITION

Social cognition is reasoning about social situations and social relationships. A child is not born with the capacity to understand self and others. As children gain more social experience and develop cognitively, they are better able to understand that they, and others, have personalities, feelings, thoughts, and relate to each other in social role relationships. Social cognition influences social interactions and social behavior.

Developmental psychologists have identified one of the key concepts that underlies social cognition. This concept is called a **theory of mind**. A theory of mind is the understanding that people have mental states and that the content of these mental states guides their behavior. Actions are guided by beliefs, emotions, and goals. If I look in my closet for a pair of shoes, I must believe that the shoes are in the closet. Baron-Chen and his colleagues developed the **false**

belief task to assess children's theory of mind. In this task, a child witnesses a confederate place a marble in a basket and then leave the room. While the confederate is out of the room, the experimenter moves the marble from the basket to a box. When the confederate returns to the room, the child is asked where he or she thinks the confederate will look for the marble. Most four-year-olds will correctly say that the confederate will look in the basket. Four-year-olds understand that since the confederate thinks the marble is in the basket, that is where he or she will look. They have a theory of mind. They also found that 80 percent of autistic children got the task wrong, leading them to hypothesize that autistic children have what they called mind blindness.

A theory of mind begins with joint attention seen in children beginning around nine months of age. Joint attention is when a child and caregiver simultaneously direct their attention to the same object. An infant this age will point to an object then turn to the caregiver to see that he or she is looking at the object. This behavior indicates that the child knows the other person has perceptual experiences too. More sophisticated understandings of a theory of mind appear in the second year. Children's pretend play also signifies an understanding that there is a difference between reality and pretend. Pretending is creating false beliefs in a sense. Beginning between two and three years of age, children refer to their mental states in their speech. "I want to. . . ." indicates the child understands his action is driven by a desire. They are also capable of deception and may try to fool someone by planting a false belief. A child may try to play a joke on Mommy by telling her that he or she ate all the cookies, when in fact he or she did not.

Social cognitive ability affects things like peer acceptance and popularity. A child who is not skilled in social cognition may often misinterpret the motives of other people. This child, for example, might push a child who accidentally bumped into him or her. Aggressive children tend to misinterpret the motives for other people's behavior.

PERSON PERCEPTION

Before interacting with other people, infants have to develop a sense of self, that is, the understanding that they are separate from other people. To determine if a child has **self-recognition**, Lewis and Brooks-Gunn developed the **mirror test of self-recognition**. Children ages 9 to 24 months of age were seated in front of a mirror after the experimenter surreptitiously placed rouge on their cheek. Infants at least 18 months of age rubbed their own cheek when they saw the reflection rather than rub the mirror as younger infants did.

The concept of self contributes to a child's ability for self-control. Toddlers are capable of compliance, obeying others' wishes, and **delay of gratification**. Delay of gratification is the ability to exert self-control and wait for an anticipated reward or goal or put off a desired activity for a later time.

Children who are younger than seven or eight who are asked to describe themselves and other people will use the physical attributes of a person before using psychological characteristics like personality attributes. Young children might describe themselves as being a boy or girl, having a certain color hair, and having twelve dolls or two bicycles. By the age of eight or so they describe themselves and others as being funny or smart. At age 11 or 12 children begin to make social comparisons of their own characteristics, traits, and abilities with their peers. They may judge themselves to be smarter than others or not as smart as others. Social comparison plays a key role in Erikson's model of psychosocial development, which is discussed in more detail in Chapter 11, Personality and Emotions. Adolescents' descriptions of themselves and others get more complex as they are able to consider more dimensions of psychological and personality characteristics.

ROLE-TAKING SKILLS

Role-taking skills also develop as the child has more social experiences and develops cognitively. These role-taking skills are also critical to the child's ability to interact with others. According to Piaget, children are egocentric between the ages of two to six or seven years. They lack the ability to take the perspective of the other. Between ages six and eight, children understand that people have different viewpoints but are not capable of judging how other people view them. Between ages 8 and 10 children understand that there is a view of the self and a view of the other. They view themselves a certain way and they view other people a certain way. They further understand that the other person's view of them can be different from their view of themselves and vice versa. Between 10 and 12 children can take the perspective of a third party. For example, they can understand how a third person views their relationship with a second person. Adolescents acquire the ability to take a societal perspective. They can understand that a group has certain views and beliefs.

GENDER ROLE DEVELOPMENT

Gender roles are our set of expectations about appropriate activities for females and males. Gender is independent of biological sex and **sexual orientation**. There is a **feminine** gender role, **masculine** gender role, and **androgyny**. **Gender stereotypes** are restrictive views about which gender role men and women should adopt. In our culture, the stereotypic view is that females are feminine and males are masculine. Elements of the stereotypical feminine gender role include being caring, nurturing, and compliant. Elements of the stereotypical masculine role are being aggressive, dominant, and competitive. The androgynous gender role combines the best elements of the other two gender roles.

Developmental psychologists studying gender development have discovered that children have to acquire **gender stability**, the understanding that biological sex remains the same throughout life and **gender constancy**, the understanding that one's biological sex is not changed by changes in appearance. Daddy does not become a girl when he dresses up like a female on Halloween. These concepts are necessary for the child to develop a gender identity, an internalized view of the self as feminine, masculine, or androgynous.

Gender typing starts early in life. This is the process of socializing children about what roles are appropriate for males and females in the society. Differences in toys, clothing, and how people treat them communicates these gender concepts. Research has shown that even preschoolers believe that males and females have different characteristics. They also believe it is inappropriate to act like a member of the other gender. Young school-age children are very restrictive about gender roles but become more flexible and tolerant of violations of gender stereotypes. Adolescents regress to being more inflexible about gender roles and conform to gender stereotypes. Adults tend to adopt stereotypical roles when they have children but the androgyny shift hypothesis argues that in mid-life people start to become more androgynous.

Theories that explain gender role development include:

Social Learning Theory	Proposes that children learn gender roles because they are rewarded for appropriate behavior and punished for inappropriate gender role behaviors. Children also watch and imitate the behaviors of others.
Cognitive Theory	Kohlberg argued that children learn about gender the same way that they acquire other cognitive concepts (see Piaget's theory for more detail). First, preschool children acquire **gender identity**—that is, they identify themselves as male or female. Then children classify others, activities, objects, etc., as male or female. Once these gender concepts are acquired, children engage in gender-typed behavior—they prefer same-gender playmates, activities, etc. Kohlberg also proposed that preschool children lack **gender constancy**. That is, they do not understand that a person's gender stays the same despite changes in outward physical appearance.

Psychoanalytic Theory	Freud's theory proposes that children establish their gender role identity as a result of identification with their same sex parent during the Phallic stage.

KOHLBERG'S THEORY OF MORAL DEVELOPMENT

Lawrence **Kohlberg** developed a model of moral development based on an individual's responses to difficult moral questions called moral dilemmas. Kohlberg's theory attempts to explain how children develop a sense of right or wrong. Kohlberg was influenced by Piaget's theory and therefore felt that moral development was determined by cognitive development.

Kohlberg's theory describes how individuals pass through a series of three levels of moral development, each of which can be broken into two sublevels, resulting in a total of six stages.

Level I. Preconventional Morality		
Stage 1.	Punishment orientation	A person complies with rules during this stage in order to avoid punishment.
Stage 2.	Reward orientation	An action is determined by one's own needs.
Level II. Conventional Morality		
Stage 3.	Good-girl/Good-boy orientation	Good behavior is that which pleases others and gets their approval.
Stage 4.	Authority orientation	Emphasis is on upholding the law, order, and authority and doing one's duty by following societal rules.
Level III. Postconventional Morality		
Stage 5.	Social contract orientation	Flexible understanding that people obey rules because they are necessary for the social order but that rules can change if there are good reasons and better alternatives.
Stage 6.	Morality of individual principles orientation	Behavior is directed by self-chosen ethical principles. High value is placed on justice, dignity, and equality.

Criticisms of Kohlberg's theory of moral development include that it may be better at describing the development of male morality than of female morality. Carol Gilligan conducted similar studies of reasoning about moral dilemmas, but in comparing males to females found that females tended to apply a **morality of care** versus a **morality of justice** when reasoning about moral issues. A morality of care is basing decisions about morality by considering the impact of actions on other people or on social relationships. Kohlberg's model suggested that a morality of justice was the most developmentally advanced type of morality. His model has also been criticized by those who argue that development may not be as orderly and uniform as his theory suggests. For instance, it is not unusual to find individuals who are reasoning at several adjacent levels of moral reasoning at the same time. Also, Kohlberg's theory describes moral reasoning but does not predict moral behavior.

The development of more advanced moral reasoning in children is assisted by parents' use of induction. Parents use induction when they explain to a child how his or her behavior can negatively impact others. For example, a parent might explain to a child that it was bad to take a toy from another child because it made the other child sad. Punishing a child for bad behavior or withdrawing affection are both less effective means of teaching morality.

INTERPERSONAL RELATIONSHIPS

Attachment

Attachment is the close emotional relationship between an infant and his or her caretakers. Ethologist Konrad Lorenz studied attachment in animals. He found that ducklings attach to their mother duck after birth. They follow their mother duck, a behavior Lorenz called **imprinting**. Lorenz also found that there was a critical period for imprinting to develop. In fact, ducklings will imprint on any moving object (including Lorenz himself) if they are exposed to that object during a critical period of days after hatching. If the exposure does not occur during this time period, the ducklings never imprint. Ethologists suggest that infant attachment to a caregiver is analogous to imprinting in ducklings and that attachment is adaptive for an infant since the infant is dependent on caregivers for survival.

Complete social isolation prevents the development of attachment and socialization in primates. Monkeys raised in complete social isolation either display fear or aggression when suddenly placed in the companionship of peers.

Harry **Harlow** conducted a seminal study with monkeys to study the formation of attachment. To test the hypothesis that infants attach to a caregiver for survival, Harlow conducted an experiment to see which of two surrogate mothers the infant monkeys attached to. One surrogate mother fed the monkeys. A bottle with a nipple was placed in a wire-mesh structure and was the wire-mesh mother. The other surrogate was a cloth-covered wire-mesh structure. This was the cloth mother. Infants attached to the cloth mother even though they were fed by the wire-mesh mother. Harlow concluded that the warmth and comfort given by the cloth mother was the necessary condition for the attachment relationship.

Human infants come prepared with attachment behaviors, that is, behaviors that elicit caregiving. Initially, infants attempt to attract the attention (usually through crying, smiling, etc.) of no one in particular. Between 6 and 10 weeks of age, an infant begins to smile in the presence of a caregiver. Prior to this time, an infant's smile is merely a reflexive response.

Eventually infants develop the ability to discriminate familiar from unfamiliar people. Shortly thereafter, they may cry or otherwise become distressed when preferred caregivers leave the room. This is referred to as **separation anxiety**. Separation anxiety may begin as early as six months of age, but it usually peaks around 18 months and then gradually declines. Mary Ainsworth and her colleagues found they could distinguish three categories of attachments based on the quality of the infant-caregiver interactions. They developed a method of measuring the quality of the attachment relationship in what is known as the **Ainsworth Strange Situation**. They had mothers and infants come into a lab room and then observed the infants' behaviors when the mother left the room and upon their return. Although this method has been criticized as measuring the quality of attachment in an artificial setting, it remains the most frequently used technique in studies of attachment. Based on their reactions in the Strange Situation, infants are classified as either having a secure or insecure attachment. Insecure attachment is further divided into three categories.

Secure Attachment	Children use parent as secure base from which they explore the new environment. They become upset when their mother leaves the room but are glad to see her and go to her when she returns.

Insecure Attachment

Anxious-Ambivalent	Children tend not to use the parent as a secure base (and may often cling or refuse to leave their mother). They become very upset when she leaves and may often appear angry or become more upset when she returns.
Avoidant	Children seek little contact with their mother and are not concerned when she leaves. Usually avoid interaction when the parent returns.
Disorganized-Disoriented	Children alternatively approach and avoid contact with their mother. They appear confused about whether to seek or avoid her. Often appears in abused children.

Parents of securely attached infants are often found to be more sensitive and responsive to their child's needs. Some studies have found a relationship between attachment patterns and children's later adjustment. For instance, one study found that securely attached infants were less frustrated and happier at two years of age than were their insecurely attached peers. Some researchers have suggested that in addition to **sensitive parenting**, temperament, genetic characteristics, and goodness of fit may be important for both the type of attachment bond formed and a child's later developmental outcome. Psychologists studying adult relationships have shown a relationship between the quality of infant attachments and later adult relationships. Securely attached infants develop the capacity to have secure adult attachments. Adults who had insecure infant attachments tend to have insecure adult relationships.

Peer Relationships

Infants up to the age of two generally spend their time on solo missions. They play by themselves. Their play tends to be **unoccupied** or **functional play** such as moving a truck back and forth on the floor. Even if they are playing in a room with other children, they are engaged in **parallel play**. Parallel play is when two children are playing side by side but have little to no interaction. Play gradually becomes more social. **Associative play** is when two or more children are playing in proximity to each other and may share toys but do not share a common goal. **Onlooker play** is receiving enjoyment by watching other people play. Children engaging in **cooperative play** share a common goal. Cooperative play often is rule-governed. Between ages two and seven children seek the company of their peers regardless of sex.

During the elementary school years, children desire same-sex friendships. Boys and girls often antagonize each other during these years. These children tend to play in groups but start to pair off into sets of best friends.

Peer acceptance and rejection in childhood has significant influences on children's development. **Rejected children** are at risk for dropping out of school, having delinquent or criminal behavior, and needing mental health services. Children who are less aggressive and more cooperative tend to be most well liked. Predictors of popularity in children include good social-cognitive skills, above-average intelligence, being good natured, having positive self-perceptions, and having a good sense of humor. Rejected children can be either rejected-aggressive or rejected-withdrawn. Rejected-aggressive children are actively disliked by their peers. Rejected-withdrawn children are ignored or invisible to their peers. Experiences in the family, parenting style, attachment quality, and exposure to aggressive or non-aggressive models influence children's social competence. Many of these factors are discussed in Chapter 10, Family, Home, and Society.

In adolescence same-sex and opposite-sex friendships occur as well as dating relationships. Friendships are very important in adolescence as the need to be accepted by peers gets stronger as adolescents spend more time with friends than family. The need to be accepted leads to **conformity** and capitulating to peer pressure.

Friendship groups vary in size. A **clique** is a small collection of close friends who spend a substantial amount of time together. A **crowd** is a collection of several cliques and typically is mixed-sex. Membership in a clique tends to be very restrictive and what is acceptable behavior, dress, etc., is strictly defined. Opposite-sex friendships occur with greater frequency than in childhood and may help heterosexual adolescents prepare for dating relationships.

Adult friendships remain equally important to the quality of one's life as compared to children and adolescents. In fact, adults who are single report a great need for friendship and companionship. Many single adults report feeling lonely. Erikson argued adults have a need for intimacy and if they do not fulfill this need, they face feelings of isolation. Developmental psychologists have spent a great deal of time studying mate selection and relationship satisfaction to better understand how relationships form.

INTERPERSONAL ATTRACTION

Interpersonal attraction refers to those factors that contribute to a relationship being formed. One theory of interpersonal attraction is social exchange theory. Social exchange theory views human interactions in economic terms. According to this theory, when two people meet, they each calculate the costs and benefits of developing a relationship. If the benefits outweigh the costs, then the two people will be attracted to each other. Other theories of attraction suggest that there are key dimensions on which we evaluate others. These factors influence whether we develop a relationship with another person.

Friendship

Studies of friendships have found three factors that are important in determining who will become friends.

Similarity	People are generally attracted to those who are similar to themselves in many ways—similar in age, sex, race, economic status, etc.
Proximity or Propinquity	It is easier to develop a friendship with people who are close at hand. Proximity also increases the likelihood of repeated contacts and increased exposure can lead to increased attraction—the mere exposure effect. In a classic study at Massachusetts Institute of Technology, Festinger found that friends of women who lived in married student housing were most likely to live in the same building. In fact, half of all friends lived on the same floor.
Attractiveness	Physical attractiveness is a major factor in attraction for people of all ages. We tend to like attractive people. Research in social psychology indicates that physical appearance is the most important determinant of first impressions. It also contributes to effectiveness in persuading others to change their beliefs.

Love

Overall, the same factors connected with friendships (similarity, proximity, and attractiveness) are also related to love relationships.

Similarity	Dating and married couples tend to be similar in age, race, social class, religion, education, intelligence, attitudes, and interests.
Proximity	We tend to fall in love with people who live nearby.
Attractiveness	We tend to fall in love with people whose attractiveness matches our own according to the matching hypothesis.

Researchers believe that love is a qualitatively different state than merely liking someone. Love includes physiological arousal, self-disclosure, all-encompassing interest in another individual, fantasizing about the other, and a relatively rapid swing of emotions. Unlike liking, love also includes passion, closeness, fascination, exclusiveness, sexual desire, and intense caring.

Some researchers have distinguished two main types of love.

Passionate or Romantic Love	Predominates in the early part of a romantic relationship. Includes intense physiological arousal, psychological interest, sexual desire, and the type of love we mean when we say we are "in love" with someone.

| Companionate or Affectionate Love | The type of love that occurs when we have a deep, caring affection for a person. |

Robert Sternberg has proposed a triangular theory of love that consists of three components:

Intimacy	The encompassing feelings of closeness and connectedness in a relationship.
Passion	The physical and sexual attraction in a relationship.
Decision/ Commitment	The initial cognition that one loves someone and the longer-term feelings of commitment to maintain the love.

According to Sternberg's theory, complete love only happens when all three kinds of love are represented in a relationship. Sternberg called this consummate love. Fatuous love is based on passion and commitment only and is often short-lived. Research has shown that successful romantic relationships that last for many years are based on the expression of love and admiration, friendship between the partners, a commitment to the relationship, displays of affection, self-disclosure, and offering each other emotional support.

PROSOCIAL AND ANTISOCIAL BEHAVIOR

Aggression

Hostile aggression is defined as intentionally inflicting physical or psychological harm on others. **Instrumental aggression** is using aggressive behavior to achieve a goal, but is not intended to harm. **Relational aggression** is a form of hostile aggression that is aimed at damaging other people's social relationships. About one-third of studies show that males are more aggressive than females, and the differences are larger with children than adults and with physical rather than verbal aggression. The consistency in the differences between males and females has led some theorists to suggest aggression is due to a biological difference between males and females. This is a nature view of aggression. Cross-cultural research on gender differences in aggression has shown that males are more aggressive than females in each of the cultures studied, but the differences between the two groups vary—smaller in some cultures and larger in other cultures. Therefore, while there may be a biological component, culture clearly influences aggressive behavior.

The frustration-aggression hypothesis states that frustration produces aggression and that this aggression may be directed at the frustrater or displaced onto another target, as in scapegoating. However, frustration does not always cause aggression.

According to social learning theory, people learn to behave aggressively by observing aggressive models and by having their aggressive responses reinforced. For instance, parents who are belligerent with others or who use physical punishment to discipline their children tend to raise more aggressive offspring. Also, exposure to role models in the mass media, especially television, can influence aggression. Some research demonstrates that adults and children as young as nursery-school age show higher levels of aggression after they view media violence.

Altruism

Altruism, or **prosocial behavior**, is the selfless concern for the welfare of others that leads to helping behavior. Altruistic behavior is observed in children as young as 13 months of age. Research has found that individuals who are high in **empathy**—an emotional experience that involves a subjective grasp of another person's feelings—are more likely to help others in need. According to the empathy-arousal hypothesis, empathy has the power to motivate altruism. How children develop empathy is discussed in Chapter 11, Personality and Emotions.

RISK AND RESILIENCE

Developmental psychologists have learned a great deal about what factors lead to some infants who are born at risk being able to survive and thrive. Infants at risk are those infants who come into the world facing challenges like those who have low birth weight or genetic defects or encounter challenges in their lives, like neglected or abused children. **Resilience** is the term used for whatever qualities or characteristics an infant has who is at risk but overcomes those risks. Resilient children tend to have above average intelligence, are sociable, and have an easy temperament. But most important for this discussion of social development is the fact that resilient children have the unconditional love of at least one person in their life. Unconditional love is love that is not only given as a reward or withdrawn as a punishment. To be loved unconditionally is to be loved as a person and not for what you do.

CHAPTER 10

Family, Home, and Society Throughout the Life Span

Chapter 10

Family, Home, and Society Throughout the Life Span

Urie Bronfenbrenner pointed out that development takes places within sociocultural systems or contexts. Bronfenbrenner's bioecological approach suggests there is a reciprocal determinism between the child and the environment. A child's biological makeup determines some of the characteristics of the child like potential intelligence. However, if the child is raised in a non-stimulating environment or by parents who are neglectful, the child may not reach his or her full potential. Following his lead, developmental psychologists have studied the influence of sociocultural contexts on development.

Bronfenbrenner constructed a model depicting the systems of development and their interrelationships as a series of embedded, concentric circles. The innermost circle is the microsystem. These are the systems in which a child directly participates. Examples of microsystems are the family, day care, or school. A child's experience in one microsystem affects his or her experiences in another microsystem through the mesosystem. A child whose parents are divorcing may start doing poorly in school. The exosystem is where interrelationships between events in contexts in which the child does not directly participate affect the child. A parent who is experiencing stress at work may interact less with his or her child at home. Finally, the macrosystem affects each of the other systems. The macrosystem is the outermost area that encircles all of the other systems in the model. This is the sociocultural context and it contains the values and attitudes shared by the members of the culture. For example, parenting customs vary across different cultures. These customs affect the child's experiences in the microsystem of the family. Another example is social attitude regarding mothers working outside the home. Before it was more socially acceptable for a mother to work outside the home, having a working mother had different influences on the child's experiences.

This chapter examines the major systems of child development including the family and society. The contemporary theoretical perspective on the family is also a systems theory.

FAMILY

Family systems theory is the theoretical perspective that views the family as an organized, whole unit with integrated parts. Members of the family adopt roles that are reciprocally determined interrelationships like mother-child, father-child, and mother-father. The behavior of each family member affects the whole system, and relationships between two or more members of the family affect the system as a whole. The father-child or the mother-child relationship can impact the mother-father relationship. In this perspective, the child influences the family system as much as the family influences the child.

There are different family structures other than the traditional nuclear family. The **beanpole family** is a household that consists of multiple generations of the same family as in when grandparents live in the home. The **blended** or **reconstituted family** is a family structure that is the result of remarriage. Also there are single-parent families. More households are non-traditional today due to the high rate of divorce and remarriage, and the increasing numbers of same-sex parent households and single-parent households.

Today, many households are headed by dual-working parents raising concern regarding the degree of supervision children have after school and the amount of time parents spend with their children. **Latchkey children** are children who go home to an empty house after school. Many latchkey children suffer no ill effects, but these are the children whose parents monitor them through cell phone calls and who establish rules for what the child can and cannot do. Second, research clearly shows that it is the quality of time parents spend with their children that affects their development, not the quantity of time. Working parents who come home and engage in meaningful activities with their children have well-adjusted and competent children. Also, fathers in these households participate more in child care than those in households with stay-at-home mothers.

FAMILY LIFE CYCLE

Family systems theory also describes a family life cycle. Theorists in this perspective view the family unit as moving through a sequence of phases analogous to a stage model of the developing individual. The phases are married couple without children, first child, family with preschool children, family with school-age children, family with teenagers, family launching young adults, family without children, and aging family (retirement to death). Family roles are affected by the phase of the family and marital satisfaction changes across the phases. Marital satisfaction is at its peak before the first child, decreases thereafter until the launching phase, where it begins to increase again. The **launching phase** is when young adult children leave the home. This used to be called the **empty nest stage**. Psychologists described the empty nest as a period of crisis for parents, particularly for mothers, but recent survey research indicates that most parents enjoy a renewal in their relationship and are very satisfied during the launching phase.

This model, however, assumes a traditional view of the family as headed by a heterosexual couple who marry, have children, and remain married to each other throughout the entire family cycle. Obviously, this model does not apply to the many non-traditional families in our society today.

PARENTING STYLES

Diana **Baumrind** conducted a longitudinal study of parenting and developed a system of classifying parenting styles. She found that she could classify parents into three styles and that there are predictable developmental outcomes for children raised with each parenting style. A fourth parenting style, neglectful/uninvolved has subsequently been added to the classification system which is described below.

Authoritative Parents	Affectionate and loving.
	Provide control when necessary and set limits.
	Allow children to express their own point of view—engage in "verbal give and take."
	Their children tend to be self-reliant, competent, and socially responsible.
Authoritarian Parents	Demand unquestioning obedience.
	Use punishment to control behavior.
	Less likely to be affectionate.
	Their children tend to be unhappy, distrustful, ineffective in social interactions, and often become dependent adults.
Permissive Parents	Make few demands.
	Allow children to make their own decisions.
	Use inconsistent discipline.
	Their children tend to be immature, lack self-control, and explore less.

Neglectful/ Uninvolved Parents	Do not pay attention to the needs of the child.
	Provide no discipline or guidance.
	Provide no love or affection.
	Their children are at risk for anti-social behavior.

These four parenting styles can be compared on two dimensions: demandingness/control and acceptance/responsiveness. Authoritarian parenting is high on demandingness/control and low on acceptance/responsiveness. Authoritative parenting is high on demandingness/control and high on acceptance/responsiveness. Permissive parenting is low on demandingness/control and high on acceptance/responsiveness. Neglectful/uninvolved parenting is low on demandingness/control and low on acceptance/responsiveness.

Longitudinal research has also shown that parents' style of parenting changes across the stages of family life. They may adopt one style when children are young, but then adjust this style as the children age and approach the launching phase.

SIBLING RELATIONSHIPS

Sibling relationships are important to the social development of the child. Children who grow up with siblings have an advantage over their only-children peers when they begin forming friendships. Only-children are less socially accepted compared to their counterparts with siblings. However, an issue in sibling relationships is **sibling rivalry**. Sibling rivalry is the competition that can arise between siblings. This competition tends to rise through childhood as school-age children experience more things on which they can compete, but tends to decrease in adolescence as teenagers spend less time in the home and more time with friends. The best way to describe sibling relationships is as a relationship characterized by ambivalence. Siblings can be very close, benefit from interactions with each other, yet fiercely argue and fight. Older siblings are often caregivers for younger siblings and serve as role models and teachers.

ADOLESCENT-PARENT RELATIONSHIPS

The quality of the adolescent-parent relationship depends on the degree to which parents and adolescents successfully renegotiate this relationship. A major task of adolescence is achieving autonomy, the ability to make decisions independently. In order to accomplish this task, adolescents need to make attempts to be independent even if these attempts sometimes fail. If parents are too restrictive and continue to control their adolescents' lives as much as when they were children, adolescents will not have the opportunity to develop independence. Parents tend to give greater autonomy as the adolescent shows more responsibility. Therefore, adolescents must show responsibility if they expect to be given more freedom to make their own decisions, and parents must expect to give adolescents more freedom to be independent. The authoritative parenting style leads to the best outcomes with adolescents as it did with younger children. Parents who provide rules with consistent consequences for violations, reason with their teenagers, allow their teenagers a voice, and continue to provide warmth and affection have teenagers most likely to become autonomous and well-adjusted.

ADULT-PARENT RELATIONSHIPS

The majority of adult children have continued strong relationships with their aging parents and these relationships become more mutual, comparable to friendships, rather than parent-child relationships. Adult children continue to have significant contact with their aging parents even if they do not live together or in close proximity. As parents age they may rely on middle-aged adult children for their care, a change that has been referred to as role-reversal. The **middle generation sandwich** or squeeze is when adult children are responsible for the care of aging parents as well as their own children. This is a source of significant stress on middle adults and the weight of the responsibility tends to fall more heavily on daughters and daughters-in-law of aging parents. The growth of the assisted care industry in the United States has helped to ease the burden on adult children. Many assisted living facilities are well-designed facilities that provide a high quality of life and a continuous level of care for elderly residents.

GRANDPARENTHOOD

The grandparent role is a source of great satisfaction for middle and older adults. While there are differences in styles of grandparenting and degrees of grandparent involvement, grandchildren, their parents, and the grandparents themselves, all benefit from the grandparenting role in the family.

INFLUENCES OF DIVORCE AND SINGLE-PARENTHOOD

There have been three major trends facing the developing family over the past three decades: an increase in divorce, an increase in single-parent families, and an increase in working mothers. Because every household is different, it is difficult to generalize the effect of divorce or single-parenting on the family. There are general trends, however, that do appear.

Certain factors contribute to the stability of family members involved in divorce or single-parenthood. A parent who is secure and rewarded in the workplace deals better with the situation. A positive network of friends and family provides support, lending a more positive aspect to the situation. When both parents play a role in raising the child, there is a more positive outcome. The quality of the relationship with the non-custodial parent is a key factor that predicts outcomes of divorce. The better the quality of this relationship, the better the children's developmental outcomes. The degree of post-divorce conflict in turn predicts the quality of the relationship with the non-custodial parent.

There are five aspects that affect the development of a child dealing with divorce. They are the levels of stress and amount of support at the time of the divorce; the sex of the child; the age of the child; the amount of time since the change; and the parents' response to the change.

SOCIAL CLASS AND CULTURE

Parents from different social classes tend to adopt different parenting styles and customs, and value different developmental outcomes for their children. Lower- and working-class parents tend to adopt the authoritarian parenting style more than middle- and upper-class parents, because they tend to value obedience. Obedience to authority may be valued because parents assume their own children will be working in blue-collar jobs in which they are required to be compliant. They usually express less affection toward children and perhaps this is due to the greater number of stressors they have in their lives from economic hardships and the poor environments in which they are forced to live. They also are less educated and therefore may lack knowledge about how to parent more effectively.

Culture influences parenting style as well. The pattern of influence of culture is complex. First, there are reliable differences in parenting style across to the two broad types of cultures, collectivistic and individualistic. A collectivistic culture values the greater good, and members who work toward the goals of the group, like the family, versus individual goals are rewarded. Individualistic cultures are the reverse. Members of these cultures value and reward individual achievement and promote competition among individuals. The Hispanic and Japanese cultures are collectivistic, while European-American culture is individualistic. Parents who are Hispanic or Japanese tend to be authoritarian in their style of parenting because those cultures value respect and obedience to authority. European-American parents tend to be authoritative in their orientation because they value the developmental outcomes of independence and autonomy.

The relationship between parenting style and culture is more complex, though. As described earlier, the authoritarian parenting style has been associated with poor outcomes in studies conducted in the United States. However, the developmental outcomes of the authoritarian parenting style depend on how that style is viewed within the culture. In other words, if authoritarian parenting is viewed as an indication that parents love and care about their children, as it is in the Chinese culture, the developmental outcomes are positive.

MEDIA INFLUENCE

In addition to the family, the media, particularly television and computers, have a significant effect on children's development. Research has shown that preschoolers engage in television viewing more than any other activity other than sleeping. Children between the ages of 2 and 11 watch an average of over 22 hours of television per week. This average declines by only two hours or so for those who are 12 to 17 years old. Educational television programs have been found to have a positive effect on children's cognitive development and prosocial behavior. However, as Bandura and his colleagues showed in a classic experiment, children will imitate an aggressive model that they see on television. Children who watch more violent television are more aggressive than their counterparts. Younger children are also frightened by the content of some television shows and do not understand the difference between reality and fiction. Television viewing is also negatively correlated with the amount of family interaction and communication.

Computer technology is both potentially beneficial and harmful. The World Wide Web provides children access to a great deal of appropriate and educational, as well as inappropriate and harmful, information. Computer video games can be very violent and unlike merely observing violence in a television program, violent video games reward children's violent behavior. Players earn points by killing or destroying. Use of the computer, like television viewing, has the capacity to decrease the time family members spend interacting with each other.

CHILD ABUSE AND NEGLECT

Child abuse (physical or emotional) and **child sexual abuse** are found in all cultures and across all socioeconomic classes. Child **neglect** is failure to protect children from harm or failure to meet their biological and medical needs. Studies of child mistreatment have found a link between temperament and abuse. The difficult temperament is the hardest of the three temperaments for caregivers to deal with and perhaps that is why children with this temperament are at greater risk for abuse. Sexual offenders tend to target children who are isolated and needy. Offenders play on these children's vulnerabilities and may gain the trust of children because they are socially isolated and crave attention.

Young infants who are abused or neglected often develop a syndrome called failure to thrive, which is discussed in more detail in Chapter 14, Atypical Development. Victims of child sexual abuse frequently develop post-traumatic stress disorder and engage in sexualized behavior. They may be promiscuous and behave in an overly seductive way. A smaller number develop serious psychological disorders, such as multiple-personality disorder. These disorders are also discussed in Chapter 14.

Parents are most often the abuser. Parents who abuse their children tend to have a history of abuse themselves, have little social support and low self-esteem, and are hypersensitive to their children's bad behavior. Studies have shown that abusers have significantly higher levels of emotional arousal under stressful conditions compared to non-abusers. Intervention programs that focus on social support for these parents tend to be most successful.

DEATH AND DYING

Elisabeth **Kubler-Ross** provided the first psychological model of death and dying. She studied death and dying by conducting in-depth interviews with terminally-ill patients. Her interviews with people who were coming to terms with their own death led her to propose a stage model of death and dying. The first stage in this model is **denial** in which the patient refuses to accept the diagnosis and prognosis of death. A person in this stage may spend a lot of time and money seeking other medical opinions. The next stage is **anger**. When the person has no recourse but to accept the prognosis as true, he or she reacts with anger. They are angry at God, at the medical profession, and even perhaps at significant others. After the anger phase, the person enters the stage of **bargaining**. He or she tries to find ways to delay the inevitable. An example is a person saying "Let me live to see my daughter's wedding." Both anger and bargaining take a toll on the dying patient and, when neither reaction seems to change the person's situation, a period of **depression** ensues. Kubler-Ross reported that terminally-ill patients do finally come to accept their impending death. In the final stage of **acceptance**, they may participate in planning for their own funeral and put their affairs in order. Critics argue that all people do not progress through these stages in the same order or at all, and that all dying patients do not come to accept their death.

Grief (or **bereavement**) is the distressful responding to the death of a loved one. Psychologists argue that grief is a process that proceeds through the same stages as in Kubler-Ross's model of death and dying. Again, researchers caution that the grief process is very individual, may not proceed through these stages, and is greatly affected by the circumstances of the loved one's death. Culture also affects how people deal with death and the dying process. Each culture has death and bereavement rituals, attitudes toward death, and expectations for the behavior of those who are bereaved.

Anticipatory grief is grief that begins before the loved one's death. Family members often begin the grief process when they learn that a loved one has a terminal illness.

Medical advancements now make it possible to extend a person's life through artificial means. Examples of these measures are resuscitation, oxygen ventilation, and feeding tubes. Medical ethics is a field that has emerged to deal with the ethical and moral dilemmas that arose as a result of these end-of-life measures. Family members often have to make decisions about end-of-life treatments because the patient is incapacitated. Many people believe that it is unethical to keep a person alive who has no quality of life and no hope of recovering. **Euthanasia**, actively assisting the death of a terminally-ill person who has a very poor quality of life, is equally controversial. In order to help family members make decisions about end-of-life care, it has become common practice for people to have a **living will**. A living will is a legal document that outlines the individual's wishes with regard to end-of-life care. Often the document dictates that no extreme measures be used if there is no hope for recovery.

A **hospice** is a comprehensive support program for terminally-ill patients and their families. The goal of a hospice is to help the dying person have a pain-free death in a comfortable environment, preferably the home, surrounded by their loved ones.

CHAPTER 11

Personality and Emotions

Chapter 11

Personality and Emotions

Personality is a psychological construct defined as the relatively stable and characteristic set of traits and behaviors of an individual. There is a debate, however, between personality theorists, who believe a person's behavior in any situation is greatly influenced by a stable and internal personality and theorists who believe behavior is more situationally controlled and there really is no such thing as personality. The fundamental attribution error that people regularly make reflects the fact that most people agree with the personality theorists. The fundamental attribution error is the tendency to assume that another person's personality or beliefs cause his or her behavior. We underestimate the power of external factors in controlling behavior and overestimate the power of internal factors. Furthermore, personality theorists disagree on whether personality shows more stability than change throughout the life span.

Two influential theories of personality development are Freud's psychoanalytic theory and Erikson's psychosocial theory. Developmental psychologists suggest that a rudimentary form of personality called **temperament** is found in newborns. Temperamental differences among newborns suggest that personality is, in part, influenced by nature as well as shaped by experience.

Developmental psychologists also study emotional development. An emotion is a conscious experience or feeling that has a stimulus component, a cognitive component, a bodily or physiological component, and a behavioral component. Emotional development includes becoming able to express different emotions, regulating emotional responses, and interpreting the emotions of the self and others.

TEMPERAMENT

Temperament refers to a child's characteristic mood and activity level. Even young infants are temperamentally different from one another. The New York Longitudinal Study (1956), carried out by Stella Chase, Alexander Thomas, and Herbert Birch, is a research project that investigated temperament.

The New York Longitudinal Study followed 140 children from birth to adolescence. Thomas, Chess, and Birch interviewed parents when the infants were between two and three months of age and rated the infants based on activity level, rhythmicity, approach/withdrawal, adaptability, intensity of reaction, and quality of mood. They found that infants could be classified into different groups based on temperament.

Easy Infants (40%)	Adaptable to new situations.
	Predictable in their rhythmicity or schedule.
	Positive in their mood.
Difficult Infants (10%)	Intense in their reactions.
	Not very adaptable to new situations.
	Slightly negative mood.
	Irregular body rhythms.
Slow-to-Warm-Up Infants (15%)	Initially withdraw when approached, but may later "warm up."
	Slow to adapt to new situations.
Average Infants (35%)	Did not fit into any of the above categories.

Thomas, Chess, and Birch found that temperament was fairly stable over time. For instance, they found that 70 percent of the difficult infants developed behavior problems during childhood, while only 18 percent of the easy infants did so. There were, of course, individual differences in whether specific children showed continuity or dramatic changes in their temperament over time.

Although early temperament appears to be highly biologically determined, environment can also influence temperament. Researchers have used the term "goodness of fit" to describe an environment in which an infant's temperament matches the opportunities, expectations, and demands the infant encounters.

FREUD'S PSYCHOANALYTIC THEORY OF PERSONALITY DEVELOPMENT

Freud argued that childhood experiences determine adult personality, unconscious mental processes influence everyday behavior, and conflict causes most human behavior. According to Freud, each adult personality consists of an id, an ego, and a superego.

Freud's Personality Components

Personality component	When it develops	How it functions
Id	Present at birth	Pleasure principle; unconscious instincts; irrational; seeks instant gratification; contains the libido
Ego	Around six months	Reality principle; mediates id and reality; executive branch
Superego	Around six years	Morality principle; personal conscience; personal ideals

According to Freud, the id is unconscious and has no contact with reality. It works according to the pleasure principle—the id always seeks pleasure and avoids pain. The id contains the libido or sexual energy. The ego evolves from the id and deals with the demands of reality. It is called the executive branch of personality because it makes rational decisions. The reality principle describes how the ego tries to bring individual id demands within the norms of society. The ego, however, cannot determine if something is right or wrong. The superego is capable of determining if something is right or wrong because it is our conscience. The superego does not consider reality, only rules about moral behavior.

According to Freud, behavior is the outcome of an ongoing series of conflicts among the id, ego, and superego. Conflicts dealing with sexual and aggressive impulses are likely to have far-reaching consequences because social norms dictate that these impulses be routinely frustrated.

Freud considered personality to be like an iceberg—most of our personality exists below the level of awareness just as most of an iceberg is hidden beneath the surface of the water. Freud referred to the hidden part of our personality as the unconscious. Through a process he called repression, unwanted thoughts are pushed down into the unconscious. Even though Freud felt that many thoughts, memories, and desires were unconscious, they nonetheless influence our behavior.

The conscious part of our personality consists of whatever we are aware of at any particular point in time. The preconscious, according to Freud, contains material that is just below the surface of awareness but can be easily retrieved. An example of preconscious awareness would be your mother's birthdate. You were not thinking of your mother's birthdate but can if you need or want to.

Defense mechanisms are unconscious methods used by the ego to distort reality and thereby protect us from anxiety. Anxiety can result from the irrational pleasure demands of the id or from the superego causing guilty feelings about a real or imagined transgression. The major defense mechanisms are described in Chapter 2, Theories of Development.

Stages of Psychosexual Development

Freud believed that our adult personality is formed through five stages of psychosexual development. In each stage, pleasure that satisfies the id comes from a different erogenous zone or part of the body where the pleasure originates. In each stage there is a **psychosexual crisis** because the ego (and later in development, the superego) must find socially acceptable ways to satisfy the id.

Freud's Psychosexual Stages

Stage	Age	Erogenous zone	Description
Oral	0–1 year	Mouth	Stimulation of mouth produces pleasure; infant enjoys sucking, biting, and chewing. Weaning is major task or conflict.
Anal	1-3 years	Anus	Toilet training is major task. Expelling and retaining feces produces pleasure.
Phallic	3–6 years	Genitals	Self-stimulation of genitals produces pleasure. **Oedipal** (for boys) and **Electra** (for girls) **complexes** occur—children have erotic desires for opposite-sex parent as well as feelings of fear and hostility for same-sex parent. Successful resolution of this conflict results in **identification** with same-sex parent.
Latency	6–12 years	None	Sexual feelings are repressed. Social contacts beyond immediate family are expanded. Focus shifts to school and same-sex friendships.
Genital	Puberty onward	Genitals	Establishing intimate, sexual relations with others is main focus.

According to Freud, children experience conflicts between urges in their erogenous zones and societal rules. **Fixation** can result when these urges are either frustrated or overindulged in any one erogenous zone. Fixation results in one's personality becoming permanently locked in the conflict surrounding that erogenous zone.

Freud felt that the first three psychosexual stages were the most important for personality development. Examples of possible personality traits resulting from fixations in the first three psychosexual stages are presented here.

Freud's Psychosexual Stages

Stage	Examples of traits related to fixation
Oral	Obsessive eating Smoking Drinking Sarcasm Overly demanding Aggressiveness
Anal	Extreme messiness Overly orderly Overly concerned about punctuality Fear of dirt Love of bathroom humor Anxiety about sexual activities Overly giving Rebelliousness
Phallic	Excessive masturbation Flirts frequently Excessively modest Excessively timid Overly proud Promiscuity

ERIKSON'S PSYCHOSOCIAL THEORY OF PERSONALITY DEVELOPMENT

Erik Erikson proposed eight stages of social-emotional/personality development. He is one of the few theorists to discuss development throughout the life span—infancy through old age. Erikson was trained as a psychoanalytic or Freudian theorist. Erikson's theory, however, is very different from Freud's. For instance, Erikson believed that personality continues to develop over the entire life span (not just through childhood). Also, Erikson did not stress unconscious motives or desires. However, like Freud, Erikson did feel that events that occur early in development can leave a permanent mark on one's later social-emotional development.

A description of Erikson's eight stages of psychosocial development follows. Each stage represents a specific task or dilemma called a **psychosocial crisis** that must be resolved with some degree of success for further development.

Childhood

Trust versus Mistrust (Birth-1 year)

Infant's needs must be met by responsive, sensitive caretakers. If this occurs, a basic sense of trust and optimism develops. If not, mistrust and fear of the future results.

Autonomy versus Shame and Doubt (1–3 years)

Children begin to express self-control by climbing, exploring, touching, and toilet training. Parents can foster a sense of autonomy by encouraging children to try new things. If restrained or punished too harshly, shame and doubt can develop.

Initiative versus Guilt (3–6 years)

Children are asked to assume more responsibility. Through play, children learn to plan, undertake, and carry out a task. Parents can encourage initiative by giving children the freedom to play, to use their imagination, etc. Children who are criticized or discouraged from taking the initiative learn to feel guilty.

Industry versus Inferiority (6–11 years)

In elementary school, children learn skills that are valued by society. Success or failure while learning these skills can have lasting effects on a child's feelings of adequacy.

Adolescence

Identity versus Role Confusion

The development of identity involves finding out who we are, what we value, and where we are headed in life. In their search for identity, adolescents experiment with different roles. If we establish an integrated image of ourselves as a unique person, then we establish a sense of identity. If not, role confusion results and can be expressed through anger and resentment.

Young Adulthood

Intimacy versus Isolation

At this time we are concerned with establishing intimate, long-term relationships with others. If we have successfully resolved the identity crisis, then we can be warm and open with others. If we are unsure of our identity or if we have developed an unhealthy identity, then we may avoid others or keep them at an emotional distance.

Adulthood

Generativity versus Stagnation

This stage centers around a concern for the next generation. Successful development shows adults sharing their life-acquired wisdom and caring for the growth of the community. Complacency in this stage leads to stagnation and potentially to depression and loneliness.

Late Adulthood

Ego Integrity versus Despair

If a person looking back on his or her life can believe that it has been meaningful and relatively successful, then a sense of integrity develops. If all that is seen is wasted opportunities and meaninglessness, then the person will be disgusted. Despair will follow disgust if the person feels it is too late to change.

Erikson believed that the way each psychosocial crisis is resolved affects the person's ability to successfully resolve the next crisis. For example, basic trust is necessary for a toddler to explore his or her world to gain a sense of autonomy. A toddler who leaves the second stage with a sense of shame or self-doubt rather than autonomy, will hesitate to plan activities and hence will not develop initiative. Self-identity is necessary before a intimate relationship can be formed, and so on.

SELF-CONCEPT AND SELF-ESTEEM

As children progress through the early stages of personality development they develop a sense that they are a separate being or self. By about age three they have an immature **self-concept** that describes who they are in physical, non-psychological terms. A child may describe himself or herself as being tall and having blond hair. In middle childhood, children's self-concept contains more psychological characteristics and also becomes more realistic as children understand their strengths and weaknesses.

Children's perception of their strengths and weaknesses comes from making **social comparisons** to their peers. Bandura used the term **self-efficacy** for children's perception of their ability to succeed at a task. Children with low self-efficacy may be very competent but do not believe they are competent.

During the initiative versus guilt and industry versus inferiority stages of psychosocial development, children need opportunities to take on tasks for which they have a high probability of success. Self-efficacy comes from experiencing success and perceiving one's successes as comparable to peers. Bandura suggested parents and teachers can help by persuading children to try new tasks and telling them they can succeed. He also suggested that a child who is very emotionally aroused before a task (excited or nervous) can either have the arousal cause him or her to perform better or worse. An optimal level of arousal might be the most advantageous.

Self-esteem is the perception of one's worth. Children's self-esteem judgments are influenced by self-concept and self-efficacy. These are all closely related constructs. Self-esteem is affected by the quality of children's attachment relationships with caregivers, their social competence, school achievement, and how they are viewed by society. Children from minority groups who suffer social prejudice may have lower self-esteem. Parents can prevent this affect of prejudice by helping children develop a strong ethnic identity and pride in their ethnic group.

Cross-cultural research on self-esteem has shown significant differences in levels of self-esteem in children from different cultures. Chinese and Japanese children have been shown to have lower self-esteem than American children. The difference in how these cultures value collectivism versus individualism may explain the differences.

ADOLESCENT IDENTITY FORMATION

The major task of adolescence is forming an adult identity. This period of life has been described as one of storm and stress. Cross-cultural research on the adolescent stage of development has shown variations in the length of adolescence as well as the experiences of adolescents. There is some evidence that the biological changes associated with adolescence produce some universals of experiences and stress. However, in some cultures, adolescence is nonexistent or only a brief phase. Some cultures have a ceremonial rite of passage into adulthood so that a child becomes an adult in the same day, whereas in others, the stage is long and stressful. In Western cultures the formation of an adult identity is typically lengthy and stressful. Adolescence is viewed as a **moratorium period**, a period of time given to adolescents to explore different identities and prepare for adulthood. Adolescents are not still children, but also not yet adults, during this moratorium.

Marcia has studied adolescents' identity formation. Based on that research, Marcia developed a model that classifies adolescents into four identity status groups based on whether or not they have experienced an identity crisis and whether or not they have made an identity commitment. Marcia, as well as Erikson, argues that a healthy identity is formed only after the adolescent has explored many different options. An adolescent becomes an adult when he or she has made a commitment to an adult identity. Choosing the wrong identity will lead to an identity crisis later on in adulthood.

The four statuses are 1) **identity moratorium** (identity crisis and no commitment), 2) **identity diffusion** (no identity crisis and no commitment), 3) **identity foreclosure** (no identity crisis and a commitment), and 4) **identity achievement** (identity crisis and a commitment).

Longitudinal research on self-concept and self-esteem shows different patterns. Some report a dip in self-esteem from age 12, others show stability in self-esteem from grade five through adolescence. It may be the case that self-esteem, once formed, has a tendency to be stable but can be affected by positive or negative experiences. Getting involved in drug use is an example of such a negative influence. Male adolescents tend to have higher levels of self-esteem compared to females. This may be due to the fact that males have better body images than females.

ADULT PERSONALITY

Developmental psychologists suggest that adults' lifestyle and satisfaction are influenced by their adult personality style. In the past, theories of adult development disagreed about what lifestyle was associated with the best adjustment and satisfaction in adulthood. **Activity theory** suggested that adults who remained active and connected with other people were more satisfied. **Disengagement theory** suggested that satisfied older adults followed a natural tendency to become less engaged in society and to focus inward. The latter theory flowed from Erikson's description of the crisis of old age, integrity versus despair. In fact, research shows that there are four adult personality styles that determine preferred lifestyle. The integrated type is an adult who has chosen to be very active and is satisfied, has chosen to engage in a few activities and is satisfied, or has disengaged voluntarily and is satisfied. The armored-defended type is an older adult who remains active in the hope of maintaining abilities and is satisfied, or disengages after experiencing losses and is satisfied. The passive-dependent type is an older adult who is very emotionally needy and satisfied if he or she has others to lean on, or disengaged, rocking chair adults who have low satisfaction. The unintegrated/disorganized type is an adult who has lost or never had normal psychological functioning.

EMOTIONAL DEVELOPMENT

Theories of Emotions

Robert Plutchik proposed that emotions evolved because they help a species to survive. He felt that emotions are inherited behavioral patterns and are modified by experience. Emotions have four components: external stimuli that are interpreted by the person, feelings, physiological arousal, and behavioral responses.

Various theories have attempted to explain the experience of emotions. William James and Carl Lange proposed that people experience physiological changes and interpret these changes as emotions. In other words, emotions follow behavior and not vice versa. For instance, you feel afraid after you begin to perspire. (You do not perspire because you are afraid.) Walter Cannon and a colleague, P. Bard, felt that the physiological changes in many emotional states were identical. Because of this, people cannot determine their emotional state only from their physiological state. The Cannon-Bard Theory argues that emotion occurs when the thalamus sends signals simultaneously to the cortex and to the autonomic nervous system.

Stanley Schachter's view of emotion is a cognitive approach. It is referred to as the Schachter-Singer Theory. This theory proposes that emotion occurs when physiological arousal causes us to search for reasons for this arousal. We examine the environment for an explanation for this arousal. Emotions are determined, therefore, by labeling our arousal based on what is occurring in our environment.

Ekman and his colleagues studied people's ability to judge emotions based on facial expressions in photographs of adults. They found that there are six facial expressions corresponding to six basic emotions that people can recognize and that this interpretation of facial expressions is universal. The six different universal facial expressions include happiness, anger, disgust, sadness, fear, and surprise. Adults are somewhat successful at recognizing emotional expressions in photographs of infants as well.

Based on studying infant facial expressions, some psychologists argue that infants are born with the emotions of interest, distress, and disgust. Joy develops between four and six weeks; anger, surprise, sadness, fear, and shame between three and eight months; and contempt and guilt in the second year. Critics argue that infants may experience all of these emotions before they can express them.

Psychologists do agree that there is a biological component to emotion, but that emotions are also affected by experience. Learning theory suggests that emotional responses are learned through classical and operant conditioning. An example is when a child develops a fear of dogs. Children do not evidence an innate fear of dogs but many children become afraid of them. Classical conditioning theory would explain the fear of dogs as a conditioned response. If a child sees a dog and at the same time experiences an unconditioned fear stimulus like a loud bark, the dog (CS) becomes associated with the loud noise (UCS). Observational learning also produces fears in children who observe their own parents' fear responses.

The goal of emotional development is to have a balance between emotional expression and emotional control. Emotional control is associated with social competence and prosocial behavior. Children need help in learning how to control their emotions. Parents who reward temper tantrums are not helping children gain control. Parents who do not allow children to express any emotion are also not helping their children's emotional development. Children develop more emotional control as they engage in more activities with peers. In fact, children control their emotions most when with peers, less when they are with family, and the least when they are alone.

Empathy is the ability to understand what another person is feeling. Empathy often motivates prosocial behavior and is a key factor in moral reasoning. Between one and two years of age, infants show signs of empathy. A two-year-old might bring his or her own teddy bear to a friend who is crying.

Daniel Goleman has recently proposed a psychological construct called emotional intelligence (EQ). He argues that children as well as adults vary in intellectual capacity to interpret their own and other people's emotions. Competence in correctly identifying one's own or another person's emotional state leads to a better understanding of motivation. People with high E.Q.'s are more socially competent and successful. Goleman made the controversial prediction that E.Q. better predicts success in life than I.Q.

ATTRIBUTION STYLES AND ACHIEVEMENT MOTIVATION

Attribution style is the term for the characteristic way an individual interprets the causes of his or her behaviors, successes, and failures and the behaviors, successes, and failures of other people. People tend to take credit for successes and good behavior, and blame others or situational variables for mistakes and failures. However, we don't extend that consideration to others. When people make mistakes, we hold them totally responsible and discount any situational variables that may have influenced them.

Weiner proposed an attribution theory of motivation which related attribution style to achievement motivation. He distinguished four causes to which people attribute success and failure: effort, ability, task difficulty, and luck. A person who consistently attributes success and failure to effort and ability has an **internal locus of control**. People who consistently attribute success and failure to luck and task difficulty have an external locus of control. Children with an internal locus of control have higher academic achievement than those with an **external locus of control**. What is particularly problematic is when a child has a very stable external locus of control. This child has developed the perception that no matter what he or she does on any task, he or she is helpless to control the outcome. Studying for a test and working harder in school are perceived as being useless. Equally problematic is if a child has a stable internal locus of control but perceives himself or herself as lacking ability.

Achievement motivation is also influenced by child-rearing practices and values in the home. Parents may be more likely to have children with a high achievement motivation if they give their children responsibilities, stress independence, and praise them for genuine accomplishments. Children's achievement motivation is positively affected by experiences with feeling mastery. Children with a mastery orientation thrive on challenges and tend to stick with difficult tasks. They have feelings of pride and competence. The opposite orientation is the **learned helplessness** orientation.

Children of parents who set very high standards for their achievement, but also communicate to them that they are not capable of achieving those standards, show signs of learned helplessness. Learned helplessness is a syndrome first observed by Seligman. Seligman placed animals in an experimental chamber from which they could not escape. Animals who received electric shocks through the floor of the chamber first tried to escape but they eventually stopped trying. Even when an escape route became available to them, they could not learn to escape. Parents who communicate high standards but little confidence in the children's abilities produce children who do not try to succeed and avoid challenges.

CHAPTER 12
Learning

Chapter 12

Learning

Learning is defined as a relatively permanent change in behavior as a result of experience, practice, or both. Learning theorists have described several different learning mechanisms including **habituation**, **classical conditioning**, **operant conditioning**, and **observational learning**.

HABITUATION

Habituation is the most rudimentary form of learning. This form of learning is observed when an organism's response to a continuous stimulus decreases over time. If a person is employed in a factory in which a loud noise sounds at regular five-minute intervals, that person will initially respond with a startle response of a certain magnitude but then, over continued exposure, his or her response will diminish.

CLASSICAL CONDITIONING

Classical conditioning always involves a reflexive or respondent behavior. This means that classical conditioning produces an automatic response to a stimulus. Classical or respondent conditioning occurs when a neutral stimulus that does not trigger a reflexive behavior is conditioned so that it will elicit an automatic response. Conditioning occurs because the neutral stimulus has been associated with a stimulus that automatically triggers a response.

It appears that both humans and animals may be biologically prepared to learn some associations more readily than others. The associations that are more readily learned may be ones that increase chances for survival.

Ivan Pavlov (1849–1936), a Russian physiologist, classically conditioned dogs using the salivary reflex. Dogs normally respond to food by salivating. They do not have to be conditioned to salivate to food. Dogs do not, however, automatically salivate to the sound of a bell ringing. This is what Pavlov conditioned them to do. He would ring the bell, present the food, and the dogs would salivate. He repeated this procedure until the bell alone would cause the dogs to salivate. They had learned to associate the sound of the bell with the presentation of food.

The terms used to describe classical conditioning include:

Unconditioned Stimulus (UCS)—The stimulus that automatically produces a reflex. (In Pavlov's study, this was the food.)

Unconditioned Response (UCR)—An automatic response to the UCS; a natural response that does not require conditioning for it to occur. (In Pavlov's study, this was salivation to the food.)

Conditioned Stimulus (CS)—A neutral stimulus that does not normally elicit an automatic response; only after pairing it repeatedly with the UCS does the CS come to elicit a conditioned response. (In Pavlov's study, this was the bell.)

Conditioned Response (CR)—The learned response that occurs when the CS is presented alone, without the UCS. (In Pavlov's study, the CR was salivation that occurred to the bell alone; no food was present.)

The standard classical conditioning paradigm is:

	UCS (food)	$\rightarrow$	**UCR** (salivation)
CS + (bell)	**UCS** (food)	$\rightarrow$	**UCR** (salivation)
	CS alone (bell alone)	$\rightarrow$	**CR** (salivation)

Step 2 is repeated until the CS alone will prompt the CR.

After classical conditioning has taken place, the conditioned stimulus (CS) must be paired with, or reinforced by, the unconditioned stimulus (UCS) at least some of the time or else the conditioned response (CR) will disappear. The process of eliminating the conditioned response (CR) by no longer pairing the unconditioned stimulus (UCS) with the conditioned stimulus (CS) is called extinction. Extinction will take place, therefore, if the conditioned stimulus (CS) is presented repeatedly without the unconditioned stimulus (UCS). Extinction is a method that is used intentionally to eliminate conditioned responses (CR).

Stimulus **generalization** occurs when a conditioned response (CR) occurs to a stimulus that only resembles or is similar to the conditioned stimulus (CS) but is not identical to it. For instance, Pavlov's dogs were classically conditioned to salivate to a bell (the CS), but if the first time they heard a buzzer they also salivated, this would be stimulus generalization. They were never conditioned with the buzzer, but they responded because the sound resembled that of the bell.

Stimulus **discrimination** occurs when the differences between stimuli are noticed and, thus, the stimuli are not responded to in similar ways. For instance, stimulus discrimination would occur if Pavlov's dogs did not salivate to the sound of the buzzer, even if it sounded similar to the bell. This would indicate that the dogs could discriminate these two sounds and, as a result, respond differently to each.

Researchers have used humans as well as animals in classical conditioning studies. In humans, emotional reactions occur sometimes as a result of classical conditioning because emotions are involuntary, automatic responses. For instance, phobias (intense, irrational fears) may develop as a result of classical conditioning.

The most famous classical conditioning study using a human subject was one conducted by American researcher John Watson (1878–1958). Although this study is considered unethical today and some have suggested that it is more myth or legend than fact, most textbooks mention the Little Albert study when discussing classical conditioning. Little Albert was an 11-month-old infant who initially was not afraid of laboratory white rats. Watson classically conditioned Albert to fear these rats by pairing the presentation of the rat with a loud noise that scared the infant. The diagram of this study would be:

Noise → **Fear response**
(UCS)   (UCR)

Rat + **Noise** → **Fear response**
(CS)   (UCS)   (UCR)

eventually,

Rat alone → **Fear response**
(CS)   (UCR)

Higher-order conditioning occurs when a new neutral stimulus is associated with a conditioned stimulus (CS) and eventually comes to produce the conditioned response (CR). If after Albert was classically conditioned, a dog was always paired with the rat, eventually Albert would display the fear response to the dog. A diagram of this higher-order conditioning example would be:

Rat alone → **Fear**
(CS)   (CR)

Dog + **Rat** → **Fear**
(new stimulus) (CS)   (CR)

eventually,

Dog alone → **Fear**
(CS)   (CR)

OPERANT AND INSTRUMENTAL CONDITIONING

In operant or instrumental conditioning, responses are learned because of their consequences. Unlike classical conditioning, the responses learned in operant/instrumental conditioning are voluntary.

Reinforcers are consequences for behavior and can be anything that increases the likelihood that a behavior will be repeated. Reinforcers can be positive or negative. Both positive and negative reinforcers have the potential to increase behaviors. Positive reinforcers are rewards or other positive consequences that follow behaviors and increase the likelihood that the behaviors will occur again in the future. Giving your dog a biscuit each time he sits on command is an example of **positive reinforcement**.

Negative reinforcers are anything a subject will work to avoid or terminate. Nagging behaviors are examples of **negative reinforcement** because we often will do something (anything!) to stop the nagging. For instance, a parent who buys a child a candy bar to stop a child's nagging in the grocery store is responding to negative reinforcement. Escape conditioning occurs when a subject learns that a particular response will terminate an aversive stimulus. The parent who buys a nagging child candy has escaped the nagging by purchasing candy.

Reinforcers can also be primary or secondary. Primary reinforcers are necessary to meet biological needs and include such things as food, water, air, etc. Secondary reinforcers have acquired value and are not necessary for survival. Grades, money, a pat on the back, etc., are examples of secondary reinforcers.

Extinction occurs in operant conditioning by removing the reinforcer. For example, the dog stops receiving dog biscuits for sitting or the child gets no candy for nagging. Once these reinforcers are removed, both sitting and nagging should decrease and/or be eliminated. Spontaneous recovery can also occur in operant conditioning.

How easily an operant response is extinguished is dependent, in part, on how often that response was reinforced, or its schedule of reinforcement. A continuous schedule of reinforcement happens when each and every response is reinforced (100 percent of the time). Each time your dog sits on command, he receives a biscuit. Behaviors that are continuously reinforced are easier to extinguish than behaviors that are not reinforced 100 percent of the time.

Behaviors that are not reinforced each time they occur are on an intermittent, or partial, schedule of reinforcement. There are four possible partial schedules of reinforcement:

Fixed ratio schedule: Reinforcement is given after a fixed number of responses (e.g., every third time your dog sits, he receives a biscuit). Being paid on a piece-rate basis is an example of a fixed ratio schedule. The fixed ratio schedule produces a high rate of responding with a slight pause after each reinforcement is given. Fixed ratio schedules produce the fastest rate of extinction because the subject realizes quickly that reinforcement has stopped.

Variable ratio schedule: Reinforcement is given after a variable number of responses. Thus, on one occasion, reinforcement may occur after 10 responses and on another occasion after 50, etc. The rate of reinforcement depends upon the rate of responding: the faster, the more reinforcers received. This schedule produces steady, high rates of responding and is extremely resistant to extinction. Slot machines are based on variable ratio schedules.

Fixed interval schedule: Reinforcement is given after the first response after a given amount of time has elapsed. This may mean a reinforcer every five minutes, for example. Being paid once per month is another example. Fixed interval schedules produce a low rate of responding at the beginning of each interval and a high rate toward the end of each interval.

Variable interval schedule: Reinforcement is given after the first response after a varying amount of time has elapsed. Pop quizzes often occur on a variable interval schedule. The variable interval schedule produces a steady, slow rate of responding.

In general, the ratio schedules produce higher response rates than the interval schedules. Variable schedules are usually harder to extinguish than are fixed schedules because variable schedules are less predictable.

American behaviorist B. F. Skinner (1904–90) devised a chamber, known as a **Skinner box,** to study the effects of various schedules of reinforcement on the behavior of small animals such as rats and pigeons. During acquisition, or learning, each time a lever in the Skinner box was pressed, a food pellet was dispensed into a food dish. A speaker or light signal was also used to indicate conditions of reinforcement or extinction. In some studies, the grid floor was electrified, and the electric current could be turned off by pressing the lever. The speaker or lights signaled when the current would be turned on and, in avoidance trials, the animal had a certain amount of time to press the lever to avoid the shock.

Shaping involves systematically reinforcing closer and closer approximations of the desired behavior. When a rat is first placed in the Skinner box, it doesn't know that pressing the lever will result in a food reward and may never press the lever on its own. Lever pressing can be conditioned through shaping—each step closer to the lever results in a food reward.

Discriminative stimuli serve as cues that indicate a response is likely to be reinforced. The light in the Skinner box can be a discriminative stimulus.

When the light is on, lever pressing results in a food reward. When it is off, lever pressing is not reinforced. The animal will eventually learn to discriminate and to press the lever only when the light is on.

Punishment is also an operant conditioning technique. The goal of punishment is to decrease behavior. Punishment involves the presentation of an aversive stimulus, or undesirable consequence, after a behavior has occurred. Something negative can be added or something positive can be taken away. Receiving a ticket for speeding and being placed on house restriction are two examples of punishment.

Timing is very important for punishment to be effective—the sooner the punishment is delivered after the undesired behavior occurred, the better the learning. Even very short delays can reduce the effectiveness of punishment. Punishment must also be severe enough to eliminate the undesirable response.

Punishment may have undesirable side effects. Punishment often provides a model of aggressive behavior, and the person punished may learn that aggression is a method for solving problems. Punishment alone does not teach appropriate behavior. The person providing the punishment can become a feared agent to be avoided. Punishment can get out of hand and become abusive. Many behaviorists today suggest that punishment be avoided as a method used for conditioning. Instead, they recommend the use of extinction to weaken an inappropriate response and reinforcement to increase appropriate behaviors.

OBSERVATIONAL LEARNING

Observational learning or social learning theory occurs when we learn new behaviors by watching others. This is sometimes called social learning or **modeling**.

Observational learning is guided by four processes.

Attention—Attention must be paid to the salient features of another's actions. Prestige or status of a model can influence whether another's actions are noticed.

Retention—Observed behaviors must be remembered in order to be carried out.

Reproduction of Action—We must be able to carry out the behavior that we observed.

Motivation—There must be some reason for carrying out the behavior. Observing someone being rewarded for a behavior increases the likelihood that the behavior will be performed.

Vicarious learning occurs when we learn the relationship between a response and its consequences by watching others. Vicarious reinforcement occurs when we observe the model receiving reinforcement. Vicarious punishment happens when we observe the model being punished for engaging in a behavior.

The classic research on observational learning was conducted by Albert Bandura and his colleagues. This research included children watching and imitating an adult's aggressive behavior toward a Bobo doll. Bandura found that children learned the aggressive behavior even when the adult was not reinforced for this behavior. Later research indicated that children who watched an aggressive model being reinforced were much more aggressive in a similar situation than children who saw the model punished for the aggressive actions. Through his research, Bandura has demonstrated that both classical and operant conditioning can take place through observational learning—by observing another's conditioning.

LEARNING AND DEVELOPMENT

The mechanisms of learning described above are viewed as remaining the same throughout development. Learning, therefore, is believed to be a continuous versus discontinuous developmental process. Very young infants show habituation and can be conditioned with either classical or operant conditioning techniques. Observational learning, however, does not emerge until later. This is because of the greater cognitive demands for attention, memory, and deferred imitation of observational learning.

CHAPTER 13

Schooling, Work, and Interventions

Chapter 13

Schooling, Work, and Interventions

DAY CARE

Even though more children than ever before are attending day care, there have been relatively few well-controlled studies that have looked at the effects of day care on development. Summarized below are the most consistent findings to date.

Children who attend day care usually score higher than children who do not attend day care on tests of intelligence. Non-day care children, however, usually catch up once they enter kindergarten and elementary school.

Children in day care tend to be more socially skilled—more cooperative, more confident, and better able to take the perspective of another. Day care children also tend to be more aggressive and noncompliant (less likely to carry out an adult's request). Some have suggested this is because day care children have learned to think for themselves, not a symptom of maladjustment. There is a slight tendency for day care children to be classified as insecurely attached (36 percent versus 29 percent for home care children). Although statistically significant, some have questioned the practical significance of a 7 percent difference.

PRESCHOOL

Preschools that overemphasize academics do not always have the expected results. Children from these programs may experience a temporary advantage in achievement when they start kindergarten but they do not maintain these gains over children who did not attend preschool. They actually have lower **achievement motivation** and are more negative about school. The best preschool programs balance play and academics. In particular, preschool programs are beneficial to children from impoverished backgrounds.

APPLICATION OF COGNITIVE DEVELOPMENTAL PRINCIPLES WITHIN THE SCHOOL

It is one thing for teachers to have command of their subject matter. It is a given that English teachers will be able to write well, that math teachers will be able to compute and calculate, that science teachers will know and understand science, and so forth. However, it is something else—and something at least as important—that teachers know how to teach.

When teachers understand learners, that is, when teachers understand developmental processes common to all learners and how environmental features and learning styles—varied and diverse—affect learning, then teachers are better able to design and deliver effective instruction. Although there may be some intuitive aspects to teaching (and it seems that some people were born to teach), teaching skills can be acquired through processes of introspection, observation, direct instruction, self-evaluation, and experimentation.

How teachers teach should be directly related to how learners learn. Theories of cognitive development describe how learners learn new information and acquire new skills. There are many theories of cognitive development, two of which will be included in this review: the Piagetian theory and the information processing theory.

Piagetian theory describes cognitive development in discrete and predictable stages. Piaget believed that cognitive development could not be speeded up, but subsequent research showed that given familiar materials to interact with, children can reason at higher levels. It is important for teachers to understand the differences in how different-aged children think. A teacher who is working with children in the concrete operations stage should provide concrete objects for the children to manipulate. They are very capable of logical reasoning with concrete tasks and concrete objects but not abstract concepts.

Therefore, teachers who understand this theory can provide students with developmentally appropriate instruction. This theory also describes learners moving from simpler ways of thinking to more complex ways of problem solving and thinking. For teachers, there are many important implications of this theoretical perspective. For example, teachers must create enriched environments that present learners with multiple opportunities to encounter new and unfamiliar stimuli—be they objects or ideas.

Teachers must also provide learners with opportunities to engage in extended dialogue with adults; according to Vygotsky's theory, conversational interactions with adults are a key component in cognitive development. Teachers encourage children's cognitive development when they reveal their own complex ways of thinking and solving problems to students. Vygotsky also would predict more effective learning takes place when tasks are presented in a natural context.

On the other hand, information-processing theories of human development take a different approach to describing and understanding how learners learn. Based on a computer metaphor and borrowing computer imagery to describe how people learn, information-processing theories begin by determining the processing demands of a particular cognitive challenge (or problem to solve). This necessitates a detailed task-analysis of how the human mind changes external objects or events into a useful form according to certain, precisely specified rules or strategies; this is similar to the way a computer programmer programs a computer to perform a function. Thus, information processing theories focus on the process, how the learner arrives at a response or answer.

A brief analysis of one information-processing theory will serve to illustrate this point. Sternberg's (1985) triarchic theory of intelligence is a theory taking into account three features of learning. Those three features are (1) the mechanics or components of intelligence (including both higher-ordered thinking processes, such as planning, decision making and problem solving, and lower-ordered processes, such as making inferences, mapping, selectively encoding information, retaining information in memory, transferring new information in memory, and so forth); (2) the learner's experiences; and (3) the learner's context (including the adaptation to and the shaping and selecting of environments).

According to Sternberg, learners' use of the mechanics of intelligence is influenced by learners' experiences. To illustrate, some cognitive processes (such as those required in reading) become automatized as a result of continued exposure to and practice of those skills. Learners who come from homes in which parents read and where there are lots of different reading materials tend to be more proficient readers; certainly, learners who read a lot become more proficient readers. Those learners who are exposed to reading activities and who have ample opportunities to practice reading have greater skill and expertise in reading. In a cyclical manner, students who have skills in reading like to read. Conversely, those who lack reading skills don't like to read. Students who don't like to read, don't read; thus, their reading skills, lacking practice, fail to improve.

An information-processing approach acknowledges that not only are individuals influenced by their environments which they then adapt to, but individuals also are active in shaping their own environments. In other words, a child who wants to read but who has no books at home may ask parents to buy books, may go to the library to read, or may check out books to read at home.

Information-processing theory is of interest to educators because of its insistence on the idea that intelligent performance can be facilitated through instruction and direct training. In sum, intelligent thinking can be taught. Sternberg has urged teachers to identify the mental processes that academic tasks require and to teach learners those processes. He challenges teachers to teach learners what processes to use, when and how to use them, and how to combine them into strategies for solving problems and accomplishing assignments.

Teachers who wish to follow Sternberg's advice might choose to begin teaching by identifying instructional objectives, that is, what students should be able to do as a result of instruction. Second, these teachers would analyze the objectives in terms of identifying the instructional outcomes, the tasks or assignments that students can perform as a result of achieving the instructional objectives. Third, teachers would analyze instructional outcomes in terms of the cognitive skills, or mental processes, required to perform those tasks or assignments. After following these three steps and identifying instructional objectives, instructional outcomes, and cognitive skills involved, the teachers would be ready to conduct a preassessment (or pretest) to determine what students already know.

Instruction is then based on the results of the preassessment, with teachers focusing on teaching directly the cognitive skills needed in order for students to perform the task(s). Following instruction, teachers would conduct a post-assessment (or post-test) to evaluate the results of instruction. Further instruction would be based on the results of the post-assessment, that is, whether or not students had achieved expected outcomes and whether or not teachers had achieved instructional objectives.

Regardless of which theoretical perspective is adopted by teachers, and teachers may sometimes find themselves taking a rather eclectic approach and borrow elements from several theoretical bases, it is helpful for teachers to consider if they are structuring their classrooms to satisfy learners' needs or merely their own needs as teachers. Furthermore, if the teacher's goal is to increase teaching effectiveness by facilitating learners' knowledge and skill acquisition, then teachers will engage continuously in a process of self-examination and self-evaluation.

TEACHING READING

There has been a long-standing debate whether the whole language or **phonics approach** is the best way to teach reading. The **whole language approach** to reading instruction teaches reading by having children interact with written passages or whole books, compared to the phonics approach which emphasizes teaching children the associations between letters and sounds. Research suggests that the phonics approach is the better approach, although children must eventually be able to read for meaning. Research on the phonics method has also led to the development of phonics-based intervention programs for dyslexic children.

LEARNING STYLES

Psychologists have observed that people have different, preferred ways of processing new information. If new information is indeed processed through these preferred channels, learning is more successful. The three **learning styles** that have been identified are visual, auditory, and kinesthetic. Teachers are encouraged to assess students' learning styles and then develop instructional strategies to match their styles. However, it is often difficult to tailor instruction to each student's learning style in a classroom with 20 students. An alternative approach is for teachers to present material in different ways to accommodate all three learning styles.

APPLICATION OF LEARNING THEORY WITHIN THE SCHOOL

Skinner's operant conditioning theory has many applications to applied settings like the classroom. An intervention strategy called behavior modification was derived from Skinner's theory. Behavior modification is the use of reinforcement to shape behavior. Effective classroom management strategies flow from this approach. Teachers are more effective at controlling classroom behavior if they consistently reinforce students for good behavior and ignore bad behavior. Disruptive classroom behavior tends to be reinforced by the attention it brings to the disruptive student. A strategy for dealing with disruptive behavior without unintentionally reinforcing it is called **time out**. Time out involves removing the student from the setting for a specific period of time. Punishing or being verbally abusive toward a disruptive student is not effective in changing the behavior and creates a negative classroom atmosphere.

ACHIEVEMENT MOTIVATION

Like parents, teachers play a role in children's achievement motivation. Two achievement orientations have emerged from research in child development. These are the **mastery orientation** and the **learned helplessness orientation**. The mastery orientation is attributing successes to one's own ability and effort. Children with this orientation seek rather than avoid challenges. A learned helplessness orientation causes a child to avoid challenges because of the perception that no matter what, they will never succeed. Children need to have experiences with success and the associated feeling of mastery to develop a mastery orientation. Teachers can help provide such opportunities for children and communicate their confidence in the child's competence and ability to succeed. Teachers can also help children correctly interpret the results of their attempts so that the child believes he or she had control over and was responsible for a success.

INTERVENTION PROGRAMS AND SERVICES

Childhood intervention programs were originally developed by United States government and private educational agencies acting on the supposition that intelligence is strongly influenced by environment, and therefore poor and culturally deprived people are at a great disadvantage academically. The best known of these intervention programs is **Project Head Start**. In accordance with the theory of environmental influence, underprivileged children ready to enter first grade—about five years old—were given experience with toys, books, and games with which most middle-class children are familiar. It began as a summer program and lasted eight weeks.

Project Head Start was not completely successful. The children made immediate gains in I.Q., but these gains were unstable: the children's I.Q.s returned to the pre-intervention level as soon as the program ended. Opponents of Head Start, who believe that intelligence is determined genetically, used this information to support racist claims that blacks had less innate intellectual ability than did whites.

Owing to its poor organization, however, Head Start was destined to fail from its inception. It simply was not designed to play an important enough role in the lives of the children. Mainly, the children's experience in the program was isolated from their family environments. The enrichment did not extend to the rest of the family, the unit that has the most significant influence on a child. In addition, an eight-week intervention program cannot compensate for the cultural deprivation a five-year-old minority child has experienced. Intervention programs must begin earlier, last longer, and make more complete changes in a child's life.

The new philosophy of Head Start intervention is to involve the mothers of the children in the programs: mothers are taught how to be effective teachers. This kind of intervention has been extremely successful. Children's I.Q. scores rise, thus lessening the disparity in group I.Q.s. Moreover, there is a secondary benefit to this kind of intervention. When a mother is involved as the teacher, her self-esteem is raised, her cooperation increases, she becomes closer to her child, and she can spread her learning to other mothers in the area.

TRAINING IN PARENTING SKILLS

Studies show that behaviors, positive and negative, are passed down through generations. Often subconsciously, a parent reacts to a situation in the manner in which he or she saw his or her parent respond. This is particularly threatening in the case of abusive or neglectful behavior.

Today, it is commonly believed that the best way to end a cycle of poor parenting is through parental retraining. Parents are taught through discussion and role play how to deal successfully with stressful situations arising in the family. These situations vary from dealing with a crying baby to dealing with a rebellious teenager using inappropriate language. Because their initial response was learned vicariously through watching their parents, the adults need to be retrained in the more appropriate methods of parenting. Parenting classes have proven effective for both male and female parents.

CAREER DEVELOPMENT AND RETIREMENT

One aspect of the identity formed in adolescence is a career identity. It is often difficult and stressful for an adolescent/young adult to decide on a career. Ginzberg suggested that career choice develops over a three stage process. The first phase is the fantasy phase in which young children talk of career goals like becoming a fire fighter or a doctor. During adolescence, teenagers consider careers but start to calculate in their perceived abilities and traits as well as the likelihood of getting a job in that career. This is the tentative phase. Adolescents can explore the match between their personalities and abilities and different careers using the model developed by John Holland. Holland conducted research on the relationship between personality traits and characteristics of different occupations. Based on this research, he developed a system to match personality types with occupational types.

The final phase in Ginzberg's theory is the realistic phase. Between the ages of 18 and 22, adolescents/young adults select the career or a few career options that they further pursue. Many men and women are still changing careers and making decisions about their careers in their mid-30s.

Career counselors understand career development as a life-long process. Research shows that most people will change jobs numerous times and/or pursue different careers in adulthood. They emphasize the need for extensive career exploration in adolescence and young adulthood and encourage individuals to intentionally plan the entire course of their careers.

Retirement, the final phase in career development, also should be a planned process. Research suggests that people who are highly satisfied with their retirement years have opportunities to engage in meaningful activities. Planning for retirement economically can increase the likelihood that a retired person will be satisfied during this phase of life.

CHAPTER 14
Atypical Development

Chapter 14

Atypical Development

GENETIC DISORDERS

There are several genetic diseases that are passed to offspring in the genes they inherit from biological parents. These include **Huntington's disease, phenylketonuria (PKU), sickle cell anemia, cystic fibrosis**, and **Tay-Sachs disease**. Huntington's disease is genetically transmitted via a dominant gene on chromosome four. This gene causes nervous system deterioration and is fatal. Since it is a dominant gene trait, a child who inherits the gene will definitely have the disease. PKU is caused by a pair of recessive genes which cause a child to be unable to metabolize phenylalanine. This disease is typically managed with a diet free of phenylalanine, but without this controlled diet, a build up of phenylalanine in the system will cause intellectual disability and hyperactivity. Sickle cell anemia is also caused by two recessive genes. People with this disease have abnormally shaped red blood cells that carry less oxygen than normal through the circulatory system. People with this disease have trouble breathing when they exert themselves and often die of kidney failure by adolescence. There are more carriers of sickle cell among the African-American population than the general population. Cystic fibrosis is also caused by a pair of recessive genes and is a disease that causes a build up of mucous in the lungs and is eventually fatal. Like Huntington's disease, Tay-Sachs disease causes nervous system degeneration and is fatal. Unlike Huntington's, Tay-Sachs is carried by a pair of recessive genes.

Genetic disorders are also caused by chromosomal abnormalities in the fetus. Examples include **Down's syndrome, Klinefelter syndrome**, and **Turner syndrome**. Down's syndrome, which causes intellectual disability, distinctive facial features, and stubby limbs, is due to inheriting an extra chromosome at the 21st level. Klinefelter and Turner syndromes are sex chromosomal abnormalities which produce males and females who are sterile and who do not develop normal secondary sex characteristics. Klinefelter syndrome occurs in males who have inherited an additional X sex chromosome (XXY) and Turner syndrome occurs in females who have inherited only one X (XO).

DRUGS, DISEASES, BIRTH COMPLICATIONS, AND AT-RISK NEWBORNS

Teratogens, like drugs and diseases that are part of the prenatal environment, can cause fetal death, fetal defects, or problems like low birth weight (**small-for-date babies**) that place newborns at risk. Drugs taken by pregnant women pass through to the fetal bloodstream and can cause the fetus to have birth defects or to be born addicted to the drug. These drugs include nicotine, alcohol, and narcotics like cocaine. Mothers who smoke while pregnant have higher rates of miscarriages and tend to have low birth weight or **preterm infants**. Their infants have retarded growth, although many eventually catch up. Maternal smoking is also associated with **sudden infant death syndrome**, the sudden and unexplained death during infancy typically occurring during sleep. Alcohol consumed in large quantities causes **fetal alcohol syndrome** (FAS). Children with FAS have an intellectual disability, distinctive facial abnormalities, and abnormal head size. Pregnant women who use narcotics run the risk of having addicted babies who experience withdrawal symptoms at birth which can be fatal (for example, convulsions). Cocaine can cause spontaneous abortions, preterm birth, low birth weight, irritability at birth, and retarded growth.

An important lesson was learned about prescription drugs and prenatal development in the 1950s. The prescription drug **thalidomide** was marketed as a drug that controlled nausea and was taken by many pregnant women in the 1950s. Unfortunately, the drug caused birth defects. Many children born to these women had defective limbs, feet, hands, and ears, or were born without limbs.

Several diseases can be transferred from the mother to the fetus during prenatal development. In order for a disease to infect the fetus, it must be capable of passing through the semi-permeable placenta into the fetal bloodstream. **Rubella (German measles)** is a disease that passes through this membrane and causes birth defects in 60 to 85 percent of babies if they are infected during the first eight weeks of pregnancy. Defects include vision and hearing loss, heart defects, cerebral palsy, and intellectual disability. **Syphilis** can be passed this way as well and can lead to miscarriage or birth defects depending on the timing of exposure. Syphilis is more damaging in the middle and late stages of pregnancy. **AIDS** can be passed on to the fetus through the placenta but this is less likely if the mother is taking AIDS medication. AIDS can also be transmitted during the birthing process if there is an exchange of blood between the mother and baby or through breastfeeding. Both of the latter two means of transmission are prevented today through the use of medications during birth and through bottle feeding. Genital herpes passes the placental barrier and can cause brain damage or death if the fetus is exposed in the first trimester. A baby can also be infected with herpes by a vaginal delivery. Mothers with genital herpes usually have cesarean deliveries to avoid infecting the child.

Another prenatal teratogen has to do with the **Rh factor** in blood. People either have or do not have an Rh factor in their blood. Those who do not are called RH– and those who do are RH+. In the past, one common cause of intellectual disability was an Rh incompatibility between the mother and her fetus. An RH– mother's immune system would attack the cells of an RH+ fetus. This is prevented today by an inoculation given to the mother that prohibits this immune system response.

Birth complications place the fetus at risk for serious problems. One problem during the birth can be a reduced flow of oxygen to the fetus because either the umbilical cord, which transports oxygen from the mother to the baby, gets crimped or mucous builds up in the throat and nostrils of the baby. The condition of oxygen deprivation during the birthing process is called **anoxia**. If anoxia is prolonged, the baby may develop **cerebral palsy**. Cerebral palsy is a neurological disorder that is characterized by a lack of muscle control and coordination.

Some infants who are neglected or abused or have protracted separations from attachment figures may develop a syndrome called **failure to thrive**. These infants do not develop normally, become grossly underweight, and show signs of depression. Most rebound once they are removed from the home, but some never grow to normal size and suffer social and cognitive deficits.

EXTREMES OF INTELLIGENCE

Two basic extremes of intellectual performance are demonstrated on the extreme left and right of the normal distribution for intelligence.

In order to be considered **mentally retarded**, an individual must meet all three of the essential features described below:

1. Intellectual functioning must be significantly below average. Today intelligence test scores of below 70—or two standard deviations below the mean—are considered significantly below average.

2. Significant deficits in adaptive functioning must be evident. Adaptive functioning refers to social competence or independent behavior that is expected based on chronological age.

3. Onset must be prior to age 18.

Four general categories or ways of classifying intellectual disability include the following:

Categories of Intellectual Disability

Category	Percentage	I.Q. range	Characteristics
Mild	80 percent	50 – 70	May complete sixth grade academic work; may learn vocational skills and hold a job; may live independently as an adult.
Moderate	12 percent	35 – 49	May complete second grade academic work; can learn social and occupational skills; may hold a job in a sheltered workshop.
Severe	7 percent	20 – 34	May learn to talk or communicate; through repetition may learn basic health habits; often needs help for simple tasks.
Profound	1 percent	less than 20	Little or no speech; may learn limited self-help skills; requires constant help and supervision.

There are hundreds of known causes of intellectual disability. Many of them are biological, genetic, chromosomal, prenatal, perinatal, and postnatal in origin. Intellectual disability can also result from environmental influences, such as sensory or maternal deprivation. In some cases (especially mild intellectual disability), the cause of an individual child's intellectual disability is unknown. **Behavior modification** techniques have been used successfully to teach severe or profoundly retarded children simple tasks.

Giftedness is often defined as having an intelligence of 120 to 130 or higher (or having an I.Q. in the upper two to three percent of the population). Lewis Terman began a longitudinal study of gifted children in the 1920s. That is, he and others followed the lives of these children as they grew up and became adults. The study will not be completed until the year 2010. The average intelligence score was 150 for the approximately 1,500 children in this study. The findings of this study have challenged the commonly held belief that the intellectually gifted are emotionally disturbed and socially maladjusted. In fact, just the opposite was found. As adults, this group was also more academically and professionally successful than their non-gifted peers.

Learning disabilities are diagnosed in children whose performance in school is significantly different from their assessed level of competence. Learning disabilities occur in the areas of reading, math, and writing. Learning disabilities are believed to be caused by brain processing deficits. **Dyslexia** is one of these disorders that affects children's ability to read. Many dyslexics have trouble discriminating speech sounds. Phonics-based intervention programs that provide practice in sound discriminations produce improvements in this ability. Other dyslexics have a visual discrimination problem and have difficulty distinguishing letters that are similar in appearance or they read words backwards.

ATTENTION DEFICIT/HYPERACTIVITY DISORDER

Children diagnosed with **attention deficit/hyperactivity disorder (ADHD)** have some combination of the three characteristic symptoms, inattention, impulsivity, and hyperactivity. Boys are diagnosed with ADHD three times more often than girls consistently throughout the world. Girls tend to have inattention but not hyperactivity or impulsivity. Males with ADHD are often also diagnosed with a conduct disorder. Most children with ADHD have social and academic difficulties and continue to have attention difficulties throughout their life. Seventy percent or so of children diagnosed with ADHD take stimulant medication to control the symptoms. Studies have found that a combination of medication and behavioral therapy to teach children and parents how to control the symptoms yields the best treatment outcomes. The causes of ADHD appear to involve both nature and nurture. Identical twins have a high concordance rate (if one twin has ADHD, the other twin also tends to have it) suggesting a genetic factor. However, low birth weight, prenatal exposure to nicotine, and several family risk factors have also been identified as potential causes of ADHD.

AUTISM SPECTRUM DISORDERS

Autism spectrum disorders or pervasive developmental disorders are characterized by deviant social development, deviant language development, and repetitive behavior. Autistic children vary in the severity of their symptoms along a continuum. An autistic child does not seek out social interactions or respond much to human contact. Many either do not speak or use disordered language. Their speech may be highly repetitive. Autistic children need consistency and may be very upset by change. They show an obsessive attachment to some objects and seem to be calmed by repetitive behavior like rocking. Behavior modification programs that use conditioning techniques have been successful in teaching language and social skills to autistic children. Intervention programs begun early have been found to have very good outcomes, particularly when parents are involved in the training program.

Researchers hypothesize that autism is caused by a disturbance in the executive function. This is the function in the prefrontal lobe of the cortex that integrates information. Another hypothesis is that autistic children have damaged brain stems. The brain stem controls the ability to direct attention. Recent research suggests a genetic cause for autism spectrum disorders. Many, but not all, autistic children have been found to have a specific gene called HOXA1. Identical twins' concordance rates for autism is around 92 percent (roughly speaking, in 92 percent of identical twin pairs in which one twin has autism, so does the other) and around 10 percent for fraternal twins.

ANTISOCIAL BEHAVIOR

Aggression, conduct disorder, oppositional defiant disorder, and criminal behavior or delinquency are examples of **antisocial behavior**. According to Dodge's social-information processing model, aggressive children and adolescents show deficits in how they process information to determine the motives for other people's actions and to choose how to respond. Very aggressive youth tend to assume hostile intent even when there is little information to support that conclusion, set a goal of getting even with the other person rather than resolving conflict, and have a bias toward selecting aggressive responses compared to non-aggressive alternatives.

Other research has shown that delinquent and violent youth tend to come from coercive home environments. In these homes, parents use coercive means to get obedience and compliance, and often parents and children are locked in a power struggle. Highly aggressive children tend to be rejected by their peers and have difficulties in school. This in turn tends to cause them to drop out of school which puts them at further risk for antisocial behavior.

EATING DISORDERS

Anorexia nervosa and **bulimia nervosa** are two eating disorders that are most prevalently found in adolescent females. Anorexia nervosa is characterized by refusal to maintain at least 85 percent of one's expected body weight, a fear of gaining weight, and a distorted body image. About one percent of adolescent females have anorexia. This eating disorder is very serious and can be fatal. Bulimia nervosa is characterized by binge/purge cycles. Bulimics consume a large amount of food and then purge with laxatives or by vomiting. This is also a serious and life threatening disorder and is found in about five percent of female college students. Bulimics also have an extreme fear of being fat and a strong drive for thinness.

The causal mechanism for eating disorders is complicated. There is some evidence for a genetic factor but that may not be expressed unless there are environmental triggers. These triggers may include difficulty dealing with the stresses and physical changes of adolescence, living in a culture that values thinness, emotional or sexual abuse, perfectionism, low self-esteem, self-directed anger, and having overprotective, enmeshed parents.

OTHER MAJOR PSYCHOLOGICAL DISORDERS

The following disorders are other major psychological disorders that are defined in the **Diagnostic and Statistical Manual of Mental Disorders (DSM)** published by the American Psychiatric Association. The DSM is the standard source used to diagnose disorders.

Anxiety Disorders

Anxiety disorders are characterized by intense feelings of apprehension and anxiety that impede daily functioning. Approximately 8–15 percent of adults in this country are affected by anxiety disorders. Different types of anxiety disorders include generalized anxiety disorder, panic disorders, **phobias**, and **obsessive-compulsive** disorders.

Dissociative Disorders

Dissociative disorders are characterized by a loss of contact with portions of consciousness or memory, resulting in disruptions in one's sense of self. They appear to be an attempt to overcome anxiety and stress by dissociating oneself from the core of one's personality and result in a loss of memory, identity, or consciousness. The major dissociative disorders are multiple personality disorder, psychogenic amnesia, and psychogenic fugue.

Mood Disorders

Mood disorders (affective disorders) involve moods or emotions that are extreme and unwarranted. These disturbances in emotional feelings are strong enough to intrude on everyday living. The most serious types of mood disorders are major depression and bipolar disorders.

Personality Disorders

Personality disorders are patterns of traits that are long-standing, maladaptive, and inflexible and keep a person from functioning properly in society. Behavior often disrupts social relationships.

Post-Traumatic Stress Disorder

Post-traumatic stress disorder (PTSD) is characterized by recurring nightmares, flashbacks, and feelings of helplessness and anxiety after exposure to a traumatic experience. PTSD is frequently seen in people who have experienced combat or sexual abuse. About one-third of victims of child sexual abuse develop PTSD.

Schizophrenic Disorders

Schizophrenia is a serious psychotic disorder (i.e., one is out of touch with reality). Schizophrenia is not the same as multiple personality disorder, described previously with the dissociative disorders. Schizophrenia includes disorders of thought. Schizophrenics display problems in both how they think and what they think.

Schizophrenic thinking is often incoherent. For instance, they sometimes use neologisms, or words that only have meaning to the person speaking them (e.g., the word "glump"). Loose associations, in which thought appears logically unconnected, is another characteristic that is sometimes seen. Word salad describes a jumble of words that are spoken but do not make sense. The content of a schizophrenic's thinking is also disturbed. A person with schizophrenia may also experience hallucinations and delusions.

Somatoform Disorders

Somatoform disorders are characterized by complaints of physical symptoms in the absence of any real physical illness. About 1 person in 300 has a somatoform disorder, and they are slightly more common in women than in men. Hypochondriasis and conversion disorder are the two main types of somatoform disorders.

COGNITIVE DISORDERS (DEMENTIA)

There are cognitive disorders that appear in adulthood that have common characteristics collectively referred to as **dementia**. Dementia is a progressive loss of cognitive functioning including declining intelligence, impaired memory, poor judgment, disorientation, and personality changes. The disease eventually causes death. The two irreversible dementia disorders are **Alzheimer's disease** and multi-infarct dementia. Dementia symptoms can be temporary if they are caused by things like drug interactive effects. It is important not to misdiagnosis reversible dementia as Alzheimer's or multi-infarct dementia. Furthermore, dementia is not an inevitable part of growing old as many mistakenly believe. These are diseases, not the product of aging. Approximately only 5 percent of people who are 65 or older have dementia. This rate does increase to 16 percent in those people 85 and older.

Alzheimer's disease is the most prevalent of the dementias. It can begin as early as middle adulthood so some people can live 10 or more years after their diagnosis. The rate of diagnosis increases with age. The brains of patients with Alzheimer's disease have distinctive **neurofibrillary tangles**, which are twisted neural fibers, and senile **plaques**, which are deposits of amyloid protein. Since Alzheimer's disease has different ages of onset and the progression of symptoms varies somewhat, it may be that this is not one disease but a collection of related diseases.

It is difficult to point to a single cause of Alzheimer's disease. Some research suggests a link to Down's syndrome as people with Down's syndrome reliably develop Alzheimer's in adulthood. Geneticists have indeed found a gene on the 21st chromosome that is common in members of families who have high rates of Alzheimer's disease. Other theories are that a virus that lies dormant for most of one's life causes the disease or it is caused by an immune system response that attacks the brain. Finally, since the distinctive symptom is cognitive impairment, researchers suggest the disease is caused by a deficit in a neurotransmitter (the substance that causes neural impulses to travel through the brain's neural circuits) that is necessary for learning and memory functioning. New drug treatments for Alzheimer's disease have been shown to slow the disease's progression and even improve patient's cognitive functioning.

Multi-infarct dementia is caused by a series of strokes that reduce blood flow and hence oxygen to the brain. Its progression involves sudden noticeable declines in functioning rather than the slow and steady progression of Alzheimer's disease.

PHYSICAL DISABILITIES

Children with physical disabilities can have speech disorders, visual impairments, hearing impairments, or motor skills impairment. Children with physical handicaps often are rejected by peers. They may be teased or avoided. However, many are able to overcome these hardships and develop normal social relationships. Families of children with disabilities have added stress. How families cope with this stress influences the child's adjustment as well as the family's well being. Families who use problem-focused coping, rather than emotion-focused coping, fair much better. Problem-focused coping is coping with stress by working to accurately define the source of the stress and the problems that are related to it, and then generate solutions to those problems. Emotion-focused coping is coping with stress by focusing on feelings and emotions, avoiding the actual problem or source of stress, and does not involve any active steps in finding a solution to the problem.

Speech disorders can be caused by malformations like a cleft palate, neurological damage, or hearing impairment. Hearing impairments are caused by prenatal exposure to Rubella, anoxia, or other hereditary conditions. Hearing impairments are often not diagnosed until the second year. Treatments for hearing impairments include hearing aids that amplify sound or cochlear implants that are more sophisticated hearing aids which are surgically implanted. Teaching children American Sign Language (ASL) is optimal and ought to begin as early as possible. Like learning other languages, there is a sensitive period for learning ASL. Enabling a child to have the ability to communicate within hearing (perhaps lip reading or hearing implants) and non-hearing communities (ASL) may be the optimal treatment plan for hearing impaired children.

Children with visual impairments may appear to be unresponsive to caregivers as infants and have fewer facial expressions than other infants. They usually are developmentally delayed in their physical development both in terms of fine motor and gross motor skills. Motor disabilities can be caused by congenital disease, inherited diseases like muscular dystrophy, or due to injuries.

Federal law requires that children with disabilities are mainstreamed in public schools. This law was intended to prevent discrimination against children with disabilities and to provide them with an educational experience comparable to their non-handicapped peers. However, depending on the degree of handicap, some children benefit from specialized resource rooms with teachers who have specialized training rather than from being in large classes with teachers who do not have such training. Special schools for disabled children provide an alternative to public schools.

PRACTICE TEST 1

CLEP Human Growth and Development

Also available at the REA Study Center (*www.rea.com/studycenter*)

This practice test is also offered online at the REA Study Center. Since all CLEP exams are administered on computer, we recommend that you take the online version of the test to simulate test-day conditions and to receive these added benefits:

- **Timed testing conditions** – helps you gauge how much time you can spend on each question
- **Automatic scoring** – find out how you did on the test, instantly
- **On-screen detailed explanations of answers** – gives you the correct answer and explains why the other answer choices are wrong
- **Diagnostic score reports** – pinpoint where you're strongest and where you need to focus your study

PRACTICE TEST 1

CLEP Human Growth and Development

(Answer sheets appear in the back of the book.)

TIME: 90 Minutes
90 Questions

> **DIRECTIONS:** Each of the questions or incomplete statements below is followed by five possible answers or completions. Select the lettered choice that best answers each question and fill in the corresponding oval on the answer sheet.

1. Which theoretical perspective emphasizes nature in the "nature versus nurture" controversy?

   (A) Behavioral theory

   (B) Social learning theory

   (C) Social-cognitive theory

   (D) Psychodynamic theory

   (E) Sociocultural

2. Which theorist would be most likely to expect cultural differences in development?

   (A) Vygotsky

   (B) Piaget

   (C) Freud

   (D) Skinner

   (E) Bowlby

3. To determine whether boys and girls play differently, a researcher video-taped children at play during school recess. This is an example of a

   (A) field experiment

   (B) naturalistic observation

   (C) cross-sectional study

   (D) survey

   (E) clinical interview

4. The average child begins to walk between

   (A) 7 and 8 months (D) 13 and 14 months

   (B) 9 and 10 months (E) 16 and 17 months

   (C) 11 and 12 months

5. According to Piaget, adaptation is made up of the two processes called

   (A) equilibration and accommodation

   (B) accommodation and fixation

   (C) equilibration and assimilation

   (D) operation and conservation

   (E) accommodation and assimilation

6. The fact that parents will provide less direction to a child who begins to show competence on a task, supports the theory of

   (A) Bronfenbrenner (D) Vygotsky

   (B) Freud (E) Bandura

   (C) Piaget

7. According to the information-processing approach, children's memories improve with age mainly because

   (A) they get better at organizing information

   (B) they develop additional memory storage systems

   (C) their perceptual abilities improve

   (D) they are more interested in remembering information

   (E) parents expect older children to remember information better

8. Jane digs a hole in the sandbox while Jim, who is sitting next to her, fills his bucket with sand. They share the shovels in the sandbox and talk about school. They are engaged in

   (A) cooperative play (D) nonsocial play

   (B) parallel play (E) associative play

   (C) mature play

9. Which of the following research methods is most often used to study rare or unique situations or behavior?

    (A) Survey

    (B) Case study

    (C) Cross-sequential

    (D) Correlational

    (E) Psychosocial

10. Which of the following theories describes stages of development?

    (A) Collectivist

    (B) Continuity

    (C) Discontinuity

    (D) Nature

    (E) Nurture

11. Which of the following is an example of instrumental aggression?

    (A) Sara pushes Joy out of the way so she can get a toy she wants to play with first.

    (B) Sara tells Emma not to play with Joy because she bites.

    (C) Sara is mad at her brother, so she hits her doll.

    (D) Sara yells at Emma because she knocked down her block tower.

    (E) Sara can't get the wrapper off a candy bar, so she throws it across the room.

12. According to statistics, which group commits most of the child abuse in our country?

    (A) Siblings

    (B) Day care workers

    (C) Foster parents

    (D) Parents

    (E) Stepparents

13. Which theoretical perspective assumes there is a bidirectional relationship between the person and the environment?

    (A) Behavioral

    (B) Learning

    (C) Psychobiological

    (D) Sociocultural

    (E) Nature

14. A problem with longitudinal research is

    (A) confounding age difference with birth cohort differences

    (B) a lack of control over extraneous variables

    (C) subject drop out

    (D) subject bias

    (E) researcher bias

15. Students who have developed a mastery orientation would attribute a good grade on a test to their ability, and a bad grade on a test to

    (A) the teacher   (D) lack of effort

    (B) their ability   (E) luck

    (C) bad luck

16. According to recent research, which of the following has shown a correlation with age, but is NOT found only in older people?

    (A) Insight   (D) Collectivism

    (B) Metacognition   (E) Wisdom

    (C) The executive process

17. Compared to peer groups in middle childhood, adolescent peer groups

    (A) are more likely to be mixed sex

    (B) do not last as long

    (C) are more structured and exclusive

    (D) are less structured and exclusive

    (E) are larger

18. Which of the following indicates the presence of empathy?

    (A) Mollie starts to cry whenever she sees someone else cry.

    (B) Mollie sees Jake crying and gives him a toy to help him stop crying.

    (C) Mollie laughs when she sees something funny on television.

    (D) Mollie tells her Daddy when she doesn't feel well.

    (E) Mollie goes to her room to cry so no one sees her crying.

19. Among the parenting styles that have been studied by Baumrind, which of the following is associated with the most negative impact on development?

    (A) Authoritative

    (B) Authoritarian

    (C) Permissive

    (D) Strict

    (E) Uninvolved

20. Which of the following statements about physical growth is true?

    I. Physical growth is rapid during infancy, slows during early and middle childhood, and then is rapid again during adolescence.

    II. Physical growth is rapid from infancy to its completion in middle childhood.

    III. Physical growth is rapid during infancy, and then is slow from early childhood through adolescence.

    IV. Physical growth is a steady process from infancy through childhood.

    (A) I

    (B) II

    (C) III

    (D) IV

    (E) II and IV

21. Research on the growth hormone (GH) has shown that

    (A) children with normal thyroid function will grow to be taller than their genotype with injections of GH

    (B) children who do not have GH are likely to be mentally retarded

    (C) children given early treatments of GH develop normally

    (D) children given GH treatments later can still catch up to their peers

    (E) vitamin C can simulate GH production in the body

22. Researchers have studied the impact of late versus early maturation on adolescents' adjustment. Which of the pairs below have been shown to have the best adjustment outcomes?

    (A) Early maturing boys and early maturing girls

    (B) Early maturing boys and late maturing girls

    (C) Late maturing boys and early maturing girls

    (D) Late maturing boys and late maturing girls

    (E) Adolescent adjustment is in fact NOT related to the timing of maturation.

23. One theory of biological aging suggests aging is inevitable and is caused by

    (A) carcinogens

    (B) teratogens

    (C) wear and tear from normal use

    (D) arteriosclerosis

    (E) genetic mutations

24. An effective treatment for the side effects of menopause is

    (A) antipsychotic medication

    (B) psychotropic medication

    (C) estrogen replacement therapy

    (D) testosterone replacement therapy

    (E) hysterectomy

25. Compared to women, the male climacteric is

    (A) a faster decline

    (B) a slower decline

    (C) unaffected by sex hormone levels in the body

    (D) associated with increased risk of heart disease

    (E) more uncommon

26. Osteoporosis is

    (A) a disease of the pancreas

    (B) a circulatory disease

    (C) a bone disease

    (D) a normal product of biological aging

    (E) an arterial disease caused by plaque buildup in the arteries

27. Janet's mother is terminally ill and the doctors have said her death is imminent. A hospital social worker has suggested to Janet that she contact the hospice program. The social worker most likely told Janet that hospice

    (A) would immediately stop her mother's pain medication

    (B) would persuade the doctors to keep her mother in the hospital where she can get the best medical care

    (C) would do everything possible to give her mother a pain-free death

    (D) would help Janet make the difficult euthanasia decision

    (E) would be at the hospital to establish brain death

28. Gibson's visual cliff experiment showed that

    (A) depth perception is innate

    (B) depth perception is learned

    (C) six-month-olds crawled across the visual cliff

    (D) six-month-olds did not crawl across the visual cliff

    (E) six-month-olds have an inborn fear response

29. Visual scanning experiments with infants suggest which pattern of looking?

(A) Newborns actively scan a stimulus if it is black and white but not colored, but the opposite is true in older infants.

(B) Newborns will actively scan a stimulus if it is colored but not black and white, but the opposite is true of older infants.

(C) Newborns scan the edges of a stimulus, and older infants scan the center or inside of a stimulus.

(D) Newborns do not have preferences for what they look at, but older infants do.

(E) Newborns scan a stimulus quickly, older infants scan a stimulus more slowly.

30. When you see a German shepherd 100 yards away from you in a park, you don't think it is a miniature dog because of

(A) Gestalt perception   (D) color constancy

(B) shape constancy   (E) size constancy

(C) lightness constancy

31. Which of the following is the LEAST developed in newborns?

(A) Taste   (D) Audition

(B) Touch   (E) Smell

(C) Vision

32. Speed of habituation in infancy and later IQ scores have been shown to be

(A) conversely related   (D) positively correlated

(B) diametrically opposed   (E) in a curvilinear relationship

(C) negatively correlated

33. The type of hearing loss associated with aging is loss of sensitivity for

(A) the human voice   (D) rhythmic sounds

(B) low frequency sounds   (E) tympanic sounds

(C) high frequency sounds

34. One reason older adults experience declining eye sight is

    (A) decreased flexibility of the lens

    (B) a decrease in the size of the retina

    (C) a decrease in the fibers of the optic nerve

    (D) increased pupil diameter

    (E) decreased fluid in the eyeball

35. Which of the following statements represents the learning approach to language development?

    I.   Children learn language through imitating the speech of those around them.

    II.   Children learn language through a gradual stamping in of the grammatical rules of the language.

    III. Children learn language by formulating and testing hypotheses about the meaning of words and the rules of their combination.

    IV.   Children learn language to fulfill their unconscious desire to communicate with others.

    V.   Children learn language to increase their chances of survival.

    (A) I   (D) IV

    (B) II   (E) V

    (C) III

36. Which of the following is an example of overregularization in language development?

    (A) "I and Mommy went to the store."

    (B) "Mommy went to the store with me."

    (C) "Mommy went to the store with I."

    (D) "We, Mommy and I went to the store."

    (E) "Mommy and I goed to the store."

37. Billy sees a beach ball and says "ball." He sees a basketball and says "ball." He sees a soccer ball and says "ball." Finally he sees a globe on a desk and says "ball." Calling the globe a ball is referred to as

    (A) categorization

    (B) classification

    (C) accommodation

    (D) overregularization

    (E) overextension

38. Noam Chomsky argued that the ability to learn language

    (A) is innate

    (B) shows wide individual variation

    (C) is positively correlated with intelligence

    (D) is positively correlated with creativity

    (E) differs between males and females

39. The first stage of language development is

    (A) cooing

    (B) babbling

    (C) first words

    (D) expressive speech

    (E) receptive speech

40. An indication that we are born prepared to acquire a language is the fact that

    (A) infants can discriminate among all of the speech sounds used in all of the world's languages even better than adults

    (B) children can produce complex sentences by the age of two years

    (C) newborns do not habituate to speech sounds

    (D) mothers all talk in a special way called "motherese"

    (E) we can easily acquire a new language at any age

41. Studies of intelligence in adulthood have shown

    (A) while there is some decline in information processing, there is some stability in fluid and crystallized intelligence

    (B) no intellectual decline, even in the very old

    (C) no relationship between health and intelligence test performance

    (D) no relationship between speed of information processing and age

    (E) a steady increase in both crystallized and fluid intelligence into late adulthood

42. Sibling rivalry tends to be worse during

    (A) toddlerhood   (D) early adolescence

    (B) early childhood   (E) late adolescence

    (C) middle childhood

43. Compared with children who have siblings, only children

    (A) have lower self-esteem

    (B) are less well-accepted by their peers

    (C) are less dependent on parents

    (D) do better academically

    (E) experience more parent-child conflict

44. Although the rate of divorce is high, the rate of remarriage is also high. This leads to a large number of reconstituted families referred to as

    (A) hyercomplex families   (D) custodial families

    (B) blended families   (E) extended families

    (C) cohabitating families

45. A sexual offender is more likely to target

    (A) an early maturing child

    (B) a late maturing child

    (C) a child who is emotionally needy and socially isolated

    (D) an outgoing, extroverted child

    (E) a popular child

46. One way to help children adjust to divorce is to

    (A) minimize the conflict between parents after the divorce

    (B) lengthen the time of separation before divorce

    (C) minimize their contact with the non-custodial parent

    (D) have each parent decide how to discipline the child his and her own way

    (E) be sure the amount of contact with each parent is equal

47. Researchers examining cultural influences on self-esteem have found that

    (A) Chinese and Japanese children score lower in self-esteem than American children

    (B) African American children score lower in self-esteem than Caucasian children

    (C) Chinese and Japanese children score higher in self-esteem than American children

    (D) Chinese and Japanese children have equal levels of self-esteem compared to American children

    (E) African American children score lower in self-esteem than Chinese and Japanese children

48. Children display learned helplessness if their parents

    (A) use physical punishment

    (B) always encourage them to do their best

    (C) set high standards of achievement for them, but also communicate the belief that the child is not very capable

    (D) compare them to their peers

    (E) never let them quit even when a task becomes very difficult

49. The use of a parenting technique called "induction" can help promote the development of a conscience. Which of the following is an example of induction?

    (A) "If you don't put your toys away, I will throw them out."

    (B) "If you put your toys away, you can have dessert."

(C) "Putting your toys away is a sign that you are growing up."

(D) "If you put your toys away, I will talk to you."

(E) "If you don't put your toys away, someone may trip on them, fall, and get hurt."

50. A child who laughs when Daddy dresses up as a woman for Halloween, but knows Daddy is still a boy, shows

(A) a gender schema   (D) gender constancy

(B) gender infallibility   (E) gender flexibility

(C) gender holism

51. The most important personality achievement of adolescence according to Erikson is

(A) identity   (D) personal space

(B) generativity   (E) intimacy

(C) integrity

52. In Freud's theory, resolution of the Oedipal conflict is achieved through

(A) identifying with mother

(B) identifying with father

(C) repressing aggressive tendencies

(D) rejection of father as the love object

(E) embracing one's feminine tendencies

53. The psychosocial crisis of young adulthood in Erikson's model is

(A) generativity versus stagnation

(B) intimacy versus isolation

(C) integrity versus despair

(D) autonomy versus doubt

(E) initiative versus guilt

54. Males have a higher risk of sex-linked genetic diseases like hemophilia than females do because

   (A) they have more genes than females

   (B) they have fewer genes than females

   (C) the male sex hormone provides less immunity to disorders than the female sex hormone

   (D) their Y chromosome cannot mask the effect of a trait for the disease on their X chromosome

   (E) they have only one sex chromosome

55. Which of the following is a genetic disorder that can be controlled with diet?

   (A) Encephaly

   (B) Hemophilia

   (C) Turner's syndrome

   (D) PKU

   (E) Phenotype

56. The best approach to helping profoundly deaf children is to

   (A) home school them

   (B) give them speech therapy

   (C) teach them sign language

   (D) teach them to lip read

   (E) teach them sign language and how to lip read

57. Johnny is disobedient, loud, and aggressive in the classroom and at home. He recently threatened to hit his teacher. Johnny would most likely be diagnosed with

   (A) conduct disorder

   (B) delinquent disorder

   (C) hyperactivity-impulsivity disorder

   (D) hyperactivity-inattentive disorder

   (E) bipolar depression

58. A key indicator that a child has a learning disability is

    (A) hyperactivity

    (B) impulsivity

    (C) a discrepancy between ability and performance

    (D) a low score on an intelligence test

    (E) eidetic memory

59. When asked what career he wanted to pursue, Julio said: "I am going to be a doctor just like my mother and father. I have always wanted to be a doctor. I can remember pretending to be a doctor when I was just a little kid." Julio's answer illustrates

    (A) moratorium

    (B) identity diffusion

    (C) identity confusion

    (D) identity foreclosure

    (E) identity achievement

60. Recent survey research has shown the period of time between launching the last child and retirement to be a time of

    (A) depression and sadness for parents

    (B) renewal and growth for parents

    (C) depression and sadness for mothers but not fathers

    (D) decreased activity

    (E) lowered marital satisfaction

61. The social smile first appears in infants

    (A) between 10 and 12 hours after birth

    (B) between 1 and 4 weeks of age

    (C) between 6 and 10 weeks of age

    (D) between 6 and 8 months of age

    (E) between 10 and 12 months of age

62. Research suggests it is important to plan for one's retirement because

    (A) it goes by so quickly

    (B) it will reduce the financial costs

    (C) engaging in meaningful activities during retirement is associated with happiness

    (D) you might decide to keep working instead of retiring

    (E) keeping active prevents normal aging declines from occurring

63. The ego, in contrast to the id,

    (A) mediates between wish-fulfilling desires and the outer reality

    (B) is composed of only wish-fulfilling desires

    (C) mediates between reality and internal rules

    (D) cannot mediate with the superego

    (E) is innate, not learned

64. Freud believed that the primary driving force in an individual's life was

    (A) the superego

    (B) psychosexual development

    (C) libido

    (D) bodily functions

    (E) domination

65. Which approach to psychology stresses the importance of the person's environment on development?

    (A) Psychodynamic   (D) Cognitive

    (B) Humanistic   (E) Psychobiological

    (C) Behavioristic

66. Suppose you believe that people are capable of developing personally throughout life and that, given the opportunity, they will achieve their full potential. Which approach to personality does this describe?

    (A) Humanistic

    (B) Cognitive

    (C) Psychodynamic

    (D) Behavioristic

    (E) Social learning

67. Ivan P. Pavlov is famous for his research on

    (A) teaching machines

    (B) perceptual learning

    (C) forward conditioning

    (D) classical conditioning

    (E) backward conditioning

68. The role of imitation in social learning was first systematically observed by

    (A) I. Pavlov

    (B) Bandura and Walters

    (C) Stanley Milgram

    (D) B.F. Skinner

    (E) J.B. Watson

69. Correlational studies

    (A) indicate causality

    (B) are more valid than laboratory studies

    (C) involve manipulations of independent variables

    (D) indicate a relationship between two variables

    (E) have no predictive validity

70. Which of the following effects does adrenaline have on the human body?

    (A) Constriction of the pupils

    (B) Increased rate of digestion

    (C) Accelerated heartbeat

    (D) Increased hormone production

    (E) Decreased hormone production

71. According to Piaget, a person who cannot consistently use abstract logic has NOT reached the stage of

    (A) concrete operations

    (B) preoperational development

    (C) formal operations

    (D) initiative vs. guilt

    (E) extrovert vs. introvert

Questions 72 and 73 refer to the following passage:

Suppose you are playing "Monopoly" with a group of children. These children understand the basic instructions and will play by the rules. They are not capable of hypothetical transactions dealing with mortgages, loans, and special pacts with other players.

72. According to Piaget, these children are in which stage of cognitive development?

    (A) Sensorimotor stage

    (B) Formal operations stage

    (C) Preoperational stage

    (D) Concrete operational stage

    (E) Intuitive preoperational stage

73. What are the probable ages of these children?

    (A) 8–13   (D) 7–12

    (B) 4–7   (E) 5–10

    (C) 2–4

74. Suppose you teach preschool and you break Joe's candy bar into three pieces and Mike's candy bar into two pieces. Mike complains that he received less than Joe. What does Mike lack?

    (A) Conservation   (D) Egocentrism

    (B) Constancy   (E) Accommodation

    (C) Object permanence

75. The short-term memory can hold how many items at one time?

    (A) Seven items, plus or minus two

    (B) Ten items, plus or minus two

    (C) Ten items, plus or minus five

    (D) Five items

    (E) It has unlimited capacity.

76. Which of the following problems would require divergent thinking?

    (A) Adding a column of numbers

    (B) Deciding whether to turn left or right at an intersection while driving a car

    (C) Choosing the best move in a card game

    (D) Repairing a broken typewriter

    (E) Both (A) and (D)

77. The Language Acquisition Device was proposed by

    (A) Piaget   (D) Chomsky

    (B) Bruner   (E) Mednick

    (C) Kohler

78. In linguistic terminology, the term "boy" is

    (A) a morpheme   (D) a prosody

    (B) a phoneme   (E) an example of syntax

    (C) a stereotype

79. A "normal" average I.Q. score is

    (A) 85   (D) 110

    (B) 100   (E) 140

    (C) 115

80. Which of the following does NOT describe a true relationship between environmental factors and I.Q.?

    (A) Level of parent education predicts I.Q.

    (B) Socioeconomic status predicts I.Q.

    (C) Score on the HOME scale predicts I.Q.

    (D) Parents' occupational status predicts I.Q.

    (E) Intensity of separation anxiety predicts I.Q.

81. Shortly after birth a duck will follow the first object that walks by it. This illustrates

    (A) conditioned responses   (D) imprinting

    (B) superstimuli   (E) shaping

    (C) sign stimuli

82. Which of the following is NOT a factor that influences the degree to which two people like each other?

    (A) Familiarity   (D) Conformity

    (B) Physical attractiveness   (E) Proximity

    (C) Similarity

83. Which of the following increases as a person's need for social affiliation increases?

    (A) Cognitive dissonance   (D) Depression

    (B) Fear   (E) Repression

    (C) Anxiety

84. According to social learning theory, one of the primary means of social-izing our children is

    (A) taming their instincts

    (B) developing their superegos

    (C) helping them self-actualize

    (D) observational learning

    (E) providing minimum discipline

85. According to Freud, a developmental halt due to frustration and anxiety is referred to as

    (A) depression   (D) neurosis

    (B) fixation   (E) learned helplessness

    (C) regression

86. A stimulus that elicits a response before the experimental manipulation is

    (A) a response stimulus (RS)

    (B) an unconditioned stimulus (UCS)

    (C) a generalized stimulus (GS)

    (D) a conditioned stimulus (CS)

    (E) a specific stimulus (SS)

87. In our society, money is an example of a

    (A) primary reinforcer

    (B) secondary (conditioned) reinforcer

    (C) socio-reinforcer

    (D) negative reinforcer

    (E) simple operant

88. The reinforcement schedule that produces the highest rates of performance is a

    (A) fixed-interval schedule

    (B) variable-interval schedule

    (C) fixed-ratio schedule

    (D) variable-ratio schedule

    (E) constant reinforcement

89. Mary is a bright student but she is constantly disrupting the class by trying to draw the teacher into a power struggle for control. The school psychologist might advise the teacher to do all of the following EXCEPT

    (A) not show Mary the anxiety she is causing

    (B) ignore Mary's disruptive behavior

    (C) verbally embarrass Mary until she is more cooperative

    (D) suggest she talk to Mary's parents

    (E) reinforce Mary when she engages in more productive behavior

90. The major affective disorders are characterized by

    (A) extreme and inappropriate emotional responses

    (B) severe behavior problems

    (C) disturbed speech

    (D) hyperactivity

    (E) delusions

PRACTICE TEST 1

Answer Key

1.	(D)	31.	(C)	61.	(C)
2.	(A)	32.	(D)	62.	(C)
3.	(B)	33.	(C)	63.	(A)
4.	(C)	34.	(A)	64.	(C)
5.	(E)	35.	(A)	65.	(C)
6.	(D)	36.	(E)	66.	(A)
7.	(A)	37.	(E)	67.	(D)
8.	(E)	38.	(A)	68.	(B)
9.	(B)	39.	(A)	69.	(D)
10.	(C)	40.	(A)	70.	(C)
11.	(A)	41.	(A)	71.	(C)
12.	(D)	42.	(C)	72.	(D)
13.	(D)	43.	(B)	73.	(D)
14.	(C)	44.	(B)	74.	(A)
15.	(D)	45.	(C)	75.	(A)
16.	(E)	46.	(A)	76.	(C)
17.	(C)	47.	(A)	77.	(D)
18.	(B)	48.	(C)	78.	(A)
19.	(E)	49.	(E)	79.	(B)
20.	(A)	50.	(D)	80.	(E)
21.	(C)	51.	(A)	81.	(D)
22.	(B)	52.	(B)	82.	(D)
23.	(C)	53.	(B)	83.	(B)
24.	(C)	54.	(D)	84.	(D)
25.	(B)	55.	(D)	85.	(B)
26.	(C)	56.	(E)	86.	(B)
27.	(C)	57.	(A)	87.	(B)
28.	(D)	58.	(C)	88.	(D)
29.	(C)	59.	(D)	89.	(C)
30.	(E)	60.	(B)	90.	(A)

PRACTICE TEST 1

Detailed Explanations of Answers

1.   **(D)**   The psychodynamic theory emphasizes nature in the nature versus nurture debate more than the other perspectives listed because of the emphasis on inborn, biological drives within this perspective.

2.   **(A)**   Vygotsky is the one theorist of the five who argued that culture influences cognitive development. He argued that a child's cognitive abilities develop as a result of engaging in tasks with older, more competent adults. He also argued that language affects thought.

3.   **(B)**   Since the researcher is recording behavior in a natural setting, and is not controlling or manipulating any variables, it is a naturalistic observation.

4.   **(C)**   Research on physical development shows that on average, children begin to walk on their own between 11 and 12 months of age.

5.   **(E)**   Piaget used the term "adaptation" for the process of a child adjusting to the environment. The two complementary processes involved in adaptation are accommodation, when a child constructs a new scheme that organizes a new experience, and assimilation, when a child applies an already existing scheme to understand a new experience. Piaget argued that accommodation occurs when an attempt to assimilate new information fails.

6.   **(D)**   Vygotsky used the term "guided participation" or "scaffolding" to describe the cognitive support that older adults, like teachers or parents, provide to children when they engage in a task. Adults will adjust the amount of direction and support they provide as the child shows greater mastery over the task at hand.

7.   **(A)**   The information-processing approach argues children's memory improves because children get better at organizing to-be-learned information. The better a child can organize new information, the better that information is encoded for storage in memory and later retrieval.

8.   **(E)**   The children are engaged in associative play because even though they are talking to each other while playing and sharing tools, they are not sharing the same purpose or goal.

9. **(B)**   The case study method of research is designed to collect a great deal of information about a single person or event. By its nature then, a case study yields conclusions that are difficult to generalize beyond that person or event. There is typically something very unique or special about the case that motivates a researcher to study it in such depth.

10. **(C)**   The terms "discontinuity theory" and "stage theory" are used interchangeably in this field. Theories of this type describe development as qualitative shifts in ability or behavior that take place through a series of distinct stages. Almost all stage theories argue that the stages are universal and occur in a fixed sequence.

11. **(A)**   Instrumental aggression is aggression that is used in order to achieve an end. The child in this question uses aggression as a means toward the end of getting a toy. Instrumental aggression is usually used in battles over toys and is not personal

12. **(D)**   Statistics on child mistreatment indicate that more often, among the types of offenders listed in this question, the abuser is the child's parent.

13. **(D)**   The sociocultural view of development argues there is a bidirectional relationship between the child and the environment. A child influences the people and the environments he or she interacts with, as much as those people and environments influence the child's development. For example, an infant's temperament influences the caregiver's responses to the child, and those caregiving responses in turn shape the child's behavior.

14. **(C)**   Longitudinal research involves collecting data from the same group of participants at several points in their life. One problem that threatens the validity of the findings of a longitudinal study is subject dropout. If participants drop out of the study, not only is the research sample size reduced, but the sample may become biased. For example, participants who drop out of a longitudinal study on memory may have poorer memory ability to begin with compared to those who complete the study. The findings of this longitudinal study of memory then would be biased, that is, only apply to people with good memory ability.

15. **(D)**   Those with a mastery-oriented attribution style typically attribute successes and failures to internal traits or abilities and effort. This type of person believes that he or she can be successful at tasks that are attempted and will tend to persevere through challenging or difficult tasks.

16. **(E)** Recently, researchers have begun to systematically study wisdom. Wisdom is defined as exceptional insight into the problems of life. Research has shown that, while the majority of people believe wisdom comes with age, wisdom is not a normal product of aging. The key elements that influence the development of wisdom have to do with the quality and amount of life experience, not just chronological age.

17. **(C)** Adolescent peer groups are more structured and exclusive. In other words, there are more requirements to meet for acceptance into the group and stricter rules regarding things like acceptable behavior and dress. While crowds tend to be mixed sex, adolescent peer groups do not.

18. **(B)** A key element of empathy is being able to feel what another person is feeling. Crying because someone else is crying does not necessarily indicate the child feels what the other person is experiencing. However, a child offering a toy to a crying child shows he or she feels the underlying unhappiness causing the child's crying, and he or she believes a toy will make the child feel happy.

19. **(E)** The uninvolved parenting style is characterized by the parent being low on both the acceptance/responsiveness and the control/demandingness parenting dimensions. Children raised with this style of parenting tend to engage in antisocial behavior.

20. **(A)** Statement I is true. Physical growth is not a steady process. There are growth spurts that occur in infancy and in adolescence.

21. **(C)** Research on the growth hormone (GH) has shown that as long as a child who lacks GH is given injections of the hormone early on, he or she will grow to their full height potential. If GH is given later, the child does not catch up.

22. **(B)** Early maturing boys and late maturing girls have been shown to experience better adjustment compared to their counterparts—late maturing boys and early maturing girls. Early maturing boys may benefit from having larger physical stature than their late maturing peers, and early maturing girls may have difficulty adjusting to puberty and the concomitant physical changes in their bodies. Other people may treat early maturing girls as if they were older than their age. Because of this, they may be faced with higher expectations for their behavior than they are capable of meeting.

23. **(C)** The wear and tear theory of biological aging suggests that aging of the body is inevitable because of wear and tear on it from normal use. This theory suggests that, like a machine, over time the body will wear out.

24. **(C)**   Estrogen replacement therapy (ERT) has been used successfully to treat symptoms of menopause in women. The therapy works to replace the female hormone, estrogen, which decreases substantially in a woman's body during menopause. ERT seems to treat symptoms like hot flashes quite well. Controversy exists, however, over the side effects of ERT. Some research suggests there is an increased risk of uterine cancer in women given long-term ERT (or breast cancer if the estrogen is given along with another hormone called progestin in therapy called hormone replacement therapy or HRT).

25. **(B)**   The male climacteric is a less noticeable physiological process than the female climacteric. Changes that occur are caused by a decline in testosterone level and are very gradual. These changes include reduced sperm production, reduction in the size of the testes, and enlargement of the prostate gland. These changes do not prevent a male from fathering a child.

26. **(C)**   Osteoporosis is a bone disease caused by a decline in bone density. Bones become very brittle and may spontaneously fracture. Osteoporosis is the result of a calcium deficiency and is found in greater frequency among post-menopausal women.

27. **(C)**   Hospice is a program that supports terminally ill patients and their families through the dying process. The goal of hospice is to provide a pain-free death for the dying patient in as comfortable a setting as possible.

28. **(D)**   Eleanor Gibson's classic visual cliff experiment showed that six-month-old infants would not crawl across a "visual cliff." The visual cliff was created by placing a Plexiglas cover, half clear and half checkerboard, across the top of a checkerboard box. For a person with depth perception, there appeared to be a drop off or "visual cliff" half way across the top. The experiment did not show conclusively that depth perception was innate, because six-month-old infants have already had experience exploring their environment and may have learned to see depth from this prior experience.

29. **(C)**   Visual scanning experiments with infants have shown that newborns will scan the edges of a stimulus while older infants will scan the interior of a stimulus. This might suggest that newborns are born prepared to scan edges to organize the perceptual field into objects. Older infants may be able to do that more rapidly and hence spend their time looking for details found within the edges.

30. **(E)**   Size constancy is the perceptual ability to perceive size accurately by adjusting for changing distance. Perception theorists would argue that, by using binocular and monocular cues to distance, we make an

unconscious inference that the German shepherd is 100 yards away. Although the size of the retinal image produced by looking at a dog that far away would be quite small, the size of the retinal image of the dog multiplied by the dog's distance yields the perception of a normal-sized German shepherd. Size constancy is achieved by multiplying retinal image size times distance.

31. **(C)** Vision is the least developed sense in newborns. Visual acuity is normally between 20/200 and 20/400 at birth.

32. **(D)** Habituation is a form of learning that has shown to be present in newborns and is measured by length of looking at a stimulus. Habituation is seen when an infant looks away or stops looking at a stimulus. When a previously seen stimulus is shown along with a novel stimulus, newborns will look longer at the novel stimulus. Speed of habituation in newborns has been shown to positively correlate with later I.Q. scores.

33. **(C)** The hearing loss most associated with aging is a decrease in sensitivity to high frequency sounds.

34. **(A)** A decreased flexibility in the lens of the eye due to normal biological aging is one reason for declining eyesight among the aged. The lens of the eye must be able to change shape from concave to convex in order to properly refract light waves to the retina on the back of the eye. When the lens cannot make these accommodations, light waves are either refracted short of the retina or beyond the retina.

35. **(A)** The learning approach to language development argues that we learn a language through imitation. We imitate the speech of those around us and, in turn, these speech utterances are positively reinforced by caregivers. Therefore, language is described as verbal behavior acquired through the general laws of learning within this theoretical approach.

36. **(E)** Overregularization is when a child who is learning a language produces speech errors that are due to exceptions to grammatical rules. The child's speech error indicates she or he assumes grammatical rules are regular and without exception. For example, one grammatical rule of the English language is to add an -ed to form the past tense of a verb. To overregularize English grammar rules, a young child would say "goed" instead of the irregular "went."

37. **(E)** Overextension is when a child learning a language applies a category label, e.g., "ball," to an object that does not belong to the category but

may share some similar features of category members. A globe is not a member of the "ball" category although it does share some characteristics of balls.

38. **(A)**   Noam Chomsky argued that humans are born prepared to acquire a language. He suggested that the human brain is pre-wired for language acquisition. He used the term language acquisition device (LAD) metaphorically to describe this pre-wiring. Evidence for this theory includes the fact that language learning is universal in humans; language learning proceeds through stages that are universal; there appears to be a sensitive period for learning language; infants can discriminate among all the speech sounds used in all of the world's languages; and children show an understanding of syntax in their speech production that does not appear to be directly taught to them. An example of the latter is speech errors of overregularization.

39. **(A)**   Cooing is the first stage of language development. Cooing appears about the same age in babies across cultures.

40. **(A)**   An indication that we are born prepared to learn a language is the fact that infants can discriminate among all the speech sounds of all of the world's languages and do so even better than adults. Being able to discriminate speech sounds means infants can perceive differences between sounds such as *pa* and *ba*.

41. **(A)**   Studies of intelligence in adulthood have shown that fluid and crystallized intelligence show stability until very late adulthood. Fluid intelligence is closely related to reasoning and thinking, while crystallized intelligence is general knowledge that has been acquired. While research does show a steady decline in the speed of processing of information, these two types of intelligence appear to be stable through most of adulthood in adults who are disease free.

42. **(C)**   Sibling rivalry tends to be worse during middle childhood as opportunities for competition and comparison increase during these years.

43. **(B)**   Only-children are less well-accepted by their peers compared to their counterparts who have siblings. A possible reason for this is that children may develop social skills from interacting with their siblings before the school years. Only-children may not have as much opportunity to interact with other children in such an intensive way as children who have siblings.

44. **(B)**   The term "blended family" refers to complex familial structures that are the results of remarriages.

45. **(C)** Sexual offenders tend to target children who are isolated and needy. Offenders play on these children's vulnerabilities and may gain the trust of children because they are socially isolated and crave attention.

46. **(A)** Minimizing conflict after a divorce has been shown to help children's adjustment, because conflict after a divorce tends to interfere with the non-custodial parent's involvement with the children. Good non-custodial parenting is one of the factors associated with children's positive adjustment after divorce.

47. **(A)** Cross-cultural research on self-esteem has shown significant differences in levels of self-esteem in children from different cultures. Chinese and Japanese children have been shown to have lower self-esteem than American children.

48. **(C)** Children of parents who set very high standards for their achievement, but also communicate to them that they are not capable of achieving those standards, show signs of learned helplessness. Learned helplessness is a syndrome first observed by Seligman. Seligman placed animals in an experimental chamber from which they could not escape. Animals who received an electric shock through the floor of the chamber first tried to escape, but they eventually stopped trying. Even when an escape route became available to them, they could not learn to escape. Children of parents who communicate high standards but little confidence in the children's abilities, produce children who do not try to succeed.

49. **(E)** Induction is a parenting technique used to teach children morality. A parent is using induction when she explains to the child how the child's actions may negatively affect other people. Providing an explanation for a behavior rule that encourages the child to think of others may induce independent moral reasoning in the child.

50. **(D)** Gender constancy is the understanding that a person cannot change his maleness or her femaleness by simply changing how he or she looks. Prior to the development of this understanding, young children believe that a male who dresses as a female is now a female and vice versa. Gender constancy is similar to the cognitive structure of conservation described by Piaget in his theory of cognitive development. A child who says that a tall, thin beaker does not contain the same amount of liquid as a short, wide beaker when the beakers in fact have the same amount of liquid is being fooled by the perceptual characteristics of the containers. A lack of gender constancy is explained the same way. Young children think Daddy has changed into a female when he dresses up as a female because the child is focusing on the perceptual characteristics of the father's appearance.

51. **(A)** Erikson suggested that identity development was the most important task of adolescence. The psychosocial crisis of this stage is identity versus identity confusion. An identity is the idea of who you are and what you will be like as an adult member of society. Erikson believed a healthy identity is the result of exploration and that it is normal for adolescents to experience stress about finding their identity.

52. **(B)** According to Freud, boys in the Oedipal stage of personality development experience an unconscious conflict because they have an unconscious sexual desire for their mother and at the same time, unconsciously fear reprisal and punishment from their father-rival. Freud argued that this Oedipal conflict is resolved through a process of identification. He believed children unconsciously resolve the conflict by replacing the sexual desire for mother with identification with father. Boys show this process of identification through modeling the father's behavior and by a preference for father over mother.

53. **(B)** Erikson argued that the psychosocial crisis of young adulthood was intimacy versus isolation. Young adults are highly motivated to be with a romantic partner. Erikson suggested a need to be with a significant other occurs at this time because the young adult has achieved a sense of identity and is now prepared to share his or her self intimately with another person. True intimacy is achieved when two people share a deep commitment, love and trust each other. This strong emotional bond cannot be achieved if one or both partners cannot trust and/or do not have a strong sense of self. Isolation is experienced when a young adult has not found a romantic partner. Erikson argued the social norm for adults was to be in an intimate relationship, so those who are not will feel lonely and isolated.

54. **(D)** Males are at greater risk of inheriting sex-linked genetic diseases because they have only one X chromosome. Females who have two X chromosomes have a greater chance of having a dominant gene to protect them from a genetic disease that is carried on a recessive gene on X chromosomes. Males who inherit a recessive gene on the X chromosome for a genetic disease have no chance of having a dominant gene to protect them. So while a female may be a carrier but not have the genetic disease, males who have the recessive gene will have the disease.

55. **(D)** Phenylketonuria (PKU) is a genetic disease caused by the body's inability to break down phenylalanine. The disease is controlled by a diet kept free of phenylalanine.

56. **(E)** The best approach to teaching deaf children language is to teach them sign language and how to lip read. This approach has the benefit of

helping the deaf child communicate among hearing people as well as communicate within the sign language community.

57. **(A)** Johnny is showing behaviors that meet the diagnostic criteria for conduct disorder. Conduct disorder is diagnosed when a child acts out and is aggressive in many situations and settings. A child with a conduct disorder is disobedient and aggressive.

58. **(C)** To screen for learning disabilities, children are given assessments to determine level of ability and level of performance. If the child's test results indicate a discrepancy between ability and performance, that child will likely be diagnosed with a learning disability.

59. **(D)** Marcia's model of identity development in adolescence classifies adolescents into four identity status groups based on whether or not they have experienced an identity crisis and whether or not they have made an identity commitment. The four statuses are: 1) identity moratorium (identity crisis and no commitment), 2) identity diffusion (no identity crisis and no commitment), 3) identity foreclosure (no identity crisis and a commitment), and 4) identity achievement (identity crisis and a commitment). Julio is an example of an adolescent who has adopted an identity too soon and never experienced an identity crisis. He is therefore showing identity foreclosure.

60. **(B)** The stage of parenthood when parents are launching children from the home is reportedly a time of growth and renewal for parents. Recent surveys of parents in this phase of parenthood break the myth that the "empty nest" phase usually brings on a period of depression and sadness.

61. **(C)** Between 6 and 10 weeks of age, an infant begins to smile in the presence of a caregiver. Prior to this time, an infant's smile is merely a reflexive response.

62. **(C)** Planning for retirement can help make retirement more satisfying if the planning includes finding opportunities for meaningful activities for the retired person.

63. **(A)** The ego is the intermediary between the id and reality. It develops between the ages of eight months and eighteen months, as the child acquires an understanding of what is possible in the outer world. The ego also distinguishes between long-range and short-range goals and decides which activities will be most profitable to the individual. The id and ego work together to determine the individual's goals.

64. **(C)** Freud believed that the primary driving force in an individual's life is the sexual urge (the libido). His theory of motivational development was particularly concerned with sexual gratification, as it changed in relation to the child's body. His theory of the personality structure (the id, ego, and superego) also deals with the sexual urge. The ego has to channel the libido into behaviors that are acceptable to the superego and fit within the constraints of the outer world.

65. **(C)** The behaviorist approach to psychology stresses the control that the environment has on development. In this view, behavior is shaped by reinforcement and punishment. It is argued that environmental stimuli control behavior.

66. **(A)** The humanistic approach, as exemplified by the work of Rogers, stresses the process of self-actualization. The cognitive approach stresses the construction of meaning, interpretations, and beliefs. The Freudian psychodynamic approach stresses unconscious conflicts. The behaviorist approach, as seen in Skinner's writings, stresses environmental stimulus control of behavior. Lastly, Bandura's social learning theory stresses the importance of modeling and vicarious reinforcement.

67. **(D)** Ivan P. Pavlov (1849–1936) virtually discovered the phenomenon of classical conditioning and was the first to investigate it systematically. In Pavlov's experiments with the salivating response of his dogs, he established the basic methodology and terminology still used today in classical conditioning experiments. Pavlov referred to food as the unconditional stimulus (UCS) because it naturally and consistently elicited salivation, which he called the unconditioned response (UCR). Pavlov later taught dogs to salivate to a bell. This was accomplished by presenting the bell just prior to presenting the food. After a series of such pairings, the dogs would salivate in response to the bell. In this case, the bell was a conditioned stimulus (CS) and the salivation in response to the bell was a conditioned response (CR). Hence, Pavlov's research elucidated the process of classical conditioning.

68. **(B)** Bandura and Walters conducted a classic experiment in which children shown videotapes of adults hitting and kicking a doll, later imitated the adults' aggressive behavior. The children also hit and kicked the doll.

69. **(D)** In a correlational study, a researcher measures two variables in a group of participants in order to determine if a relationship exists between the two variables. If a consistent pattern appears in the pairs of scores, for example, pairs of scores are very similar, or paired scores go in predictable, opposite directions, a correlation is established.

70. **(C)**   Adrenaline is a hormone that stimulates the sympathetic nervous system. One of the many resulting effects of adrenaline on the body is the stimulation of the heart. When stimulated, the sympathetic branch to the muscles of the heart causes the heart to beat more rapidly and vigorously. Thus, adrenaline has the effect of accelerating and strengthening the heartbeat.

71. **(C)**   The stage of formal operations is noted for the ability of the individual to deal with abstract problems and concepts. It usually begins around puberty but research shows that some people never develop these skills and continue to function at the level of concrete operations for life.

72. **(D)**   Based on the description of the way these children understood the game rules, one could determine that they are in the concrete operational stage of development. This stage emphasizes concrete understanding of rules and logical thinking as it relates to real concrete objects. Abstract and hypothetical thinking are largely undeveloped.

73. **(D)**   The concrete operational stage lasts from ages seven to twelve years. This is the usual age span, but it may be shorter or longer in an individual child.

74. **(A)**   Conservation is a Piagetian concept of recognizing the identity of number, mass, and volume despite transformations that alter their perceptual properties. Mike lacks conservation of mass in not realizing that his candy bar is equal to Joe's despite the perceptual difference of two versus three pieces. Learning conservation is a key indicator of progression from the preoperational to the concrete operations stage of development. However, learning conservation in one domain, such as mass, does not imply that other domains, such as volume, are understood.

75. **(A)**   Short-term memory (STM) is very limited in its capacity. It can only hold about seven items (plus or minus two items) of information at a time. This brief memory span requires deliberate rehearsal to prevent a specific memory from decaying over time.

76. **(C)**   In choosing the best move in a card game, one must be able to generate a number of possible solutions; therefore, divergent thinking is the process being utilized. Divergent thinking requires flexibility, fluency of ideas, and originality.

77. **(D)**   Noam Chomsky believes that children are born with a certain "something," a certain genetic predisposition that enables them to learn grammar. Chomsky called this predisposition the Language Acquisition Device

(LAD). It is believed to exist at birth. Chomsky used this concept to explain the relative ease with which normal children learn grammar.

78. **(A)**   A morpheme is the smallest unit of meaning in a given language. In English, morphemes can be whole words such as "boy," prefixes such as "anti-," or suffixes such as "-ing." There are more than 100,000 morphemes in English.

79. **(B)**   A "normal" I.Q. score is considered to be about 100, while 98 percent of the people who take I.Q. tests fall in the range between 60 and 140. Someone who scores above 140 is considered a genius.

80. **(E)**   There are many early childhood environmental factors that have been shown to correlate with later I.Q. I.Q. is more malleable than many people believe. All of the factors in this question influence I.Q. except for the intensity of separation anxiety.

81. **(D)**   Konrad Lorenz observed that newborn ducks would follow him if they saw him before encountering their mother. He termed this phenomenon "imprinting" and argued that it illustrated the importance of instinctual behavior. This concept, along with sign stimuli that release fixed patterns, comprised some of the central ideas of ethology.

82. **(D)**   Research on social attraction indicates that proximity is important for the obvious reason that social interaction is more likely when two people live nearby. Physical attraction and similarity are critical factors. All else being equal, the greater the familiarity, the greater the social attraction.

83. **(B)**   The need for social affiliation or a desire to be with other people is great when we are afraid. In a classic series of studies, Stanley Schachter manipulated the fear level of college women by leading them to believe they would receive electric shocks in a laboratory experiment. He then measured whether the women preferred to wait for the experiment to begin either alone or with others. Cognitive dissonance has no known effect on affiliation. Anxiety in general may or may not affect social affiliation, whereas depression decreases the desire to be with others.

84. **(D)**   According to social learning theory, we learn new behaviors by observing other people who serve as models for us. Choices (A) and (B) represent the Freudian approach, while choice (C) comes from the humanistic approach.

85 **(B)**   According to Freud, fixation results from abnormal personality development. Freud stated that a person feels a certain amount of frustration and anxiety as he passes from one stage of development to the next. If that

frustration and anxiety become too great, development may halt and the person becomes fixated at the stage he is trying to grow out of. For example, an overly dependent child is thought to be fixated. Development ceased at an early stage preventing the child from growing up and becoming independent.

86. **(B)** In classical conditioning the stimulus that elicits a response before any conditioning begins is called the unconditioned stimulus. It reliably elicits the unconditioned response (UCR) before the experiment. During the experimental manipulation, the unconditioned stimulus (UCS) is paired with a conditioned stimulus (CS) that originally does not elicit a response. After several such pairings the subject will emit a conditioned response (CR) to the conditioned stimulus (CS) that is very similar to the unconditioned response (UCR). After this conditioned response (CR) is learned, the unconditioned stimulus (UCS) may be removed, but the subject will keep responding to the conditioned stimulus (CS).

87. **(B)** Conditioned, or secondary reinforcement, occurs when the reinforcing stimulus is not inherently pleasing or reinforcing, but becomes so through association with other pleasant or reinforcing stimuli. Money is an example of a secondary (conditioned) reinforcer. Coins and paper currency are not in themselves pleasing, but the things they buy are pleasing. Therefore, an association is made between money and inherently pleasing primary reinforcers, such as food and drink. Hence, the term "conditioned reinforcer" is used.

88. **(D)** The variable-ratio schedule elicits consistently high rates of performance even after prolonged discontinuance of the reinforcement. In fact, once an operant learning response has been established with a variable-ratio reinforcement schedule, it is difficult to extinguish the response.

89. **(C)** Power struggles with authority figures occur for a variety of reasons. Relying on verbally abrasive responses to punish usually results in alienation of the student and deterioration of class atmosphere. All of the other responses are positive ways of dealing with Mary.

90. **(A)** Affective disorders are characterized by a disturbance of mood accompanied by related symptoms. Mood is defined as a prolonged emotional state that colors the whole psychic life and generally involves either depression or elation. In affective disorders, mood tends to be at one extreme or the other. The patient may be depressed, may be manic, or may exhibit bipolar symptoms, an alternation between depression and mania.

PRACTICE TEST 2

CLEP Human Growth and Development

Also available at the REA Study Center (*www.rea.com/studycenter*)

This practice test is also offered online at the REA Study Center. Since all CLEP exams are administered on computer, we recommend that you take the online version of the test to simulate test-day conditions and to receive these added benefits:

- **Timed testing conditions** – helps you gauge how much time you can spend on each question
- **Automatic scoring** – find out how you did on the test, instantly
- **On-screen detailed explanations of answers** – gives you the correct answer and explains why the other answer choices are wrong
- **Diagnostic score reports** – pinpoint where you're strongest and where you need to focus your study

PRACTICE TEST 2

CLEP Human Growth and Development

(Answer sheets appear in the back of the book.)

TIME: 90 Minutes
90 Questions

> **DIRECTIONS:** Each of the questions or incomplete statements below is followed by five possible answers or completions. Select the lettered choice that best answers each question and fill in the corresponding oval on the answer sheet.

1. Which of the following questions would be best answered using a correlational research design?

    (A) Is there a relationship between depression and age?

    (B) Are people more depressed before or after retirement?

    (C) Does exercise cause a decrease in depression?

    (D) How depressed are 14-year-olds?

    (E) Does drug addiction cause depression?

2. One of the main contributions of Freud's theory is its emphasis on

    (A) the unconscious

    (B) genetics

    (C) the environment shaping behavior

    (D) reinforcement

    (E) adult development

3. If you want to increase the number of times your child does the dishes, Skinner would say you need to

    (A) yell at your child when she does not do the dishes

    (B) give your child a cookie when she does the dishes

    (C) leave your sink full of dishes until your child does them

    (D) ask her to do the dishes

    (E) simultaneously present a reward and dirty dishes several times

4. Who is the person who identified personality types associated with occupational choice?

    (A) Bowlby   (D) Marcia

    (B) Ainsworth   (E) Holland

    (C) Bronfenbrenner

5. Which hormone has been shown to have a negative effect on the body's immune system?

    (A) Estrogen   (D) Adrenalin

    (B) Androgen   (E) Progesterone

    (C) Testosterone

6. Which of the following is a condition caused by a reduced supply of oxygen to the baby during delivery?

    (A) Anoxia   (D) Dysphoria

    (B) Presbyopia   (E) Mitosis

    (C) Apraxia

7. According to Kubler-Ross, the final stage of adjustment to death and dying is

    (A) mourning   (D) depression

    (B) renewal   (E) relief

    (C) acceptance

8. According to Daniel Goleman, which of the following may be a better predictor of success than I.Q.?

    (A) Drive   (D) Practical intelligence

    (B) Creativity   (E) Sociability

    (C) Emotional intelligence   (F) Aptitude

9. Preschoolers spend most of their waking hours engaging in which one of the following activities?

    (A) Eating

    (B) Playing with adults

    (C) Talking with other preschoolers

    (D) Watching television

    (E) Gross motor play

10. Which of the following terms is used to describe a household that has multiple generations of the same family living in it?

    (A) Blended   (D) Beanpole

    (B) Mixed   (E) Stratified

    (C) Complex

11. A person with an internal locus of control tends to attribute

    (A) success to luck

    (B) success to ability and effort

    (C) failure to bad luck

    (D) failure to a lack of effort

    (E) both (B) and (D)

12. All of the following are potential teratogens EXCEPT

    (A) illegal drugs taken by a pregnant woman

    (B) over-the-counter drugs taken by the mother during pregnancy

    (C) the emotional state of the mother

    (D) the emotional state of the father

    (E) environmental pollutants

13. Object permanence in the beginning of the sensorimotor stage is

    (A) not apparent

    (B) present in rudimentary form

    (C) characterized by active searches for missing objects

    (D) fully developed

    (E) characterized by a visual search rather than a motoric search for missing objects

14. Which of the following is a sign of habituation?

    (A) Looking time decreasing

    (B) Looking time increasing

    (C) Smiling decreasing

    (D) Respiration rate increasing

    (E) Yawning

15. Which of the following measures would be found on the Bayley Scales of Infant Intelligence?

    (A) Auditory and visual attention to objects

    (B) Reflexive response to touch

    (C) A measure of verbal ability

    (D) Temperament

    (E) Puzzle completion

16. The stage of adolescence might be best characterized as

    (A) a biologically determined period

    (B) a cultural creation

    (C) a legal fiction

    (D) an outdated historical concept

    (E) both biologically and culturally determined

17. According to Piaget, when a child is confronted with a new experience or idea that does not fit his or her present level of understanding, the child experiences

    (A) a cognitive collapse   (D) disorganization

    (B) disequilibrium   (E) fixation

    (C) preoperations

18. One of the most powerful attachment behaviors of infants is

    (A) the perceptual preference for looking at colorful objects versus black and white objects

    (B) the social smile

    (C) reciprocal interweaving

    (D) the tonic neck reflex

    (E) the Babinski reflex

19. Given the thought processes of elementary aged children, cognitive theory would recommend teaching them geography by

    (A) giving them map or globe pieces that they can manipulate and put together

    (B) showing them slides of various places around the world

    (C) having them memorize the names of the countries on each continent

    (D) having them listen to lectures from people from different countries

    (E) frequent drill and practice with country names

20. An example of the achievement of object permanence would be when an infant

    (A) flushes a favorite toy down the toilet

    (B) laughs when an adult makes a silly noise

    (C) refuses to go to sleep until Mommy and Daddy come home to say good night

    (D) looks up in the sky in response to thunder

    (E) counts to ten

21. Which of the following is a sign of secure attachment?

    (A) A strong reluctance to leave mother to play with new toys

    (B) Ignoring mother when she returns to the room

    (C) Crying when mother leaves the room and not being comforted by her return

    (D) Periodically searching for mother after she leaves the room

    (E) Hugging mother's leg when she returns to the room

22. Which of the following best fits the definition of a symbol?

    (A) A cup   (D) Wind chimes

    (B) A red traffic light   (E) A bark of a dog

    (C) The sound of laughter

23. The desire to be "good" and to obey the rules characterizes which stage of Kohlberg's theory?

    (A) Postconventional   (D) Morality of care

    (B) Conventional   (E) Morality of justice

    (C) Preconventional

24. According to Erikson, psychologically healthy middle-aged adults are likely to

    (A) engage in reflection on their lives in order to come to terms with unresolved conflicts

    (B) be concerned with personal advancement in their careers

    (C) develop a deep concern about making a contribution to society and passing on something of value to younger generations

    (D) focus on the establishment of intimate relationships with others

    (E) focus on their identities

25. Which of the following statements reflects Kohlberg's "conventional morality"?

    (A) "Do your own thing."

    (B) "Scratch my back and I'll scratch yours."

(C) "Rules were made to be broken."

(D) "Buckle up. It's the law."

(E) "All men were created equal."

26. Which sort of reasoning would likely make the most sense to a preconventional child?

(A) "Don't hit Jimmy because you should never hurt anyone."

(B) "Don't hit Jimmy because it's against the rules."

(C) "Don't hit Jimmy because you will get into trouble with the teacher."

(D) "Don't hit Jimmy because there are better ways to get what you want."

(E) "Don't hit Jimmy because he will hit you back."

27. The goals of social development in adolescence include

(A) identification with mother   (D) moral ascendancy

(B) identification with father   (E) separation-individuation

(C) symbiosis

28. A child sees a sparrow and says "bird." Then she sees a penguin and says "bird." According to Piaget, the child is using the process of

(A) scheming   (D) accommodation

(B) semantic networking   (E) conditioning

(C) assimilation

29. If a goat is separated from her kid immediately after delivery, she rejects it when reunited. But if the separation occurs ten minutes after delivery, no rejection occurs. This illustrates the developmental concept called

(A) critical period   (D) individual difference

(B) mother-infant synchrony   (E) maturation

(C) lack of permanence

30. Which of the following is an example of transductive reasoning?

    (A) Every child I see wears clothes; therefore, all children wear clothing.

    (B) Children who are good get candy; therefore, if I am good, I will get candy.

    (C) If I say I don't understand something, Daddy will explain it to me.

    (D) If you make the room dark, it will cause night to come.

    (E) If I eat a lot of candy, I will feel sick.

31. The evolutionary psychology perspective tries to

    (A) find effective ways to speed up maturation

    (B) understand the historical origins of human behaviors

    (C) understand how nutrition can influence physical growth

    (D) eliminate bad traits from the human gene pool

    (E) discover humans' closest animal relatives

32. In Bronfenbrenner's ecological theory, interactions between children and their parents take place in the child's

    (A) microsystem   (D) exosystem

    (B) macrosystem   (E) endosystem

    (C) mesosystem

33. Erikson's approach to development differed from Freud's approach in that Freud

    (A) emphasized social influences on development

    (B) did not discuss intra-psychic conflict

    (C) de-emphasized the role of animal instincts in controlling human behavior

    (D) emphasized the conflict between dreams and wish fulfillment

    (E) considered psychological development to be complete in adolescence

34. One weakness of the case study approach to research is

    (A) an inability to generalize results to a larger group

    (B) the researcher cannot get the subject's perspective

    (C) the researcher cannot quantify data that is collected from the subject

    (D) it is artificial

    (E) the researcher cannot measure any variables

35. The only research method that can identify cause-and-effect relationships is

    (A) correlational research

    (B) case study research

    (C) experimental research

    (D) observational research

    (E) twin study research

36. Which of the following research designs is considered the best to use to study development?

    (A) Cross-sectional   (D) Experimental

    (B) Lagged   (E) Correlational

    (C) Longitudinal

37. Changes in the brain after birth

    (A) rarely, if ever, occur

    (B) mainly occur in the frontal lobe

    (C) include the separation of the cerebral lobes

    (D) include a pruning back of neural connections

    (E) include cross sequencing

38. The fact that you and your spouse have brown eyes does not guarantee your offspring will also have brown eyes. This is due to which principle of genetic transmission?

   (A) Dominant   (D) Dizygotic

   (B) Recessive   (E) Chromosomal

   (C) Zygotic

39. Genetic abnormalities may be detected prenatally using

   (A) fibrosis   (D) X-rays

   (B) amniocentesis   (E) RH tests

   (C) fetal blood testing

40. A fertilized egg cell will differentiate into which of the following unless there is a Y sex chromosome present?

   (A) A female   (D) Identical twins

   (B) A male   (E) A zygote

   (C) Fraternal twins

41. Selective attention requires the ability to

   (A) focus on a stimulus   (D) think

   (B) ignore irrelevant stimuli (E) multi-task

   (C) problem solve

42. The information processing approach to the study of memory argues there are three memory storage systems. These are

   (A) sensory, primary, secondary

   (B) sensory, semantic, episodic

   (C) primary, secondary, tertiary

   (D) primary, semantic, episodic

   (E) sensory, visual, linguistic

43. The most commonly found developmental change in primary memory is

    (A) an increase in vocabulary

    (B) an increase in the number of items that can be retained in primary memory

    (C) an increase in the length of time that items can be retained in primary memory

    (D) a pruning of associations in primary memory

    (E) an increase in the organization of information in primary memory

44. In Vygotsky's theory, the term "scaffolding" described

    (A) the role of maturation in development

    (B) the role of genetics in development

    (C) older members of the community serving as guides for children's learning

    (D) how perception guides thinking in children

    (E) how knowledge of the physical world develops in children

45. Which of the following terms refers to the basic grammatical rules of a language?

    (A) Phoneme   (D) Syntax

    (B) Morpheme   (E) Syllable

    (C) Pragmatic

46. Which of the following statements is true?

> I. Infants are born with the capacity to produce all of the morphemes of all of the world's languages and retain this ability throughout adulthood.

> II. Infants are born with the capacity to produce all of the phonemes of all of the world's languages but lose this ability over time.

> III. Infants are born with the capacity to produce all of the morphemes of all of the world's languages but lose this ability over time.

> IV. Infants are born with the capacity to produce all of the phonemes of all of the world's languages and retain this ability throughout adulthood.

> V. Infants are born with the capacity to discriminate phonemes and morphemes but lose this ability over time.

(A) I   (D) IV

(B) II   (E) V

(C) III

47. One form of learning that appears in the newborn is called

(A) habituation   (D) apraxia

(B) perceptual sensitivity   (E) discrimination

(C) classification

48. Marissa's parents have raised her to respect elders, obey their rules, not talk back to them, and hardly ever ask for her opinions or point of view on matters of discipline and house rules. Based on this description, their parenting style would be classified as

(A) love oriented   (D) permissive

(B) authoritarian   (E) democratic

(C) authoritative

49. The parenting style that has been found to be associated with the best developmental outcomes for children is

    (A) disorganized

    (B) authoritarian

    (C) authoritative

    (D) permissive

    (E) democratic

50. Albert Bandura argued that children learn behaviors

    (A) without having to directly experience the behavior

    (B) by performing the behavior and then receiving reinforcement

    (C) by observing another person perform a behavior and then receive reinforcement

    (D) by doing

    (E) to avoid punishment

51. Kubler-Ross performed ground-breaking research on the experiences of people who are dying from terminal illnesses. She concluded that

    (A) dying was an individual experience; no general conclusions about how people approach their death can be made

    (B) the way a person deals with his or her impending death depends on the person's gender

    (C) the way a person deals with his or her impending death depends on the person's personality type

    (D) there are stages a terminally ill person progresses through as he or she deals with his/her impending death

    (E) terminally-ill patients are not interested in talking about death

52. The term used to describe personality in young infants is

    (A) attachment style

    (B) temperament

    (C) extroversion

    (D) autism

    (E) respondent type

53. According to Skinner, a classroom teacher who wishes to decrease students' disruptive behaviors should

    (A) ignore disruptive behaviors and reward appropriate classroom behaviors

    (B) harshly punish disruptive behavior

    (C) give children more play time

    (D) give children more tasks to keep them busy

    (E) remove distracters from the classroom

54. Which is NOT one of the factors found to contribute to resilience in babies born at risk?

    (A) Personal resources like intelligence

    (B) Having at least one person who loves them

    (C) Having a stimulating environment

    (D) Being raised in a two-parent family

    (E) Being sociable

55. There are two attribution styles that have been identified in research on personality development. These are

    (A) extroversion and introversion

    (B) openness versus a lack of openness to experience

    (C) internal and external locus of control

    (D) sociability and non-sociability

    (E) feminine versus masculine orientation

56. Which of the following statements is true?

    I.   Gender is the same as biological sex.

    II.   Feminine is to female as masculine is to male.

    III. Both males and females can be feminine or masculine.

    IV.   Gender is determined at birth.

    (A) I   (D) I and IV

    (B) II   (E) IV

    (C) III

57. Developmental psychologists who are continuity theorists

    (A) argue that development proceeds through a series of qualitatively different stages

    (B) argue that development proceeds through a series of quantitatively different stages

    (C) disagree with each other on the number of stages of development

    (D) agree that development is controlled by genetic inheritance

    (E) argue that development is best described as increases in amount or strength of abilities and not stages or qualitative shifts in abilities

58. Newborns show signs that they can discriminate among the four tastes: bitter, sweet, salty, and sour. The evidence for this ability comes from examining which of the following changes in newborns when flavored liquid is placed on their tongues?

    (A) Heart rate   (D) Moro reflex response

    (B) Respiration   (E) Grasping

    (C) Facial expression

59. Which of the following factors might predict that John, who was born with low birth weight, would develop normally?

    (A) The fact that John has a difficult temperament as an infant.

    (B) The fact that John has above-average intelligence.

    (C) The fact that John's mother is a stay-at-home mom.

    (D) The fact that John is an only child.

    (E) The fact that John is male.

60. Presbyopia refers to

    (A) infants' inability to track moving objects

    (B) changes in sensitivity to odors that gradually occur with increasing age

    (C) increasingly poor near vision that begins in middle age

    (D) newborns' preference for looking at faces

    (E) increasingly poor taste sensitivity with age

61. Teratogens have

    (A) no affect on prenatal development in the last two weeks of pregnancy

    (B) different effects on male versus female fetuses

    (C) their greatest influence on the development of systems of the body during the second trimester

    (D) effects only in nervous system development

    (E) their greatest effects in the first two weeks of pregnancy

62. Which of the following is a key element of Darwin's theory?

    (A) There is a constant competition for limited resources, like food, among members of a species.

    (B) There is a constant struggle for existence between species.

    (C) Members of species who cooperate as a group have a greater chance for survival.

    (D) All members of a species inherit the same ability to survive.

    (E) Humans and animals evolved from different ancestors.

63. Observations of children's language development indicate that

    (A) generalization is achieved before discrimination

    (B) production develops faster than understanding

    (C) understanding develops faster than production

    (D) acquisition is achieved before understanding

    (E) imitation develops slower than production

64. According to Piaget, the highest level of cognitive functioning is

    (A) sensorimotor intelligence

    (B) formal operations

    (C) concrete operations

    (D) preoperations

    (E) perceptual operations

65. Which developmental psychologist described the importance of language for the development of thought?

   (A) Sigmund Freud   (D) Jean Piaget

   (B) Lev Vygotsky   (E) Urie Bronfenbrenner

   (C) Erik Erikson

66. Research on child abuse shows that

   (A) the United States has the lowest rate of child abuse than any other country

   (B) parents who abuse their children have low I.Q.'s

   (C) most parents who abuse their children were abused themselves

   (D) parents who abuse their children experience high emotional arousal in stressful situations

   (E) abusers typically have bipolar disorder

67. A child runs into his house and expects his Daddy to know what happened to him outside. This is an example of

   (A) autistic thinking   (D) reciprocal thinking

   (B) social thinking   (E) vicarious thinking

   (C) egocentric thinking

68. One diagnostic feature of autism is the child's

   (A) delayed physical development

   (B) below average intelligence

   (C) aggressive behavior toward others

   (D) lack of interest and responsiveness to others

   (E) impulsive behavior

69. Which of the following statements is true?

    I.   One of the earliest symptoms to appear in Alzheimer's disease is a speech impairment called "word salad."

    II.   One of the earliest symptoms to appear in Alzheimer's disease is impaired motor coordination.

    III. One of the earliest symptoms to appear in Alzheimer's disease is paranoia.

    IV. One of earliest symptoms to appear in Alzheimer's disease is memory impairment.

(A) I

(B) II

(C) III

(D) IV

(E) III and IV

70. According to the information-processing approach, cognitive development is the result of

(A) improved logical thinking

(B) the construction of mental schema

(C) an increase in mental processing speed

(D) a decrease in metacognition

(E) adaptation

71. The whole-language approach to teaching reading

(A) concentrates on teaching children how to pronounce the phonemes in their native language

(B) teaches children how to write letters properly

(C) exposes children to the whole text of reading materials rather than teaching letter-to-sound combinations

(D) teaches reading by rote

(E) allows children to pretend to read whole books to increase their confidence

72. A common feature of attention-deficit hyperactivity disorder is

    (A) mood swings   (D) antisocial behavior

    (B) obsessions   (E) negativity

    (C) a lack of impulse control

73. Which level of intellectual disability is closest to the normal range of I.Q.?

    (A) Mildly mentally retarded

    (B) Trainable mentally retarded

    (C) Profoundly mentally retarded

    (D) Severely mentally retarded

    (E) Optimally mentally retarded

74. The reinforcement schedule that yields the lowest performance is the

    (A) fixed-ratio schedule

    (B) variable-ratio schedule

    (C) fixed-interval schedule

    (D) variable-interval schedule

    (E) intermittent reinforcement schedule

75. The repeated presentation of the CS without the UCS results in

    (A) spontaneous recovery   (D) higher-order conditioning

    (B) inhibition   (E) negative reinforcement

    (C) extinction

76. The Wechsler Intelligence Scale for Children differs from the Revised Stanford Binet test in

    (A) the age groups that can be tested

    (B) the distribution of verbal and nonverbal tasks

    (C) its applicability with psychotic students

    (D) its accounting for cultural background differences

    (E) its usefulness for predicting creativity

77. People who repeatedly wash their hands even when they are not dirty may be said to be suffering from

    (A) learned helplessness   (D) a phobia

    (B) a conversion reaction   (E) a compulsion

    (C) an obsession

78. The theory that we all experience a series of psychosocial crises throughout our lives was proposed by

    (A) Freud   (D) Erikson

    (B) Adler   (E) Jung

    (C) Sheldon

79. According to Freud, the main function of dreams is

    (A) to bridge the unconscious with the conscious mind

    (B) the assimilation of conscious memories into the unconscious

    (C) the release of unconscious materials into the preconscious

    (D) wish fulfillment of the individual

    (E) the release of sexual and social tensions

80. According to psychoanalytic thinking, the personality structure consists of

    (A) habits   (D) the id, ego, and superego

    (B) drives   (E) consciousness

    (C) self

81. The pituitary gland secretes all of the following hormones EXCEPT

    (A) TSH (thyroid-stimulating hormone)

    (B) ACTH (adrenocorticotrophic hormone)

    (C) FSH (follicle-stimulating hormone)

    (D) LH (luteinizing hormone)

    (E) EH (estrogen hormone)

82. The colored portion of the eye is called the

    (A) lens   (D) iris

    (B) cornea   (E) retina

    (C) pupil

83. Receptor cells that are very sensitive to color are the

    (A) ganglion cells   (D) bipolar cells

    (B) rods   (E) chromatic cells

    (C) cones

84. Children who are bilingual have been found to

    (A) have more academic difficulties than their monolingual peers

    (B) have high verbal and non-verbal intelligence scores

    (C) have lower creativity scores than their monolingual peers

    (D) have higher levels of self-esteem than their monolingual counterparts

    (E) lack an understanding of the grammar of their second language

85. The sensitive period for language acquisition refers to the fact that

    (A) humans are not emotionally stable until they can communicate effectively

    (B) after a certain age, language skills deteriorate

    (C) if a person has not acquired a language by puberty, he or she may never learn to speak appropriately

    (D) humans must acquire one language at a time

    (E) the brain needs a time frame to develop language centers

86. Mentally challenged humans frequently show language deficits. Language acquisition of simple statements and sentences is highly unlikely if the measured I.Q. is below

    (A) 100   (D) 50

    (B) 80   (E) 20

    (C) 70

87. The best demonstrations of language acquisition by apes and chimps show that they function on a level equivalent to a human

    (A) three-year-old

    (B) child between 7 and 11 years of age

    (C) adolescent between 12 and 15 years of age

    (D) adolescent between 16 and 20 years of age

    (E) adult, 21 years of age or older

88. Morphemes differ from phonemes in that

    (A) morphemes are utterances that have no meaning

    (B) phonemes carry meaning while morphemes do not

    (C) morphemes carry meaning while phonemes do not

    (D) morphemes refer to animal sounds while phonemes are sounds made only by humans

    (E) phonemes refer to speech sounds while morphemes refer to sign language gestures

89. Alfred Binet is famous for developing the first

    (A) item analysis

    (D) fixed alternative test

    (B) intelligence test

    (E) infant intelligence test

    (C) projective test

90. Children are shown a movie of an adult hitting and kicking a rubber doll. Later, they are given access to the doll. Videotapes of the children made with a hidden camera reveal that

    (A) they treat the doll like they do their own toys

    (B) they hit and kick the doll

    (C) the boys hit the doll while the girls play gently with it

    (D) the children avoid the doll

    (E) the girls console the doll

PRACTICE TEST 2

Answer Key

1.	(A)	31.	(B)	61.	(C)
2.	(A)	32.	(A)	62.	(A)
3.	(B)	33.	(E)	63.	(C)
4.	(E)	34.	(A)	64.	(B)
5.	(D)	35.	(C)	65.	(B)
6.	(A)	36.	(C)	66.	(D)
7.	(C)	37.	(D)	67.	(C)
8.	(C)	38.	(B)	68.	(D)
9.	(D)	39.	(B)	69.	(D)
10.	(D)	40.	(A)	70.	(C)
11.	(B)	41.	(B)	71.	(C)
12.	(D)	42.	(A)	72.	(C)
13.	(A)	43.	(B)	73.	(A)
14.	(A)	44.	(C)	74.	(C)
15.	(A)	45.	(D)	75.	(C)
16.	(E)	46.	(B)	76.	(B)
17.	(B)	47.	(A)	77.	(E)
18.	(B)	48.	(B)	78.	(D)
19.	(A)	49.	(C)	79.	(D)
20.	(C)	50.	(C)	80.	(D)
21.	(E)	51.	(D)	81.	(E)
22.	(B)	52.	(B)	82.	(D)
23.	(B)	53.	(A)	83.	(C)
24.	(C)	54.	(D)	84.	(B)
25.	(D)	55.	(C)	85.	(C)
26.	(E)	56.	(C)	86.	(E)
27.	(E)	57.	(E)	87.	(A)
28.	(C)	58.	(C)	88.	(C)
29.	(A)	59.	(B)	89.	(B)
30.	(D)	60.	(C)	90.	(B)

PRACTICE TEST 2

Detailed Explanations of Answers

1. **(A)**   Correlational research involves measuring two variables in a group of subjects and determining whether there is a relationship between the two sets of scores. A correlational design could be used to determine whether there is a relationship between depression and age by measuring age and level of depression in a large sample. Both responses (B) and (C) require an examination of differences, not relationships. Response (D) is a question that is best answered using a descriptive research approach like conducting a survey of a sample of 14-year-olds. The question is asking only what 14-year-olds are like. It is not a relationship or cause-and-effect question. Response (E) is a question about cause and effect. Cause-and-effect relationships cannot be identified using the correlational research design. A correlation does not mean causation because no variables are controlled or manipulated in correlational research.

2. **(A)**   Freud's theory is unique in that it emphasizes the role of unconscious thoughts and wishes in motivating human behavior. For Freud, the unconscious held innate biological urges that must be channeled into socially appropriate behavior.

3. **(B)**   Skinner described a process of learning he called operant conditioning. According to Skinner, learning, defined as changes in overt behavior, is shaped by reinforcement and punishment. Reinforcement (both positive and negative) received after a behavior is emitted will increase the probability that that behavior will be repeated under the same stimulus conditions. Punishment experienced after a behavior is emitted will decrease the probability that the behavior will be repeated again under the same stimulus conditions. Therefore, to increase the number of times your child does the dishes, Skinner would suggest you reinforce the child when she or he does the dishes. A cookie is generally considered a reward and therefore should work as a reinforcer and increase the frequency of the goal behavior.

4. **(E)**   John Holland conducted research on the relationship between personality traits and characteristics of different occupations. Based on this research, he developed a system to match personality types with occupational types.

5. **(D)** Adrenalin is a hormone secreted as part of the body's flight or fight response. It is also secreted during times of emotional stress. Consistently high levels of adrenalin can negatively impact the body's immune system.

6. **(A)** The supply of oxygen to a fetus can be disrupted during a vaginal delivery if the umbilical cord becomes crimped or if mucous builds up in the baby's throat. The condition of a depleted oxygen supply is called anoxia.

7. **(C)** Kubler-Ross was the first to systematically study terminally ill patients. Based on extensive interviews with people as they progressed through the process of dying, she formulated a stage model of adjustment to death and dying. The stages include denial, anger, bargaining, depression, and finally, acceptance.

8. **(C)** Goleman suggests that another form of intelligence, called emotional intelligence, is a person's ability to understand and adapt to emotion and emotional situations. People with high E.Q.s have an exceptional ability to understand and deal with their own emotions and the emotions expressed by other people. His controversial prediction is that E.Q. is a better predictor of success in life than I.Q.

9. **(D)** Research has shown that, second to sleeping, preschoolers watch television more than engaging in any other activity.

10. **(D)** A beanpole family has multiple generations of the same family living in the same household. Typically, this occurs because a grandparent is living in the home.

11. **(B)** A person who has an internal locus of control attribution style believes that events in his or her life are under his or her control. Therefore, both successes and failures are attributed to personal abilities, traits, or behaviors.

12. **(D)** Teratogens are substances that pass through the semi-permeable membrane of the placenta, enter the fetus's bloodstream and cause damage to the fetus. Therefore, anything that occurs in the father's body cannot, by definition, be a teratogen.

13. **(A)** The sensorimotor stage is the first stage in Piaget's model of cognitive development. Piaget demonstrated that object permanence was not present at birth and developed during the sensorimotor stage. He believed object permanence is not fully achieved until the end of infancy.

14. **(A)** Habituation is a simple form of learning that appears in newborns. Habituation is defined as decreased attention to a stimulus over time. Therefore, if a newborn habituates to a stimulus, his or her looking time will decrease.

15. **(A)** The Bayley Scales of Infant Intelligence were developed to measure levels of intelligence in infants. Prior research suggested a positive relationship between measures of attention in infants and later I.Q. scores. Therefore, measures of auditory and visual attention spans are included on the Bayley Scales.

16. **(E)** Cross-cultural research on the adolescent stage of development has shown variations in the length of adolescence as well as the experiences of adolescents. There is some evidence that the biological changes associated with adolescence produce some universals of experiences and stress. However, in some cultures adolescence is non-existent or only a brief phase. Some cultures have a ceremonial rite of passage into adulthood so that a child becomes an adult in the same day, whereas in others, the stage is long and stressful. Therefore, adolescence is both biologically and culturally determined.

17. **(B)** "Disequilibrium" is the term used by Piaget to describe the cognitive experience that occurs when assimilation fails. Assimilation is the process of understanding a new experience using already existing cognitive schema. A person is assimilating when she walks into a Burger King for the first time and acts as she has always acted in McDonald's. Disequilibrium would be experienced by the same girl the first time she went into a fancy restaurant. Disequilibrium is an important process in cognitive development because it is the experience that motivates us to modify our existing schema. We accommodate when we adjust a scheme to include new information. The scheme that is a result of this process of disequilibrium-accommodation is more mature.

18. **(B)** Attachment behaviors are behaviors emitted by the members of an attachment relationship, e.g., mother-infant or father-infant, that increase the strength of the attachment bond. As young infants' smiling develops from a reflexive facial response to an intentional, controlled "social smile," they will smile more frequently in the presence of the target of their attachment. In so doing, the infant attracts the attention of the target.

19. **(A)** Piaget argued that children develop understanding about the world through active exploration of objects. Therefore, children would benefit from a teaching approach that gives them concrete objects to manipulate.

20. **(C)** Object permanence is the concept that objects have a permanent and separate existence from our perception of them. A child who has not achieved object permanence will not actively search for a missing toy. Anything that becomes

out of sight becomes out of mind for this child. A child who wants to wait for parents to come home shows he or she has the concept of object permanence. Even though the parents are currently out of sight, they are not out of mind.

21. **(E)** Ainsworth developed a method of measuring the strength of the attachment relationship between child and caregiver called the Ainsworth Strange Situation. Although this method has been criticized by some theorists as creating an artificial situation for the child and caregiver, it is the most widely used method of assessing attachment. In the Strange Situation, a child is separated from the caregiver and his or her reactions are observed. The observers note the child's reactions when the caregiver leaves, as well as when the caregiver returns. Based upon these reactions, the child is judged to be either securely attached or insecurely attached to the caregiver. A child is judged to be securely attached if she or he is upset when the caregiver leaves, and reacts positively and seeks proximity to the caregiver upon the caregiver's return. Insecure-avoidant children do not act distressed when the caregiver leaves and avoid the caregiver upon his or her return to the room. An insecure-disorganized/disoriented child reacts in a conflicted way to the caregiver upon his or her return to the room. This child may seek contact and then move away from the caregiver. Insecure-resistant children are very distressed when the caregiver leaves and actively resist contact with the caregiver upon his or her return to the room.

22. **(B)** A symbol is something that represents something else but does not look like or relate in a rationale way to what it represents. The idea that the color red means stop is due to the symbolic relationship between the color and the idea of "stop."

23. **(B)** Kohlberg developed a theory of moral development in which he described a series of stages through which mature moral reasoning develops. In the stage of conventional morality, one makes decisions about right and wrong by applying societal laws created to control behavior. Hence, one would think being "good" means obeying the rules.

24. **(C)** In Erikson's model of personality development, the psychosocial crisis to be resolved in middle adulthood is generativity versus stagnation. Generativity is the positive resolution of this crisis and involves fulfilling one's desire to make a contribution to society and help members of younger generations of that society develop and meet their goals.

25. **(D)** According to Kohlberg's theory of how moral reasoning develops, in the conventional morality stage, decisions about right and wrong are made by applying societal laws. Thus, given the answer choices, (D) is correct because one would think it is right to buckle up because there is a law that says so.

26. **(E)** During Kohlberg's stage of preconventional morality, a child makes decisions about right and wrong based on his or her expectations of the consequences of his or her actions. Therefore, a preconventional reasoner would decide not to hit another child because he would expect to get hit back. He or she would not hit another child in order to avoid being hit back, not because it is the moral thing to do.

27. **(E)** Adolescence is a transition stage of development in which a person moves from being dependent on caregivers as a child, to becoming a separate and independent being.

28. **(C)** Assimilation is the process of understanding something new using already existing cognitive structures or schema. The child's understanding of the penguin is achieved by applying a scheme for similar looking things, i.e., "bird." In Piaget's theory of cognitive development, the process of assimilation has to be in balance with the process of accommodation which is changing an old scheme to fit new information. A child who over assimilates will not develop more mature and complex schema.

29. **(A)** The concept of critical period was introduced by the ethologists Konrad Lorenz and John Bowlby. A critical period is a restricted range of time for a characteristic or trait to develop. This question illustrates a critical period in development for a mother-infant bond to form between a goat and her kid. In humans, there is greater flexibility to develop characteristics and traits outside of critical windows of time; therefore, psychologists use the term "sensitive period" rather than "critical period" when discussing human development. For example, in human development there appears to be a sensitive period from birth to puberty during which it is easier to learn a language, but that does not mean no one can learn a language once this time period has passed.

30. **(D)** Transductive reasoning is immature reasoning about cause-and-effect relationships.

31. **(B)** Evolutionary psychology is a field that tries to trace the historical roots of human behavior. This perspective is influenced by Darwin's theory of evolution. In this perspective, behaviors in our species' repertoire are believed to have adaptive value. Evolutionary psychologists study human behavior to understand its adaptive value, as well as study the behavior of less evolved species, to develop a better understanding of human behavior.

32. **(A)** Bronfenbrenner argued that development should be studied within the contexts in which it occurs. He suggested several such contexts. A context in which a child plays a direct role is called a microsystem. The family and

school are examples of microsystems. In the ecosystem, events from different microsystems interact. The exosystem is a social context that indirectly influences the child's development, like Dad's office, and the macrosystem is the cultural context in which all the other systems are embedded.

33. **(E)** A major difference between the psychosocial model of development from Erikson and the psychosexual model of development from Freud is that Erikson's model is a life span approach. Erikson argued that development takes place throughout the entire life span. According to Freud, development was complete at puberty. Hence, Freud's focus was on the impact of early childhood experiences on personality, while Erikson argued experiences throughout our lives continue to shape our personality.

34. **(A)** The case study approach to research has strengths and weaknesses. A strength is that the researcher is able to learn a great deal about an individual case. The description of the case is detailed and deep. This can be especially helpful when the researcher is studying someone who is unique or had a unique experience. On the other hand, the findings from one case study cannot be generalized to a larger group. A goal of psychology is to understand and explain what is common to all people, as well as to understand individual differences. The case study approach does not help in attaining the first goal.

35. **(C)** Experimental research is the only type of research that can identify cause-and-effect relationships. The two key elements of the experimental approach to research are control and manipulation. In a controlled setting, an independent variable, which is the hypothesized cause, is manipulated so that it is present in one condition of the experiment but not present in another condition in the experiment. In this way, an experimenter can determine if the effect occurs if, and only if, the independent variable is present. Without this control and manipulation, researchers can only observe whether or not two variables are related, as in correlational research.

36. **(C)** There are research designs that are particularly useful in developmental research. Two of these are the longitudinal research design and the cross-sectional research design. The longitudinal method involves studying a group of participants at several points in time over a long period of time. The researcher measures changes in this group as they age. A cross-sectional study involves studying samples of participants who represent different age groups. A researcher using this design is able to show how different aged people are different from each other at one point in time but not how the same people change with age. Also, this design confounds age difference with birth cohort differences. Therefore, the longitudinal design is considered the stronger of the two designs.

37. **(D)** Studies of brain development have shown that as the human brain matures, there is a pruning back of neural connections. Neural connections that are frequently used are retained, while neural connections that were present early in development but are not used, are pruned.

38. **(B)** A recessive trait is a trait that is carried on a recessive gene. Since we inherit gene pairs from our biological parents, it is possible to inherit two recessive genes, two dominant genes, or a dominant gene-recessive gene pair. The trait on a recessive gene will be expressed only if the dominant gene is not present. The gene for blue eyes is a recessive gene. Even if both the mother and father have brown eyes, they both could be carriers of the recessive gene for blue eyes. It is therefore possible that an offspring would inherit two recessive genes and have blue eyes.

39. **(B)** Amniocentesis is one method of prenatal screening used to detect abnormalities in fetal development. Amniotic fluid is removed from the amniotic sac in the uterus and analyzed for markers of genetic diseases and abnormalities.

40. **(A)** The default is for a fertilized egg cell to develop into a female. The presence of the Y chromosome is what stops this default process and causes the fertilized egg cell to differentiate into a male. It is the biological father therefore who determines the sex of the offspring. The biological father is the only parent who can pass on a Y chromosome.

41. **(B)** Selective attention is the process in which perceptual energy is directed toward a stimulus target and kept from distracting irrelevant stimuli in the environment. Therefore, selective attention requires the ability to ignore irrelevant stimuli.

42. **(A)** The information-processing approach to studying cognitive development argues that there are three memory storage systems. These are sensory, primary, and secondary memory. Sensory memory is the temporary storage of what registers in a sensory-perceptual system like vision or audition. This is an automatic and very brief record of information lasting only a few seconds. Sensory memory is also referred to as iconic memory. Primary memory, also known as short-term or working memory, is a memory storage system that also holds information temporarily albeit for a longer period of time than sensory memory. Information can be held in primary memory for a longer period of time through the process of rehearsal. Repeating a telephone number to yourself causes the number to be retained in your consciousness. However, any interruption in rehearsal will cause the information to be lost. Secondary or long-term memory is our long-term storage system.

Memories are stored in secondary memory through the process of encoding. Information that is in primary memory that is encoded for long-term retention is moved from primary to secondary memory. Since encoding is done in primary memory, this system is also referred to as working memory. Some psychologists believe that secondary memory is a permanent storage system and that forgetting occurs not because information is lost, but because the information cannot be retrieved. The better the information to be stored is encoded, the more likely the information will be retrieved later. Secondary memory is a highly organized storage system.

43. **(B)** Researchers have studied changes in memory that occur with age. One finding is that the capacity of primary memory increases with age until it reaches full maturity of seven plus or minus two bits of information.

44. **(C)** Vygotsky described cognitive development as the result of interactions between a child and older people in his or her environment. He argued that children's thinking is supported or "scaffolded" by adults in his or her life like teachers and parents. Working with an older adult, children can solve more difficult problems than if he or she was working alone.

45. **(D)** Syntax is the term used to describe the grammatical rules of a language. Syntax guides how the elements of language are combined.

46. **(B)** A remarkable finding by psycholinguists studying language development is that newborns have the ability to produce all of the sounds or phonemes required to speak any of the world's languages. Further, this ability is lost with age. Infants will continue to form the phonemes required for their native language, and lose the ability to produce sounds of non-native languages.

47. **(A)** Habituation is a simple type of learning that appears in newborns. Habituation is a decrease in responding to a stimulus over time. A newborn will look away from a stimulus object after a period of time.

48. **(B)** Baumrind examined the relationship between parenting style and developmental outcomes. The authoritarian parenting style is seen in a parent who values strict obedience from children and uses punishment to change children's behavior. An authoritarian parent does not provide explanations for the household rules and children do not have a voice in determining those rules. They also show low acceptance/responsiveness toward the child. Authoritative parents provide guidelines and rules for behavior, but also show high acceptance/responsiveness toward the child. Harsh punishment is not used. The permissive parent provides little to no guidelines or rules for the child's behavior, but shows high acceptance/responsiveness toward the child. The uninvolved

parenting style is seen in parents who are low in control/demandingness and low in acceptance/responsiveness. These parents pay little to no attention to their child. Marissa's parents are authoritarian.

49. **(C)** Authoritative parenting has been associated with the best developmental outcomes. See the explanation for #48.

50. **(C)** Albert Bandura argued behavior is learned not only through classical and operant conditioning, but is also the result of imitation or observational learning. Bandura argued that when we observe a model being positively reinforced for his or her behavior, we are likely to imitate that model.

51. **(D)** Kubler-Ross was the first to systematically study terminally ill patients. Based on extensive interviews with people as they progressed through the process of dying, she formulated a stage model of adjustment to death and dying. The stages in order are denial, anger, bargaining, depression, and acceptance. Critics of her work argue that Kubler-Ross made death and dying a more normative process than it really is. They argue that not all dying people go through all of the stages and that some people never reach the stage of acceptance. Finally, the circumstances surrounding the dying process affect the dying person's experience.

52. **(B)** Temperament is the term used for a rudimentary form of personality in infants. Temperament is the typical style or way infants respond to people and stimulation, and their characteristic activity level. There are three temperament types, which are easy, difficult, and slow to warm up.

53. **(A)** Skinner argued that in order to shape behavior, reinforcing a goal behavior is more effective than punishing inappropriate behavior. Classroom management techniques reflect Skinner's findings. Therefore, a classroom teacher who wishes to shape a student's behavior would be advised by Skinner to ignore problem behaviors and reinforce good behavior. Attention to problem behaviors may result in inadvertently rewarding the behavior.

54. **(D)** Being raised by only one versus two parents has not been shown to influence resilience. All of the other factors have.

55. **(C)** Psychologists have studied the attributions people make for causes of experiences in life. There are two diametrically opposed styles that have emerged from this work. These are the internal locus of control style and the external locus of control style. Internals place the locus of control over events in their lives inside themselves or under their own control. Externals place the locus of control of events in their lives outside or beyond their own control.

A bad test grade is interpreted as due to a lack of effort by internals and due to the teacher making the test too difficult by externals.

56. **(C)** The term "gender" is often misapplied. In colloquial language, gender has become a substitute term for biological sex. Gender, however, is not the same as biological sex. Sex refers to one's biological make-up, i.e., male or female. Gender refers to a social role and these include masculinity, femininity, and androgyny. Biological sex and gender are independent of each other although stereotypically, males are expected to be more masculine than females, and females are expected to be more feminine than males.

57. **(E)** There is a debate among psychologists as to whether development is best described as a series of qualitative shifts or stages, or steady increases in the amount or strength of abilities. Discontinuity theorists argue for the former. Continuity theorists argue for the latter.

58. **(C)** Research on infant taste perception has relied on infants' facial expressions to indicate whether the infant can discriminate the four tastes. Reliable changes in facial expression appear in newborns presented with different flavored liquids.

59. **(B)** Having average or higher intelligence, an easy temperament, at least one person who loves you unconditionally, and being sociable have been shown to increase infant resilience in the face of risks. Low birth weight is a risk factor that can lead to developmental problems in infants. The factors listed above are associated with thriving and normal developmental outcomes in at-risk infants.

60. **(C)** Presbyopia is a vision problem associated with aging. Presbyopia is caused by a difficulty focusing on near objects. Most middle-aged adults begin to have near vision problems, but most of these problems are corrected with lenses to help properly focus light waves from near objects onto the retina.

61. **(C)** Teratogens are potentially damaging substances that cross the semi-permeable membrane of the placenta and enter the bloodstream of the fetus. Damage from teratogens rarely occurs in the first trimester or the third trimester. Most organs and systems of the body are most susceptible to damage from teratogens during the second trimester.

62. **(A)** There are several key elements to Darwin's theory of the evolution of species by natural selection. One of these is that there is a competition among members of a species for survival. The population growth of a species is always faster than the growth of the food and supplies needed to support the

species. Such limited resources produce a struggle among members of a species for survival. Another element is that members of a species inherit chance variations of the traits of the species. Some members inherit variations that increase their chances of surviving, while others inherit variations that make them less likely to survive. Members of the species who survive to maturity, reproduce and therefore keep their traits in the species gene pool. Over a very long time period, a species evolves as genes for the chance variations that did not enable survival gradually disappear from the gene pool.

63. **(C)** Children show an understanding of language that surpasses their ability to produce language. For example, an infant can follow verbal directions before uttering his or her first word.

64. **(B)** Formal operational thought is the ability to reason logically about both concrete and abstract concepts. It is therefore the highest level of cognitive development that can be achieved. While a concrete operational thinker is capable of logical thought, he or she can only reason effectively with or about concrete objects.

65. **(B)** Vygotsky concluded that language influences thought. Talking to oneself either out loud (external speech) or not out loud (internal speech) tends to occur during problem solving. Vygotsky observed that young children use external speech when working out problems. External speech occurs with more frequency in early childhood and then goes inward to become internal speech in older children and adults.

66. **(D)** Studies have shown that parents who abuse their children have stronger than normal reactions to stress. Under stressful conditions, they experience higher emotional arousal than normal. It is possible that this high level of arousal triggers aggression.

67. **(C)** Egocentric thinking is believing that what you perceive and experience is the same as what other people perceive and experience. Egocentric thinkers fail to understand that different people have different points of view. Therefore, a child who is egocentric would expect his father to have seen what happened to him, even though the father was not there.

68. **(D)** A feature of autism spectrum disorders is a lack of responsiveness to others. Autistic children do not easily form social relationships and do not respond normally to social cues. They may actively avoid social interaction.

69. **(D)** Memory impairment is one of the early symptoms of Alzheimer's disease. However, impaired memory does not necessarily mean a person has

Alzheimer's. Typically, a person in the early stages of this disease will have difficulty retrieving words.

70. **(C)**   Information processing theorists argue that improved cognitive ability is the result of an increase in processing speed in older children. The increasing speed of mental processing allows the older child to perform more mental operations at one time in working memory.

71. **(C)**   This approach to teaching reading suggests that children will learn to read faster if it is taught in the context of real reading material like a whole passage. This is contrasted with the phonics approach which argues children should be taught how to associate sounds with letters before they attempt reading materials.

72. **(C)**   Impulsivity is a common feature of children with attention deficit hyperactivity disorder (ADHD). Poor impulse control means difficulty controlling behavior and thinking before acting.

73. **(A)**   Mildly mentally retarded children have I.Q. scores between 52 and 75. This is the highest range of all the intellectual disability classifications. An I.Q. score above 75 is considered normal, with a score of 100 being the average.

74. **(C)**   In the fixed-interval schedule, reinforcement is given after a fixed period of time no matter how much work is done. This schedule has the lowest yield in terms of performance. However, just before the reinforcement is given, activity increases.

75. **(C)**   Extinction of conditioned respondent behavior occurs when the CS is presented without the UCS a number of times. The magnitude of the response elicited by the CS and the percentage of presentations of the CS that elicits responses gradually decreases as the CS continues to be presented without the UCS. If CS presentation continues without the UCS, the CR will decline to at least the level present before the classical conditioning was begun.

76. **(B)**   The Stanford Binet test has a heavy emphasis on verbal skills while the WISC uses verbal and nonverbal tasks equally.

77. **(E)**   Repeated hand washing is known as an obsessive-compulsive neurosis, although, as in other obsessive-compulsive disorders, the two components need not exist simultaneously. Repeated hand washing is termed compulsive if the person feels compelled to perform the behavior, thus interfering with more appropriate behavior. As opposed to a compulsion, an obsession is a recurring

thought rather than an action that a person cannot control or stop. This disorder is thought to arise as a defense against anxiety.

78. **(D)** Erikson determined that there were eight developmental crises in our lives corresponding to the eight developmental periods. These crises in their developmental order are (1) trust vs. mistrust; (2) autonomy vs. doubt and shame; (3) initiative vs. guilt; (4) industry vs. inferiority; (5) identity crisis; (6) intimacy vs. isolation; (7) crisis of child rearing; and (8) integrity vs. despair in old age.

79. **(D)** Freud reasoned that the dream is a hallucinatory state that structures events not as they would be in reality, but as the dreamer wishes them to be. When unconscious desires conflict with conscious restraints, however, it is necessary for the "dream work" to use symbolism to express the wish.

80. **(D)** The personality structure consists of the id, ego, and superego. According to Freud, the id is the most fundamental component of personality and is comprised of drives, needs, and instinctual impulses. It is unable to tolerate tension, is obedient only to the pleasure principle, and is in constant conflict with the superego. The superego develops out of the ego during childhood. It contains values, morals, and basic attitudes as learned from parents and society. The ego mediates between the id and superego. The ego is sometimes called the executive agency of the personality because it controls actions and decides how needs should be satisfied.

81. **(E)** The pituitary gland produces TSH, ACTH, FSH, and LH. TSH induces secretion of another hormone in the thyroid gland. ACTH stimulates the adrenal cortex to secrete cortisol. Both LH and FSH control the secretion of the sex hormones by the gonads. They also regulate the growth and development of sperm and ovum. Hence, the pituitary is in a sense a master gland that directs the hormone secretions to other glands and organs.

82. **(D)** The colored portion of the eye is called the iris. It is the tissue that surrounds the pupil and regulates its size. By contracting or dilating, the iris adjusts the amount of light entering the eye.

83. **(C)** Cones respond differentially to different color wavelengths, providing us not only with color perception but also the ability to sense fine gradations of color.

84. **(B)** Contrary to earlier research on bilingual school children, which often confounded bilingualism and socio-cultural disadvantages, bilingual

children have been found to have high verbal and non-verbal intelligence. They do not suffer academically because of being bilingual.

85. **(C)**   Humans are born prewired to acquire language. However, the environment must provide the stimulation for the brain areas associated with language to develop. Cases of children raised by animals or under conditions of extreme language deprivation (e.g., kept locked in a room and seldom spoken to) show that if a human doesn't acquire a language by puberty, they will never acquire any reasonable mastery of language, whether they are later provided with extensive remedial language training or not.

86. **(E)**   Humans with an I.Q. of 20 or less barely make reliable contact with their environments and seldom develop abilities beyond those of an infant. Retarded individuals with an I.Q. of 50 or higher can learn to comprehend and make simple statements.

87. **(A)**   Even with years of daily training, the number of vocabulary words and the complexity of the statements that apes and chimps make and comprehend are equivalent only to a human three-year-old. Most statements involve rewards such as "Give me apple." Further, they often act as if word order doesn't matter. "Give me apple," "Apple me give," and "Me apple give" are used interchangeably. In ape communications, syntax is limited.

88. **(C)**   Phonemes are the 40 or so basic sounds that all humans are capable of making. The coos and babbling of a baby are phonemes. Morphemes are the smallest units of speech sounds that carry meaning. Morphemes are whole words as well as prefixes such as "anti-" and suffixes such as "-ing."

89. **(B)**   In 1904, the French government asked Alfred Binet to construct a test that would distinguish between normal children and children with severe learning disabilities. Binet conceived of intelligence as the relationship of mental ability and chronological age. For each age up to 15 years, there is a set of characteristic abilities that develop in the normal child. If they developed earlier than average, the child is more intelligent than average; if the abilities develop later, then the child is considered to be of below average intelligence.

90. **(B)**   Children imitate what they see and hear without making value judgments. They assimilate the habits, good or bad, of those around them. Children (boys and girls) who see an adult abusing a doll imitate the behavior when given the opportunity.

ANSWER SHEETS

Practice Test 1
Practice Test 2

PRACTICE TEST 1

Answer Sheet

1. Ⓐ Ⓑ Ⓒ Ⓓ Ⓔ	31. Ⓐ Ⓑ Ⓒ Ⓓ Ⓔ	61. Ⓐ Ⓑ Ⓒ Ⓓ Ⓔ
2. Ⓐ Ⓑ Ⓒ Ⓓ Ⓔ	32. Ⓐ Ⓑ Ⓒ Ⓓ Ⓔ	62. Ⓐ Ⓑ Ⓒ Ⓓ Ⓔ
3. Ⓐ Ⓑ Ⓒ Ⓓ Ⓔ	33. Ⓐ Ⓑ Ⓒ Ⓓ Ⓔ	63. Ⓐ Ⓑ Ⓒ Ⓓ Ⓔ
4. Ⓐ Ⓑ Ⓒ Ⓓ Ⓔ	34. Ⓐ Ⓑ Ⓒ Ⓓ Ⓔ	64. Ⓐ Ⓑ Ⓒ Ⓓ Ⓔ
5. Ⓐ Ⓑ Ⓒ Ⓓ Ⓔ	35. Ⓐ Ⓑ Ⓒ Ⓓ Ⓔ	65. Ⓐ Ⓑ Ⓒ Ⓓ Ⓔ
6. Ⓐ Ⓑ Ⓒ Ⓓ Ⓔ	36. Ⓐ Ⓑ Ⓒ Ⓓ Ⓔ	66. Ⓐ Ⓑ Ⓒ Ⓓ Ⓔ
7. Ⓐ Ⓑ Ⓒ Ⓓ Ⓔ	37. Ⓐ Ⓑ Ⓒ Ⓓ Ⓔ	67. Ⓐ Ⓑ Ⓒ Ⓓ Ⓔ
8. Ⓐ Ⓑ Ⓒ Ⓓ Ⓔ	38. Ⓐ Ⓑ Ⓒ Ⓓ Ⓔ	68. Ⓐ Ⓑ Ⓒ Ⓓ Ⓔ
9. Ⓐ Ⓑ Ⓒ Ⓓ Ⓔ	39. Ⓐ Ⓑ Ⓒ Ⓓ Ⓔ	69. Ⓐ Ⓑ Ⓒ Ⓓ Ⓔ
10. Ⓐ Ⓑ Ⓒ Ⓓ Ⓔ	40. Ⓐ Ⓑ Ⓒ Ⓓ Ⓔ	70. Ⓐ Ⓑ Ⓒ Ⓓ Ⓔ
11. Ⓐ Ⓑ Ⓒ Ⓓ Ⓔ	41. Ⓐ Ⓑ Ⓒ Ⓓ Ⓔ	71. Ⓐ Ⓑ Ⓒ Ⓓ Ⓔ
12. Ⓐ Ⓑ Ⓒ Ⓓ Ⓔ	42. Ⓐ Ⓑ Ⓒ Ⓓ Ⓔ	72. Ⓐ Ⓑ Ⓒ Ⓓ Ⓔ
13. Ⓐ Ⓑ Ⓒ Ⓓ Ⓔ	43. Ⓐ Ⓑ Ⓒ Ⓓ Ⓔ	73. Ⓐ Ⓑ Ⓒ Ⓓ Ⓔ
14. Ⓐ Ⓑ Ⓒ Ⓓ Ⓔ	44. Ⓐ Ⓑ Ⓒ Ⓓ Ⓔ	74. Ⓐ Ⓑ Ⓒ Ⓓ Ⓔ
15. Ⓐ Ⓑ Ⓒ Ⓓ Ⓔ	45. Ⓐ Ⓑ Ⓒ Ⓓ Ⓔ	75. Ⓐ Ⓑ Ⓒ Ⓓ Ⓔ
16. Ⓐ Ⓑ Ⓒ Ⓓ Ⓔ	46. Ⓐ Ⓑ Ⓒ Ⓓ Ⓔ	76. Ⓐ Ⓑ Ⓒ Ⓓ Ⓔ
17. Ⓐ Ⓑ Ⓒ Ⓓ Ⓔ	47. Ⓐ Ⓑ Ⓒ Ⓓ Ⓔ	77. Ⓐ Ⓑ Ⓒ Ⓓ Ⓔ
18. Ⓐ Ⓑ Ⓒ Ⓓ Ⓔ	48. Ⓐ Ⓑ Ⓒ Ⓓ Ⓔ	78. Ⓐ Ⓑ Ⓒ Ⓓ Ⓔ
19. Ⓐ Ⓑ Ⓒ Ⓓ Ⓔ	49. Ⓐ Ⓑ Ⓒ Ⓓ Ⓔ	79. Ⓐ Ⓑ Ⓒ Ⓓ Ⓔ
20. Ⓐ Ⓑ Ⓒ Ⓓ Ⓔ	50. Ⓐ Ⓑ Ⓒ Ⓓ Ⓔ	80. Ⓐ Ⓑ Ⓒ Ⓓ Ⓔ
21. Ⓐ Ⓑ Ⓒ Ⓓ Ⓔ	51. Ⓐ Ⓑ Ⓒ Ⓓ Ⓔ	81. Ⓐ Ⓑ Ⓒ Ⓓ Ⓔ
22. Ⓐ Ⓑ Ⓒ Ⓓ Ⓔ	52. Ⓐ Ⓑ Ⓒ Ⓓ Ⓔ	82. Ⓐ Ⓑ Ⓒ Ⓓ Ⓔ
23. Ⓐ Ⓑ Ⓒ Ⓓ Ⓔ	53. Ⓐ Ⓑ Ⓒ Ⓓ Ⓔ	83. Ⓐ Ⓑ Ⓒ Ⓓ Ⓔ
24. Ⓐ Ⓑ Ⓒ Ⓓ Ⓔ	54. Ⓐ Ⓑ Ⓒ Ⓓ Ⓔ	84. Ⓐ Ⓑ Ⓒ Ⓓ Ⓔ
25. Ⓐ Ⓑ Ⓒ Ⓓ Ⓔ	55. Ⓐ Ⓑ Ⓒ Ⓓ Ⓔ	85. Ⓐ Ⓑ Ⓒ Ⓓ Ⓔ
26. Ⓐ Ⓑ Ⓒ Ⓓ Ⓔ	56. Ⓐ Ⓑ Ⓒ Ⓓ Ⓔ	86. Ⓐ Ⓑ Ⓒ Ⓓ Ⓔ
27. Ⓐ Ⓑ Ⓒ Ⓓ Ⓔ	57. Ⓐ Ⓑ Ⓒ Ⓓ Ⓔ	87. Ⓐ Ⓑ Ⓒ Ⓓ Ⓔ
28. Ⓐ Ⓑ Ⓒ Ⓓ Ⓔ	58. Ⓐ Ⓑ Ⓒ Ⓓ Ⓔ	88. Ⓐ Ⓑ Ⓒ Ⓓ Ⓔ
29. Ⓐ Ⓑ Ⓒ Ⓓ Ⓔ	59. Ⓐ Ⓑ Ⓒ Ⓓ Ⓔ	89. Ⓐ Ⓑ Ⓒ Ⓓ Ⓔ
30. Ⓐ Ⓑ Ⓒ Ⓓ Ⓔ	60. Ⓐ Ⓑ Ⓒ Ⓓ Ⓔ	90. Ⓐ Ⓑ Ⓒ Ⓓ Ⓔ

PRACTICE TEST 2

Answer Sheet

1. Ⓐ Ⓑ Ⓒ Ⓓ Ⓔ	31. Ⓐ Ⓑ Ⓒ Ⓓ Ⓔ	61. Ⓐ Ⓑ Ⓒ Ⓓ Ⓔ
2. Ⓐ Ⓑ Ⓒ Ⓓ Ⓔ	32. Ⓐ Ⓑ Ⓒ Ⓓ Ⓔ	62. Ⓐ Ⓑ Ⓒ Ⓓ Ⓔ
3. Ⓐ Ⓑ Ⓒ Ⓓ Ⓔ	33. Ⓐ Ⓑ Ⓒ Ⓓ Ⓔ	63. Ⓐ Ⓑ Ⓒ Ⓓ Ⓔ
4. Ⓐ Ⓑ Ⓒ Ⓓ Ⓔ	34. Ⓐ Ⓑ Ⓒ Ⓓ Ⓔ	64. Ⓐ Ⓑ Ⓒ Ⓓ Ⓔ
5. Ⓐ Ⓑ Ⓒ Ⓓ Ⓔ	35. Ⓐ Ⓑ Ⓒ Ⓓ Ⓔ	65. Ⓐ Ⓑ Ⓒ Ⓓ Ⓔ
6. Ⓐ Ⓑ Ⓒ Ⓓ Ⓔ	36. Ⓐ Ⓑ Ⓒ Ⓓ Ⓔ	66. Ⓐ Ⓑ Ⓒ Ⓓ Ⓔ
7. Ⓐ Ⓑ Ⓒ Ⓓ Ⓔ	37. Ⓐ Ⓑ Ⓒ Ⓓ Ⓔ	67. Ⓐ Ⓑ Ⓒ Ⓓ Ⓔ
8. Ⓐ Ⓑ Ⓒ Ⓓ Ⓔ	38. Ⓐ Ⓑ Ⓒ Ⓓ Ⓔ	68. Ⓐ Ⓑ Ⓒ Ⓓ Ⓔ
9. Ⓐ Ⓑ Ⓒ Ⓓ Ⓔ	39. Ⓐ Ⓑ Ⓒ Ⓓ Ⓔ	69. Ⓐ Ⓑ Ⓒ Ⓓ Ⓔ
10. Ⓐ Ⓑ Ⓒ Ⓓ Ⓔ	40. Ⓐ Ⓑ Ⓒ Ⓓ Ⓔ	70. Ⓐ Ⓑ Ⓒ Ⓓ Ⓔ
11. Ⓐ Ⓑ Ⓒ Ⓓ Ⓔ	41. Ⓐ Ⓑ Ⓒ Ⓓ Ⓔ	71. Ⓐ Ⓑ Ⓒ Ⓓ Ⓔ
12. Ⓐ Ⓑ Ⓒ Ⓓ Ⓔ	42. Ⓐ Ⓑ Ⓒ Ⓓ Ⓔ	72. Ⓐ Ⓑ Ⓒ Ⓓ Ⓔ
13. Ⓐ Ⓑ Ⓒ Ⓓ Ⓔ	43. Ⓐ Ⓑ Ⓒ Ⓓ Ⓔ	73. Ⓐ Ⓑ Ⓒ Ⓓ Ⓔ
14. Ⓐ Ⓑ Ⓒ Ⓓ Ⓔ	44. Ⓐ Ⓑ Ⓒ Ⓓ Ⓔ	74. Ⓐ Ⓑ Ⓒ Ⓓ Ⓔ
15. Ⓐ Ⓑ Ⓒ Ⓓ Ⓔ	45. Ⓐ Ⓑ Ⓒ Ⓓ Ⓔ	75. Ⓐ Ⓑ Ⓒ Ⓓ Ⓔ
16. Ⓐ Ⓑ Ⓒ Ⓓ Ⓔ	46. Ⓐ Ⓑ Ⓒ Ⓓ Ⓔ	76. Ⓐ Ⓑ Ⓒ Ⓓ Ⓔ
17. Ⓐ Ⓑ Ⓒ Ⓓ Ⓔ	47. Ⓐ Ⓑ Ⓒ Ⓓ Ⓔ	77. Ⓐ Ⓑ Ⓒ Ⓓ Ⓔ
18. Ⓐ Ⓑ Ⓒ Ⓓ Ⓔ	48. Ⓐ Ⓑ Ⓒ Ⓓ Ⓔ	78. Ⓐ Ⓑ Ⓒ Ⓓ Ⓔ
19. Ⓐ Ⓑ Ⓒ Ⓓ Ⓔ	49. Ⓐ Ⓑ Ⓒ Ⓓ Ⓔ	79. Ⓐ Ⓑ Ⓒ Ⓓ Ⓔ
20. Ⓐ Ⓑ Ⓒ Ⓓ Ⓔ	50. Ⓐ Ⓑ Ⓒ Ⓓ Ⓔ	80. Ⓐ Ⓑ Ⓒ Ⓓ Ⓔ
21. Ⓐ Ⓑ Ⓒ Ⓓ Ⓔ	51. Ⓐ Ⓑ Ⓒ Ⓓ Ⓔ	81. Ⓐ Ⓑ Ⓒ Ⓓ Ⓔ
22. Ⓐ Ⓑ Ⓒ Ⓓ Ⓔ	52. Ⓐ Ⓑ Ⓒ Ⓓ Ⓔ	82. Ⓐ Ⓑ Ⓒ Ⓓ Ⓔ
23. Ⓐ Ⓑ Ⓒ Ⓓ Ⓔ	53. Ⓐ Ⓑ Ⓒ Ⓓ Ⓔ	83. Ⓐ Ⓑ Ⓒ Ⓓ Ⓔ
24. Ⓐ Ⓑ Ⓒ Ⓓ Ⓔ	54. Ⓐ Ⓑ Ⓒ Ⓓ Ⓔ	84. Ⓐ Ⓑ Ⓒ Ⓓ Ⓔ
25. Ⓐ Ⓑ Ⓒ Ⓓ Ⓔ	55. Ⓐ Ⓑ Ⓒ Ⓓ Ⓔ	85. Ⓐ Ⓑ Ⓒ Ⓓ Ⓔ
26. Ⓐ Ⓑ Ⓒ Ⓓ Ⓔ	56. Ⓐ Ⓑ Ⓒ Ⓓ Ⓔ	86. Ⓐ Ⓑ Ⓒ Ⓓ Ⓔ
27. Ⓐ Ⓑ Ⓒ Ⓓ Ⓔ	57. Ⓐ Ⓑ Ⓒ Ⓓ Ⓔ	87. Ⓐ Ⓑ Ⓒ Ⓓ Ⓔ
28. Ⓐ Ⓑ Ⓒ Ⓓ Ⓔ	58. Ⓐ Ⓑ Ⓒ Ⓓ Ⓔ	88. Ⓐ Ⓑ Ⓒ Ⓓ Ⓔ
29. Ⓐ Ⓑ Ⓒ Ⓓ Ⓔ	59. Ⓐ Ⓑ Ⓒ Ⓓ Ⓔ	89. Ⓐ Ⓑ Ⓒ Ⓓ Ⓔ
30. Ⓐ Ⓑ Ⓒ Ⓓ Ⓔ	60. Ⓐ Ⓑ Ⓒ Ⓓ Ⓔ	90. Ⓐ Ⓑ Ⓒ Ⓓ Ⓔ

Glossary

A

Absolute threshold—The minimum intensity of sensory stimulation an observer can perceive.

Acceptance—The fifth and final stage in Elisabeth Kubler-Ross' model of adjustment to death and dying in which the terminally ill patient comes to realize death is imminent and there is nothing that will prevent it. During this stage the dying patient often helps plan for his or her funeral and puts his or her affairs in order.

Accommodation—Piaget's term for the process of modifying an existing scheme in order to include a new experience.

Achievement motivation—The drive to be successful at tasks that are attempted and to meet achievement standards.

Activity theory—The social theory of aging that argues the elderly are motivated to remain active and engaged in meaningful activities, but that a decline in their activity may occur as the result of a loss of social roles.

Adaptation—Piaget's term for the process of constructing cognitive schema that aid children's adjustment to the environment using the complimentary processes of assimilation and accommodation.

Adrenalin—A hormone secreted by the adrenal gland which is responsible for the body's flight or fight response. Adrenalin helps the body prepare to respond to danger; however, adrenalin is also released when an individual experiences stress. Adrenalin has a negative long-term effect on the immune system of the body and acts as a teratogen in a pregnant woman.

Affective disorders—See mood disorders.

Aggression—See antisocial behavior.

AIDS (Acquired Immune Deficiency Syndrome)—A fatal disease caused by the HIV virus that results in the deterioration of the body's immune system. Infected women can pass the disease to offspring prenatally through the placenta, during birth if there is an exchange of her blood with the baby, or through breast milk. The transmission of AIDS to newborns has decreased with the use of new medications and prevention techniques.

Ainsworth Strange Situation—The experimental paradigm developed by Ainsworth to measure the quality of the attachment relationship. This method involves observing a child's reactions when his or her caregiver leaves the room and when the caregiver returns. This method has been criticized as creating an artificial situation for the caregiver and child.

Altruism—See prosocial behavior.

Alzheimer's disease—A disease, characterized by neurofibrillary tangles and plaques in the brain of some aging individuals, that is the leading cause of dementia. Symptoms include loss of cognitive functioning, impaired judgment, and eventual death.

Amniocentesis—A test used to screen for genetic defects and chromosomal abnormalities in a fetus. The test involves removing amniotic fluid from the amniotic sac in the uterus.

Anal stage—The second stage in Freud's psychosexual model of personality development which lasts from the age of one until the age of three. Libidinal energy is focused on obtaining gratifying stimulation of the anal area in this stage. The ego appears in this stage and continues to develop throughout the remaining stages.

Androgens—Male sex hormones.

Androgyny—A gender role that combines the positive elements of both the masculine and feminine gender role.

Anger—The second stage in Elisabeth Kubler-Ross' model of adjustment to death and dying in which the terminally ill patient rages against his or her illness and may act out against caregivers and significant others.

Animistic reasoning—Characteristic of the thought of a preoperational child. Children in this stage tend to project human qualities onto inanimate objects.

Anorexia nervosa—An eating disorder characterized by exceptionally low body weight and an unrealistic fear of gaining weight.

Anoxia—A condition caused by a depleted supply of oxygen to the fetus during labor and delivery. This is normally due to a problem with the umbilical cord as the fetus is making its way down the vaginal canal. If not corrected, the lack of oxygen may cause brain damage. The damage will depend on the length of time and the amount of oxygen depravation.

Anticipatory grief—A process of reacting and adjusting to the loss of a terminally ill loved one prior to that person's death.

Antisocial behavior—Aggressive, violent, and/or criminal behavior. Influences from the family, school, and neighborhood environments (particularly low socioeconomic conditions) have been linked to antisocial behavior.

Apgar scale—A scale developed to quickly assess the condition of a neonate immediately after birth and five minutes later.

Artificial insemination—A process of fertilizing ova with sperm cells via injection. This technique can help infertile couples conceive using their own reproductive cells.

Assimilation—Piaget's term for the process of modifying an experience to make it fit into a preexisting scheme.

Associative play—An early form of play in which children are playing next to each other, interact, and may share materials with each other, but do not share a common goal.

Attention deficit/hyperactivity disorder—A disorder characterized by attention difficulties, impulsivity, and excessive motor behavior.

Attribution styles—The term used for the characteristic way a person explains his or her own behavior as well as the behavior of other people.

Authoritarian parenting style—One of the parenting styles studied by Diana Baumrind. Parents who adopt this style are strict disciplinarians who often use physical punishment. These parents are high in control/demandingness and low in acceptance/responsiveness. These parents make the household rules and children are given no voice in that process. Respect and strict obedience to adults are highly valued by this type of parent. Children raised with this parenting style tend to be anxious and withdrawn or defiant and aggressive.

Authoritative parenting style—One of the parenting styles studied by Diana Baumrind. Parents who adopt this style have household rules that often have been constructed with children having a voice in the process. Discipline is present but not harsh, and explanations for the rules, as well as the reason for the discipline, are provided to the children. These parents are high in acceptance/responsiveness and high in control/demandingness. Children raised with this parenting style have the best developmental outcomes. They tend to have high self-esteem and self-control, and be cooperative and mature.

Autism spectrum disorders—Pervasive developmental disorders characterized by impaired communication, repetitive behavior, and impaired social interaction.

Autonomy versus doubt—The second stage in Erik Erikson's psychosocial model of personality development that lasts from age one until three years. The positive resolution of the crisis is when a child develops the ability to be independent and self-reliant, rather than timid and dependent on other people.

Autosomes—All of the chromosomes except for the sex chromosomes.

B

Babbling—The second stage of language development. These vocalizations elicit responses from others in the infant's environment which in turn reinforce the child's babbling. The sounds produced during the babbling stage will be shaped into the baby's first words.

Babinski reflex—One of the neonatal reflexes present at birth. If you stimulate the bottom of a newborn's foot, he or she will reflexively spread out his or her toes.

Bandura—Psychologist who created the social learning theory. He also conducted the classic study which showed that children who previously viewed an adult model be aggressive toward a doll imitated the adult model when placed in a room with the doll.

Bargaining—The third stage in Elisabeth Kubler-Ross' model of adjustment to death and dying. In this stage, the dying person will try to negotiate for more time as in saying "Just let me live long enough to see my daughter get married."

Baumrind—One of the first psychologists to systematically study parenting styles and the effect of style of parenting on the developing child.

Bayley scales—An intelligence test developed to be used to assess intelligence in infants and young children.

Beanpole family—The term used to describe a household that has multiple generations of the same family living together.

Behavior modification—An application of operant conditioning used in educational and clinical settings. An individual's behavior is shaped using positive reinforcement. This technique has been successful when used with children with autism spectrum disorders and severe intellectual disability.

Behaviorist perspective—A theoretical perspective in psychology that defines development as changes in overt behavior. This perspective underscores the role of the environment in development and describes the developing person as passive in the developmental process. The mind is viewed as being a tabula rasa (blank slate) at birth. This perspective has its roots in the work of Ivan Pavlov, John Watson, and B.F. Skinner.

Bereavement—See grief.

Bilingualism—Being fluent in two languages.

Biological aging—The term for the biological and physiological decline that occurs with age that eventually causes death. There are several competing theories of the cause of biological aging, but most experts agree this decline is inevitable even in a relatively healthy and disease-free individual. Evidence for this claim is that there is a maximum length of life for human beings which is approximately 110 years.

Birth cohort—People born in or around the same year.

Birth cohort effects—Differences found between different birth cohorts or generations.

Blended family—See reconstituted family.

Bronfenbrenner—The psychologists who created the ecological systems theory of development.

Bulimia nervosa—An eating disorder characterized by binge eating and then purging through vomiting and/or the use of laxatives.

C

Caesarian section—An alternative birthing method which is the surgical removal of the fetus from the uterus. This is used when there is an emergency or a problem that prevents a vaginal delivery.

Case study—A method used in descriptive research to intensively study a unique situation or person.

Cataracts—The term for the clouding of the lens of the eye which causes vision problems and is associated with aging.

Cephalocaudal development—The term used for the general pattern of physical growth progressing from the head and neck down to the feet.

Cerebral palsy—A neurological disorder caused by anoxia during birth that is characterized by a lack of muscle control and coordination.

Child abuse (physical or emotional child abuse)—An assault on a child that causes physical harm (physical abuse) or causes a mental or behavioral disorder (emotional abuse).

Child sexual abuse—Fondling, having intercourse with, exhibiting to, or sexually exploiting a child through pornography or prostitution.

Chomsky—The linguist who argued humans are prepared at birth to acquire language. He argued that the human brain is pre-wired with a "language acquisition device."

Chorionic villus sampling—A prenatal screening test that can be done earlier than amniocentesis. It involves removing and analyzing fetal cells using a tube inserted in the pregnant woman's cervix.

Chromosome—The term for the biological structure in the cell that contains genes. There are 46 in each cell.

Classical conditioning—The learning process discovered by Ivan Pavlov by which a reflexive response is elicited by a new stimulus. This conditioning is accomplished by the new stimulus, called the conditioned stimulus, becoming associated with the unconditioned stimulus which initially controlled the reflex.

Classification—The ability to group items together that share a common characteristic.

Class inclusion—The ability to classify objects in a hierarchical organization with subordinate and superordinate levels.

Climacteric—The end of sexual reproductive capacity. In women this is referred to as menopause.

Clique—A small collection of close friends who spend a substantial amount of time together.

Cognitive-developmental theory—This theory describes and explains changes in thinking that occur with age. Jean Piaget is the most influential theorist within this perspective. Piaget constructed a stage model of cognitive development and he argued that these stages were universal. He suggested that a child constructs schema based on the result of his or her actions in the environment. A scheme is an organized pattern of thought or action. Schema become more logical and organized as the child progresses through the four stages, which are sensorimotor intelligence, preoperations, concrete operations, and formal operations.

Collectivist culture—Name used for cultures that value the common good rather than individual achievement.

Compulsion—A behavior that a person is compelled to perform to prevent anxiety. A person who evidences compulsive behavior often suffers from obsessive thinking and is diagnosed with obsessive-compulsive disorder.

Concrete operations—The third stage in Piaget's theory that lasts from about the age of 7 until age 11 or 12. During this stage, children develop the ability to think logically with concrete objects and concepts. These children, however, fail to reason logically about abstract concepts.

Conditioned response (CR)—The term used in Pavlov's classical conditioning theory for the motor part of a reflex which is elicited by a conditioned stimulus after classical conditioning has taken place.

Conditioned stimulus (CS)—The term used in Pavlov's classical conditioning theory for the stimulus that elicits the conditioned response after it has been repeatedly presented with the unconditioned stimulus (UCS). Pavlov argued that an associative bond forms between the UCS and CS which enables the CS to elicit the reflexive response.

Conformity—Acting the way that other people want you to act or going along with a group.

Conservation—The understanding that even though the perceptual characteristics of matter may change, the amount of it does not change if you do not add or take anything away.

Constructivism—The term used by theorists like Piaget who argue that the developing child actively constructs ideas derived from an active exploration of his or her environment.

Context specific—The principle that developmental changes are influenced by, and therefore are specific to, the sociocultural context in which the individual lives. Development varies across cultures and contexts.

Continuity theory—Any developmental theory that suggests development takes place through a series of small, incremental improvements gradually occurring over time. Development is considered to involve quantitative rather than qualitative change.

Control—The term used for a key characteristic of experiments. The experimenter tries to keep as many extraneous variables as possible constant across the experimental conditions being compared. This allows the experimenter to isolate the influence of the independent variable.

Conventional morality—The second stage in Kohlberg's theory of moral development in which decisions regarding right and wrong are made on the basis of societal laws. Moral behavior is defined as behavior that follows the laws of the society, and immoral behavior is defined as any behavior that violates the laws of society.

Convergent thinking—Thinking that works toward the one best answer to a problem.

Cooing—The first stage of language development. This stage begins with reflexive, spontaneous sounds that elicit caregivers' vocalizations. The caregiver's response reinforces the baby's cooing.

Cooperative play—A more mature form of play in which play is a coordinated and social activity guided by mutually agreed upon rules and shared goals.

Correlation coefficient—A measure of the strength and direction of a relationship between two variables. The coefficient can range from 0 to 1.00, and can be either negative (scores on the two variables tend to go in opposite directions) or positive (scores on the two variables tend to go in the same direction).

Correlational research—Research conducted in order to describe relationships between two variables measured in a large sample of participants.

Creativity—A characteristic of thinking separate from intelligence. Theorists argue a key component of creativity is divergent thinking.

Critical period—A term used by ethologists to describe a narrow window of time in which a trait or behavior must develop.

Cross-sectional design—A research method that involves comparing samples of different aged people at the same time. This method can measure differences between people of different ages, but confounds age difference with birth cohort differences.

Crowd—A collection of several cliques engaged in mixed sex activity.

Crystallized intelligence—Thinking that relies on knowledge which has been acquired through learning and experience. The use of general information like that which is acquired in school.

Culture-fair intelligence test—A goal of the intelligence testing movement is to create an intelligence test that is not biased against any group. The current tests have been shown to be biased against those from the lower socioeconomic class.

Cystic fibrosis—A genetic disease characterized by a buildup of fluid in the lungs leading to difficulty breathing and eventual death. The disease is caused by two recessive genes.

D

Darwin's theory of evolution—The theory that has influenced both evolutionary psychology and ethology. Darwin argued that species evolve slowly over a long period of time through a process of natural selection. There are four elements of Darwin's theory: 1) there is a struggle to survive among members of a species since there is a limited supply of food and other resources, 2) members of a species inherit chance variations of species' traits, 3) some variations of traits increase the chance of survival because they help the individual better adapt in his or her environment, and 4) those members who inherit adaptive traits tend to survive to maturity and reproduce thus passing on these chance variations to their biological offspring. Those who do not inherit adaptive traits tend not to survive and therefore do not reproduce and pass on their traits. Very gradually then, species evolve over time.

Defense mechanisms—Freud's term for the strategies used by the ego to reduce anxiety.

Deferred imitation—Piaget's term for the ability to represent another person's action, store this representation, and later retrieve it in order to imitate it. Piaget argued this was a sign that a child had achieved symbolic representation.

Delay of gratification—The ability to wait for an anticipated reward or goal.

Dementia—An impairment in cognitive functioning in aging individuals which can be acute or chronic. There are many causes of dementia including brain disease (chronic dementia) and drug interaction effects (acute dementia).

Denial—The first stage in Elisabeth Kubler-Ross' model of adjustment to terminal illness. She argued that the terminally ill patient at first does not accept his or her prognosis and may believe that there has been a mistake.

Dependent variable—The variable that is measured after the manipulation of an independent variable in an experiment. It is the hypothesized effect in the cause-and-effect relationship being tested.

Depression—The fourth stage in Elisabeth Kubler-Ross' model of adjustment to death and dying in which the terminally ill patient is overwhelmed by sadness and hopelessness.

Depth perception—The ability to see a three-dimensional world or depth of field.

Descriptive research—Research that is conducted in order to describe characteristics of people, places, or things. Methodologies used include case study, naturalistic observation, interview, and survey.

Difficult temperament—This is the temperament label for infants who are upset by stimulation and do not follow regular patterns of sleeping and eating.

Discrimination—The gradual process of conditioning a response to only occur to a specific stimulus, e.g., a bell of a certain tone, rather than a collection of tones that are similar in frequency.

Disengagement theory—The social theory of aging that argues elderly adults are motivated to withdraw from society in anticipation of death.

Disequilibrium—The term used by Piaget to describe the cognitive experience of imbalance that occurs when a child's experience does not fit into preexisting schema. This psychological state is the motivation for developmental change. According to Piaget, the child is motivated to return to a state of mental equilibrium or balance.

Divergent thinking—Believed to be a key component of creativity, this form of thinking involves generating many different possible solutions to a problem that has no one right answer.

Dizygotic twins—Also known as fraternal twins. These are twins that are the result of multiple ova being fertilized by different sperm and implanting in the uterus at the same time. Although they develop together in utero, these twins are similar to biological siblings.

Down's syndrome—A genetic disorder in children who inherit an extra chromosome on the 21st pair that causes intellectual disability. These children also have distinctive facial features and short, stubby limbs.

DSM (Diagnostic and Statistical Manual of Mental Disorders)—The manual used to diagnose psychological disorders.

Dyslexia—A learning disability that affects children's ability to read.

E

Easy temperament—This is the temperament label for infants who eat and sleep on a regular and predictable schedule, and who react well to new people and stimuli.

Ecological systems theory—Uri Bronfenbrenner's theory that child development occurs within multiple sociocultural systems. The child's experiences and interactions with members of these systems contribute to the child's personality, behavior, and thinking. The systems in this theory are depicted as a series of concentric circles beginning in the center with the microsystem (e.g., the family), which is the system the child directly interacts in, then the exosystem within, which the child does not directly participate but which nonetheless impacts the child's development (e.g., parent's workplace), to the outermost circle, the macrosystem, which is the larger sociocultural system.

Ego—The part of the personality structure in Freud's psychoanalytic theory that must manage the impulses of the id. The ego develops in toddlerhood and has to manage the id by finding socially acceptable ways of gratifying the id's wishes. The ego develops defense mechanisms to manage anxiety which may result from its failure to adequately control the id and meet the moral standards of the superego.

Egocentric thinking—A form of thinking typical of the preoperational child in which the child can only view the world from his or her own perspective and cannot take the perspective of others.

Electra complex—Freud's name for the unconscious conflict that arises in the phallic stage of his psychosexual model of personality development. Freud argued a female child in this phase of development is attracted to her father who she chooses as the target of libidinal energy. The child therefore unconsciously desires a sexual relationship with father, but fears reprisal from mother. According to Freud, girls have a more difficult time resolving this conflict because they have to reject their original love object, mother, and have a difficult time doing so.

Embryo—Name used for the developing baby from the third through the eighth week of pregnancy. This is the period of prenatal development called the second trimester.

Emotional intelligence (EQ)—The type of intelligence proposed by Daniel Goldman that is the ability to think about, and adapt to, emotion. People with high EQs have an exceptional ability to understand and deal with their own emotions and the emotions expressed by other people.

Empathy—The ability to feel the emotions that another person is experiencing.

Empiricist theory—An approach to language development that argues humans are born with a tabula rasa or blank slate and learn language through experience.

Empty nest (Launching phase)—The time when adult children leave the home. Historically this has been described as a period of stress for parents, particularly mothers, but recent survey research indicates this is a positive time of renewal for couples.

Encoding—The process through which information is prepared for storage in long-term memory.

Endocrine system—The physiological system of the body that contains glands which secrete hormones to stimulate growth and control the physiological functions of the body.

Erikson—The psychologist who constructed the psychosocial theory of personality development. He argued personality develops throughout the lifespan and his model contains eight stages beginning with birth and ending in old age. During each stage of development the person faces a psychosocial crisis which can be resolved in a positive or negative way. Erikson is also well known for his discussion of identity development in adolescence.

Estrogen—One of the female sex hormones secreted by the ovaries which directs the development of the female reproductive system during prenatal development and during puberty, and also stimulates the release of growth hormone.

Ethology—The term used for the approach of theorists like Konrad Lorenz and John Bowlby. These theorists compare human behavior with that of other species in order to identify the historical origins of human behavior and development. Ethologists coined the term "critical periods."

Euthanasia—The term for actively assisting the death of a terminally ill person.

Evolutionary psychology—The name of the approach in psychology that was derived from Darwin's theory of evolution by natural selection. The goal of this approach is to explain the historical origins of human behavior and how evolution has shaped human behavior and development.

Expansions—A technique observed in caregivers in which the caregiver responds to a child's vocalization by repeating it in a more complex and advanced way.

Experiment—The research method that can identify cause-and-effect relationships between variables. Two elements of an experiment are control and manipulation. An independent variable is manipulated while extraneous variables are controlled. A dependent variable is used to measure the affect of the independent variable manipulation.

External locus of control—An attribution style in which an individual characteristically believes events in his or her life are caused by forces outside of his or her control.

Extinction—Pavlov's term for the process that reverses conditioning in the classical conditioning paradigm. This is accomplished by successively presenting the conditioned stimulus (CS) without the unconditioned stimulus (UCS). Eventually the CS no longer elicits the conditioned response (CR).

F

Failure to thrive—The term for infants who do not develop normally and show signs of depression. These infants may become seriously underweight. Psychologists believe this condition is caused by a lack of comfort care as it generally occurs in children who are neglected, abused, or separated from their attachment figure.

False belief task—A test that determines if a child has a theory of mind. A child who passes this test says, for example, a person will look for a toy in a basket that person *believes* the toy is in, rather than the basket the child knows contains the toy.

Family systems theory—An approach to understanding the family that describes it as a complex whole system having interrelated members playing different interconnected roles. The action of any one member impacts the whole system.

Fast mapping—The process that Susan Carey suggested is used during the rapid vocabulary growth of the second year. Children will connect a word to an underlying meaning after only a brief encounter.

Feminine—The gender role stereotypically associated with females in our society. Stereotypic elements of this role include being caring, nurturing, and compliant.

Fetal alcohol syndrome—A collection of symptoms including facial abnormalities, small head size, and intellectual disability seen in children whose mothers consumed alcohol in large quantities while pregnant.

Fetus—Name used for the developing baby from the ninth week of pregnancy until birth. This is the period of prenatal development called the third trimester.

Field experiment—An experiment conducted in a natural setting rather than in a controlled laboratory setting. It is less artificial than a lab experiment, but also has less control than a lab experiment.

Fine motor skills—Skills that involve small coordinated movements of the hands, fingers, or toes.

First trimester—The name for the first two weeks of prenatal development. The developing zygote is most protected from negative effects of teratogens at this time.

Fixation—Freud's term for the process of remaining focused on a psychosexual crisis of a childhood stage of personality development well past the normal age of resolving that crisis.

Fluid intelligence—Thinking or problem solving that relies on the power of basic intellectual processes.

Formal operations—This is the fourth and final stage in Piaget's theory. The stage generally begins at age 11 or 12. This level of thought involves hypothetico-deductive reasoning. Adolescents develop the ability to reason logically and systematically even about abstract concepts.

Freud—Well-known father of the psychoanalytic theory. He argued that personality development takes place through a series of universal stages beginning with birth and ending in adolescence. He stressed the role of unconscious motivation and drives, such as the libido, in creating psychosexual crises during these stages. He also posed a structure of the personality which included the id, ego, and superego.

Functional play—See unoccupied play.

G

Gender constancy—The understanding that a person's biological sex does not change even if that person makes significant changes to his or her appearance.

Gender identity—The internalized view of the self as masculine, feminine, or androgynous.

Gender role—The collection of behaviors and traits that are expected for males and females in a society.

Gender scheme—An organized set of beliefs about gender a child constructs and then uses to process information and guide his or her own behavior.

Gender stability—The understanding that biological sex remains the same throughout life.

Gender stereotypes—Restrictive social views that males and females should adhere to the masculine and feminine gender roles, respectively.

Gender typing—The social process of identifying roles, traits, or objects as more appropriate for one or the other gender.

Gene—The term for the biological structure carried on chromosomes that contains the blueprint for inherited traits.

Generalization—Pavlov's term for when a conditioned response can be elicited by related conditioned stimuli, e.g., similar tone frequencies.

Generativity versus stagnation—The seventh stage in Erik Erikson's psychosocial model of personality development that lasts for the period of middle adulthood from the age of about 40 until about the age of 65. The positive resolution of this crisis is when an adult experiences the gratifying feeling of giving back to society by mentoring younger generations of that society rather than remaining self-preoccupied.

Genetic counseling—Counseling that is available to couples who are planning to have children. Partners have their genes screened for genetic disorders or abnormalities. Couples then decide whether or not they wish to have children based on the probability of their offspring having genetic abnormalities.

Genetic disorders—Disorders that are caused by genetic mutations, chromosomal abnormalities, or genes that carry the disorder.

Genital stage—The fifth and final stage in Freud's psychosexual model of personality development which begins at age 12. According to Freud, libidinal energy is channeled into work and establishing mature sexual relationships in this stage.

Genotype—The term used for the traits that are programmed in the genetic material an offspring inherits from her biological parents.

German measles—See rubella.

Giftedness—Unusually high intellectual ability (I.Q. scores above 130), creativity, or special talent.

Glaucoma—A disease of the eye caused by pressure inside the eyeball from an excess buildup of fluid. If untreated, this results in blindness.

Grasping reflex—One of the neonatal reflexes present at birth. If you stimulate the hand of a newborn, he or she will reflexively grasp and hold onto your finger.

Grief (Bereavement)—The distressful response to the death of a loved one. Some psychologists argue that the grief process involves the same stages as in Kubler-Ross' model of death and dying.

Gross motor skills—Skills that involve coordinated movements of the entire body or large parts of the body.

Growth hormone (GH)—The hormone secreted by the pituitary gland which stimulates physical growth. In the absence of GH, an infant will not develop to normal height. GH also stimulates the adolescent growth spurt.

Growth spurt—A time of very rapid physical development. There is a growth spurt during infancy and then again during adolescence.

Guided participation—Vygotsky's term for the process by which cultural values and beliefs are transmitted from adult guides to children.

H

Habituation—The most primitive form of learning. This is the process whereby attention to a stimulus decreases with continued exposure. Newborns look longer at a new stimulus compared to a familiar stimulus.

Harlow—The researcher who investigated the role of feeding in the formation of an attachment relationship. He conducted a classic experiment in which he observed the behavior of monkeys raised with two surrogate mothers, a terry cloth covered mother and a wire mesh mother. Although the monkeys were fed through a bottle in the wire mesh surrogate, they clung to the terry cloth surrogate.

Holophrase—The term for a word that stands for a sentence or more in the early speech of children. A one-word utterance, e.g., "Up," may mean "Grandma, please pick me up!"

HOME (Home observation for measurement of the environment)—The method used to assess the amount of cognitive stimulation in the home environment.

Hospice—A comprehensive support program designed to help terminally ill patients die a good death. The goals of this program are to manage the dying person's pain and enable the person to die comfortably while surrounded by loved ones.

Hostile aggression—A form of physical or verbal aggression in which there is an intent to harm another person.

Huntington's disease—A fatal genetic disease carried by a dominant gene on chromosome 4 which results in nervous system deterioration. Symptoms generally do not appear until adulthood and include slurred speech, jerky movements, personality changes, and dementia.

Hypothetico-deductive thinking—A characteristic of formal operational thinking according to Piaget. This is systematic reasoning from general concepts or ideas to specific instances.

I

Id—The part of the personality structure in Freud's psychoanalytic theory that houses unconscious drives, motives, and repressed thoughts. The id is the irrational part of the personality which must be controlled by the ego. The id is the only part of the personality present at birth.

Identification—The term used by Sigmund Freud for the process which resolves the Oedipal and Electra complexes. The child at the end of the phallic stage shifts his or her attention from the opposite sex parent to the parent of the same sex. According to Freud, the child internalizes the behavior and moral standards of the parent of the same sex which develop into the superego.

Identity achievement—The term used by Marcia to describe the identity status of adolescents who have made a commitment to an identity after experiencing an identity crisis and testing out alternative lifestyles and careers.

Identity diffusion—The term used by Marcia to describe the identity status of adolescents who have not experienced an identity crisis and have not made a commitment to an identity.

Identity foreclosure—The term used by Marcia to describe the identity status of adolescents who decide too quickly on an identity, or simply adopt an identity that others have selected for them. These adolescents have made a commitment to an identity, but have not experienced an identity crisis.

Identity versus identity confusion—The fifth stage in Erik Erikson's psychosocial model of personality development which lasts for the period of adolescence. The positive resolution of the crisis is when an adolescent develops a sense of personal identity and the idea of who he or she will be as an adult.

Imprinting—The behavior, recorded by Konrad Lorenz, of baby ducks following their mother duck as long as they are exposed to the mother within a critical time period of development. Lorenz showed that ducks would imprint on any moving object, including himself, to which they were exposed during the critical period.

Independent variable—The variable that is manipulated in an experiment. It is the hypothesized cause in the cause-and-effect relationship being tested.

Individualistic culture—Name used for cultures that value individual achievement and drive rather than the common good.

Industry versus inferiority—The fourth stage in Erik Erikson's psychosocial model of personality development which lasts from age 6 until age 11. The positive resolution of the crisis is when a child develops positive self-esteem and a sense of competence rather than incompetence.

Information processing approach—An approach to studying cognitive development that uses a computer metaphor for the mind. This approach suggests the mind is an information processing system. Developmental changes in information processing are described as being an increase in processing speed and capacity.

Initiative versus guilt—The third stage in Erik Erikson's psychosocial model of personality development which lasts from age three to age six. The positive resolution of the crisis is when a child develops the confidence to try new activities and initiate endeavors versus being self-critical.

Inner speech—Vygotsky's term for how language guides thought in an older child who talks to himself silently while solving a problem. The older child does not have to talk out loud to himself as younger children do when they are using private speech.

Insecure-avoidant attachment—The term for an insecure attachment relationship in which the child does not seek contact with the caregiver and does not show distress when the caregiver leaves.

Insecure-disorganized/disoriented attachment—The term for an insecure attachment relationship in which the child alternatively approaches and avoids the caregiver. A common response seen in abused children.

Insecure-resistant attachment—The term for an insecure attachment relationship in which the child is very difficult to console when separated from the caregiver and then is angry and resists contact with the caregiver upon his or her return.

Instrumental aggression—A form of aggression used to achieve a goal but not intended to harm another person.

Integrity versus despair—The eighth and final stage in Erik Erikson's psychosocial model of personality development that lasts for the period of late adulthood from about the age of 65 until death. The positive resolution of the crisis is when an older adult experiences the gratifying feeling that he or she has led a good and meaningful life versus experiencing regret.

Intellectual disability— Lower than average intelligence caused by many factors varies in severity and degree of impairment. Formerly known as mental retardation in DSM-IV.

Intelligence—The term used for cognitive power or ability.

Intelligence quotient (I.Q.)—A calculation that quantifies intelligence by dividing mental age by chronological age. The mean score for I.Q. is 100.

Intermodal perception—A term for the interconnectedness of our perceptual systems. An experiment has shown that neonates will look longer at a nipple which has the shape of a nipple he or she previously sucked on but did not see.

Internal locus of control—An attribution style in which an individual characteristically believes events in his or her life are caused by his or her own abilities and efforts.

Interview—A method used in descriptive research to collect information.

Intimacy versus isolation—The sixth stage in Erik Erikson's psychosocial model of personality development that lasts for the period of early adulthood from age 20 until about the age of 40. The positive resolution of the crisis is when a young adult is able to form an intimate relationship defined by trust and love versus being unconnected or alone.

In vitro fertilization—A process of fertilizing ova with sperm outside of the female body and then implanting fertilized cells into the uterus. This technique can help infertile couples conceive using their own reproductive cells.

K

Klinefelter syndrome—A sex chromosome abnormality in which males inherit an extra X chromosome (XXY). These males are sterile, develop female sex characteristics, and sometimes have lower than average language skills or some degree of intellectual disability.

Kohlberg—The psychologist who studied moral reasoning and suggested a stage model of moral development. This model contains three stages: preconventional moral reasoning, conventional moral reasoning, and postconventional moral reasoning. He presented moral dilemmas to subjects and observed differences in reasoning about these dilemmas across age groups.

Kubler-Ross—The psychologists who created a stage theory of adjustment to one's own death after conducting extensive interviews with terminally ill patients. The stages are denial, anger, bargaining, depression, and acceptance. Her theory has been criticized by psychologists who argue that all people do not go through all of the stages in her model.

L

Lamaze method (Prepared childbirth)—An alternative birthing method that involves a couple preparing for a vaginal delivery by learning and practicing breathing and other relaxation techniques to help manage the pain of childbirth without medication.

Language acquisition device—The term Noam Chomsky used for how the human brain is pre-wired for language.

Latchkey children—The term for children who have no adult supervision after school.

Latency—The fourth stage in Sigmund Freud's psychosexual model of personality development which lasts from age 6 until 12. The libido is quite inactive during this stage and there is no psychosexual crisis. According to Freud, children in this stage are focused on same sex peers, school, and play.

Lateralization—The term used to describe the fact that the left and right hemispheres of the brain control different functions. For example, the language center is located in the left cerebral hemisphere.

Launching phase—See empty nest.

Learned helplessness—The perception that one cannot alter events in one's life. This syndrome was first demonstrated by Seligman. Seligman placed animals in an experimental situation where they could not escape an electric shock. Eventually, the animals became lethargic and no longer tried to escape.

Learned helplessness orientation—Attributing failures to stable and internal personal traits, and successes to external, changeable, and uncontrollable factors. This leads to a tendency to avoid challenges and a lack of motivation to attempt difficult tasks.

Learning disabilities—Specific difficulties learning new information believed to be due to a problem in brain functioning. Children with learning disabilities often do poorly in school despite having average or higher intelligence.

Learning styles—Individual differences in the way information is processed. Some people are visual, auditory, or kinesthetic learners. Each type of learner will acquire information easier if the information is presented in a modality that matches their learning style.

Learning theory—This is the theory of language development derived from the Behaviorist perspective in psychology. Language development is described as being continuous and gradual. Development is believed to be the result of experience. Language is defined as verbal behavior which is conditioned or shaped.

Libido—The term for the sexual instinct or drive in Freud's theory of psychoanalysis.

Life expectancy—The average length of life that can be expected for a birth cohort.

Life-span perspective—Contemporary approach to development suggesting development occurs throughout the entire life span. Historically, developmental theories have suggested development is complete at adolescence. This perspective changes the view that childhood experiences shape who we become.

Living will—A legal document that outlines an individual's wishes regarding end of life care and treatment. Often the document will dictate that no extreme measures to revive or sustain life under hopeless conditions are to be used. Examples of extreme measures are resuscitation, ventilation, or use of a feeding tube.

Longitudinal design—A research method that involves studying a sample of people over a long period of time in order to measure changes that occur with age.

Long-term memory—See secondary memory.

M

Manipulation—A key characteristic of experiments. The experimenter varies the independent variable so that it is present under one condition in the experiment but not present in the other condition(s). The experimental group receives the independent variable but the control group does not.

Masculine—The gender role stereotypically associated with males in our society. Stereotypic elements of this role include being aggressive, dominant, and competitive.

Mastery-oriented attributions—Attributing successes to stable and internal personal traits or abilities, and failures to external, changeable, and uncontrollable factors. This leads to a tendency to step up to challenges and persevere through difficult tasks.

Maturation—The term used to describe biological/physical changes that occur with age.

Menarche—The first menstruation in females.

Mental age—An age assigned to a person as a result of comparing that person's intelligence test performance with norms for different age groups. This age represents that person's level of functioning.

Metacognition—Being consciously aware of one's own cognitive processing.

Middle generation sandwich—The term for the stress experienced by middle-aged adults who are both caring for their own children as well as their aging parents.

Mirror test of self-recognition—This is the technique used by Lewis and Brooks-Gunn to test for self-recognition in infants. Infants, at least 18 months of age, who have rouge surreptitiously put on their nose, will rub their nose when they look at themselves in a mirror, rather than rub the mirror, as younger infants do.

Modeling—See social learning theory.

Monozygotic twins—Also known as identical twins. These are twins that are the result of an extra division of a fertilized ovum. These twins share the exact same genetic material.

Mood disorders (Affective disorders)—Disorders characterized by abnormal affect or emotion. Examples include major depression and bipolar disorder.

Morality of care—The term used by Carol Gilligan for the style of moral reasoning found generally in females. She found that women think about other people's needs and how decisions affect interpersonal relationships when deliberating about moral dilemmas. Moral reasoning is contextualized in people with this style.

Morality of justice—The term used by Carol Gilligan for the style of moral reasoning found generally in males. Males tend to make decisions about right and wrong by applying general, universal, immutable principles of justice.

Moratorium period—The term used for a period of time given to children and adolescents to explore different identities and prepare for adulthood.

Moratorium status—The term used by Marcia to describe an adolescent who is currently experiencing an identity crisis and is testing out alternatives.

Moro reflex—One of the neonatal reflexes present at birth. This is a startle response a newborn will emit if they suddenly lose physical support.

Morpheme—The term for the basic unit of meaning in a language.

Multiple intelligences—The theory of intelligence offered by Howard Gardner that argues intelligence is not one general factor but eight different cognitive abilities. This approach to intelligence defines intelligence more broadly compared to the traditional view of intelligence.

N

Nativist theory—An approach to language development that argues humans are innately predisposed to acquire a language.

Naturalistic observation—A method used in descriptive research to collect information about a person or event. Overt behavior is observed and recorded in a natural setting.

Natural selection—The name Charles Darwin used for the process through which species evolve over time.

Nature versus nurture controversy—A debate regarding the relative influence of heredity versus experience/the environment on development. While some developmental theorists underscore one over the other, both nature and nurture influence development.

Negative reinforcement—In Skinner's operant conditioning theory, this is the term for a reward that involves removing a noxious stimulus or condition after a goal behavior is emitted. This term is formally defined by Skinner as the removal of a noxious stimulus after a behavior is emitted that increases the probability the behavior will be repeated under similar stimulus conditions.

Neglect—A parent's failure to protect a child from harm and/or meet the basic biological and medical needs of a child.

Neonate—Term used to refer to the newborn from birth to about one month of age.

Neonate preferences—Neonates come with preferences for what they look at, listen to, and taste. For example, neonates will look at the edges of an object more than the interior details.

Neurofibrillary tangles—Abnormal neural structures found in the brains of people with Alzheimer's disease.

O

Obesity—Weighing more than 20 percent than the average weight for one's age, sex, and body type.

Object permanence—A concept that develops during sensorimotor intelligence. This is the understanding that physical objects have a separate existence from the perceiver.

Observational learning—See social learning theory.

Obsession—A disturbing thought or pattern of thought that a person has difficulty controlling. People who have an obsession often develop compulsive behavior and are diagnosed with obsessive-compulsive disorder.

Oedipal complex—Freud's name for the unconscious conflict that arises in the phallic stage of his psychosexual model of personality development. Freud argued a male child in this phase of development unconsciously desires a sexual relationship with his mother but fears reprisal from his father. The resolution of this conflict occurs by the child identifying with his father.

Onlooker play—A form of play in which the child is an observer of the play activities of other children, but does not participate in the play.

Operant conditioning—A type of learning, described by B.F. Skinner, in which behavior is shaped through the use of reinforcement and punishment. A behavior which is followed by reinforcement will tend to be repeated and a behavior followed by punishment will tend not to be repeated.

Oral stage—The first stage in Sigmund Freud's psychosexual model of personality development which lasts from birth until one year. Libidinal energy is focused on obtaining gratifying stimulation of the mouth in this stage.

Osteoporosis—The term for a bone disease which is the result of a calcium deficiency in the body. Bones become very brittle and may spontaneously fracture. Osteoporosis correlates with age.

Overregularization—This is the term for applying syntactic rules as if there were no exceptions to these rules. For example, children may say "Goed" instead of "Went" because they are applying the rule that says "To make a verb past tense, add –ed."

Ovum—The term for the female reproductive cell found in the ovaries.

P

Parallel play—An early form of play in which children who are playing share the same physical space, but are engaged in individual play activities and do not interact with each other very much.

Pavlov—The behavioral psychologist who created the classical conditioning theory within the Learning theory approach. Pavlov discovered that a previously reflexive response could be conditioned to be emitted in response to a novel stimulus. He discovered classical conditioning serendipitously while conducting experiences on the salivary reflex in dogs.

Perception—The process of assigning meaning to a sensation.

Perceptual constancies—First described by the Gestalt psychologists, these are the perceptual phenomena of size constancy, shape constancy, lightness constancy, and color constancy. These involve maintaining the same percept even when the information reaching the eye has significantly changed. In size constancy, for example, an observer perceives a dog to be the same size when it stands 20 or 200 feet away.

Permissive parenting style—One of the parenting styles studied by Diana Baumrind. Parents who adopt this style are overindulgent and lenient. Children are free to make their own decisions. These parents are high in acceptance/responsiveness and low in control/demandingness. Children raised with this style tend to be non-achievers who are dependent, impulsive, and disobedient.

Phallic stage—The third stage in Sigmund Freud's psychosexual model of personality development which lasts from the age of three until age six. Libidinal energy is focused on obtaining gratifying stimulation of the genital area in this stage. It is during this stage that the Oedipal and Electra crises arise and are resolved through identification with the same sex parent. The superego develops in this stage.

Phenotype—The term used for the traits that are actually expressed in the individual rather than the sum total of inherited genetic material.

Phenylketonuria (PKU)—A genetic disorder characterized by an inability to metabolize phenylalanine. Without treatment, a child with PKU will become mentally retarded and hyperactive.

Phobia—An abnormally intense fear of an object or situation.

Phonemes—The term for the basic units of sound in a language that are needed to form meaningful units.

Phonics approach—An approach to reading instruction that teaches reading by emphasizing the connection between letters and sounds.

Piaget—Theorist who constructed a stage model of cognitive development and who argued that cognitive development is the result of the child constructing schema based on his or her activity with objects in the environment. His theory is a discontinuity theory of development which emphasizes universals in development.

Pituitary gland—Called the "master gland," this gland controls other glands in the endocrine system and secretes growth hormone (GH).

Placenta—The semi-permeable membrane that supports the developing embryo. It is the source of blood and nutrients for the baby. It also allows some harmful substances (teratogens) to pass through to the baby's bloodstream.

Plaques—Abnormal masses of toxic neural material in the brains of people with Alzheimer's disease.

Population—The entire set of people, animals, events, or things that make up the group to which a researcher is interested in applying the results of her research.

Positive reinforcement—In Skinner's operant conditioning theory, this is a type of reinforcement used to shape behavior. Positive reinforcement is presenting a reward to a person or animal after the goal behavior is emitted. This term is formally defined by Skinner as any thing that is given to a subject after a behavior is emitted that increases the probability the behavior will be repeated under the same stimulus conditions.

Postconventional morality—The third and final stage in Kohlberg's theory of moral development. People at this level make decisions about right and wrong using universal principles of justice.

Post-traumatic stress disorder (PTSD)—A psychological disorder characterized by flashbacks to a traumatic event, and feelings of anxiety and helplessness. This is often experienced in victims of crime, sexual abuse, and those who have experienced military combat.

Pragmatics—The practical rules of language use.

Preconventional morality—The first stage in Kohlberg's theory of moral development. Decisions regarding right and wrong are made on the basis of expected consequences for actions, i.e., whether or not the actor will be punished for his or her actions.

Preoperations—The second stage in Piaget's theory that lasts from about two years of age until about age seven. The child in this stage can use symbolic representations but cannot think logically.

Prepared childbirth—See Lamaze method.

Presbyopia—The term for loss of visual acuity for near objects that is associated with aging.

Pretend play—A form of play that Piaget believed signaled the development of symbolic representation. Children pretending can use an object to take the place of another absent object.

Preterm babies—The term used for fetuses born before 36 weeks gestation.

Primary memory—See working memory.

Private speech (Egocentric speech)—Vygotsky's term for how language guides thinking in young children. He argued that children talk out loud to themselves while problem solving because this speech guides their problem-solving activity.

Progesterone—One of the female sex hormones secreted by the ovaries which directs the development of the female sex system during prenatal development and during puberty, and stimulates the release of growth hormone.

Project Head Start—A federal program created to help prepare economically disadvantaged children for school. The program combines preschool education with nutritional and health care services and parental involvement in the children's education.

Prosocial behavior (Altruism)—Behavior that is done for the good of others and without any expectation of reward or personal gain.

Proximaldistal development—Term used for the general pattern of physical growth progressing from the center of the body outward to the extremities.

Psychosexual crisis—The basic motivation for personality development in Sigmund Freud's model. A sequence of four crises occurs caused by the interacting forces of the child's sexual instinct in the id and society's expectations for behavior.

Psychosocial crisis—The basic motivation for personality development in Erik Erikson's model. Eight crises occur in each of the eight stages from birth to death. Each crisis is the result of the interacting forces of the child's own physical and cognitive growth and society's expectations for the child's behavior.

Puberty—The term for the phase of development in which males and females reach sexual maturity.

Punishment—A term from Skinner's operant conditioning theory. It is anything a subject experiences after a behavior that reduces the probability the behavior will be repeated under similar stimulus conditions.

R

Random sample—The term used for a sample of the target population that has been drawn using a sampling technique that gave every member of the target population an equal and independent chance of being selected. It is therefore a representative sample of the target population rather than a biased sample.

Recall—The process of retrieving information using a general clue only.

Recasts—A technique observed in caregivers in which the caregiver repeats a child's verbalization after correcting the child's mistakes.

Reciprocal determinism—The principle that suggests development is the result of the bidirectional relationship between the person and the environment.

Recognition—The process of retrieving information by matching stored information with information presented at the time of the test. This produces the feeling of having experienced the information before.

Reconstituted family (Blended family)—The term used for families that are the result of remarriages.

Regression—The term used by Freud for the process the ego uses to displace anxiety-provoking thoughts from consciousness.

Rehearsal—The process used to maintain information in working/primary memory.

Rejected children—The term used for children who are disliked and not accepted by their peers. Some are rejected-aggressive children and others are rejected-withdrawn children.

Relational aggression—A form of hostile aggression, like gossiping, which is aimed at damaging another person's social relationships.

Resilience—The term used by developmental psychologists for the characteristic in some children that enables them to overcome early obstacles and develop normally.

Retrieval—The process of finding information in long-term memory and bringing it to consciousness.

Reversibility—The ability to mentally rewind a thought pattern.

Rh factor—A factor in blood that is present or absent in people. Those who do not have the Rh factor are called RH– and those who do have the factor are called RH+. If a pregnant woman and her fetus are not compatible (both RH– or both RH+), the mother's immune system will attack the fetus as it would any foreign body. In the past this was a common cause of intellectual disability, but damage to the fetus is prevented today by an inoculation given to a pregnant woman to prevent the immune response.

Rooting reflex—One of the neonatal reflexes present at birth. If you stimulate the cheek of a newborn, he or she will turn toward the source of the stimulation.

Rubella (German measles)—A disease that if contracted by a pregnant woman, particularly in the first 3 to 4 months of pregnancy, causes birth defects including blindness, deafness, and intellectual disability.

S

Sample—A subset of the target population who participate in a research study.

Scaffolding—Vygotsky's term for the amount of teaching support given a child as he or she moves from being less to more competent at a task.

Schema—Piaget's term for the organized patterns of thought or action that the child constructs as a result of interacting with objects in the environment. These schema become more logical and organized with age.

Second trimester—The name for the phase of prenatal development from the third through the eighth week of pregnancy. The embryo is most susceptible to the effects of teratogens during this period. Most organ systems and body parts develop during this time.

Secondary memory (Long-term memory)—The third memory storage system in the Information processing approach. Information that is encoded in working memory will be stored in this organized memory system. Some theorists argue that this is a permanent memory storage system and that forgetting is the result of failure to retrieve rather than a loss of the information.

Secure attachment—The term for a healthy relationship between a child and a primary caregiver. This relationship is characterized by a strong emotional bond between the caregiver and child, a dislike of separations, and proximity seeking. The target of a secure attachment is a source of comfort when an individual is stressed.

Selective attention—A cognitive control process that enables observers to maintain a focus on a target while ignoring other sensory information.

Selective looking—A term used to describe the preferences for looking that appear in neonates.

Self-concept—The term psychologists use for the perception a person has of himself or herself.

Self-esteem—The term psychologists use for the evaluative judgment a person makes about who he or she is.

Self-recognition—A child's ability to recognize himself or herself in a mirror.

Semantic overextension—This is the term for applying a category label, e.g., "ball," to things that are not members of the category, but share some similar characteristic(s), e.g., globe.

Semantics—The system of meaning of a language.

Sensation—The registration of information in a sense organ.

Sensitive caregiving—According to developmental psychologists, this is one requirement for a secure attachment relationship to form. This caregiving style is consistent, prompt, and appropriate responding to the child's needs.

Sensitive period—A modification of the term "critical period" to communicate the fact that humans show a greater flexibility to acquire behaviors or traits outside of a critical period of time. While a trait or behavior may be acquired more quickly or more easily during the critical period for its development, it is not impossible for it to be acquired outside of this time frame. The term "sensitive period" connotes the time frame within which a behavior or trait is more readily acquired.

Sensorimotor intelligence—The first stage in Piaget's theory of cognitive development which lasts from birth to about two years of age. Infants who are in this stage are not capable of logical reasoning, but develop object permanence and symbolic representation during this stage. Schema from this stage are organized patterns of action only.

Sensory memory—The first memory storage system in the Information processing approach. This storage system automatically holds information that has registered in a sensory system. This storage is very brief, and information will be lost unless it is transferred to working memory via the process of attention.

Sequential design—A research method that combines the cross-sectional and longitudinal designs. This method can measure changes that occur with age, differences between people who are different ages at one point in time, and can also quantify birth cohort effects.

Seriation—The ability to organize objects in order from least to most amount.

Sex chromosomes—The chromosomes (X and Y) that carry the blueprint for the offspring's biological sex. A female has an XX pair and a male has an XY pair of sex chromosomes.

Sex-linked dominant trait—A trait that is carried by a gene on a sex chromosome (X or Y) that will always appear. Someone who has this trait may have also inherited the gene for the recessive trait and would therefore be called a "carrier." An individual with the dominant trait could have inherited instead two dominant trait genes.

Sex-linked recessive trait—A trait that is carried by a gene on a sex chromosome (X or Y) that only appears in the absence of the gene for the dominant trait. Someone who has this trait did not inherit the dominant gene.

Sexual orientation—Whether a person is sexually and romantically attracted to members of the same or opposite sex.

Shaping—Skinner's term for the process of learning whereby a new behavior is conditioned. Shaping is accomplished by systematically reinforcing successive approximations of the goal behavior. Skinner created the Skinner box or operant chamber which is the apparatus used to shape behavior. A hungry or thirsty animal is placed in the Skinner box and successively rewarded with food or water, respectively, for closer and closer approximations of the goal behavior.

Short-term memory—See working memory.

Sibling rivalry—The term for jealousy and competition for the attention and affection from parents that occurs between siblings.

Sickle cell anemia—A genetic disorder of the red blood cells inherited mostly by people of African and Latino descent.

Skinner—The behavioral psychologist who created the operant conditioning theory within the learning theory approach. Skinner argued behavior is shaped through reinforcement and punishment. If a behavior is reinforced, the probability that it will occur again in the same stimulus conditions increases. Punishment, on the other hand, reduces the probability that a behavior will be repeated. Skinner's approach has been very influential in classroom management as well as in clinical approaches to treating disorders.

Slow-to-warm-up temperament—This is the temperament label for infants who are relatively less responsive to people and other stimuli in the environment.

Small-for-date babies—The term used for neonates born after the full 36 week gestation who have lower than normal birth weight, and to premature babies who have exceptionally low birth weight.

Social cognition—Reasoning about social situations and social relationships.

Social comparison—The process of comparing one's own abilities and characteristics to those of his or her peers.

Social learning theory (Observational learning)—A contemporary modification of traditional learning theory. Social learning theorists argue that changes occur in behavior as a result of modeling the behavior of others. In this way, new behaviors are acquired not through the process of shaping and direct reinforcement and punishment, but through vicarious reinforcement. Albert Bandura formulated the social learning theory. The Social Learning theory suggests that our cognitions about the behavior of others we observe influence our own behavior.

Sociocultural theory—This theory describes the influence of social and cultural forces on human development. Lev Vygotsky formulated this approach and argued that an individual's cognitive development occurs within a context of interaction between the individual and other members of the individual's culture. Hence, sociocultural values and beliefs are transmitted to younger generations in a society.

Sperm—The term for the male reproductive cell found in the testes.

Stage theory—Also known as Discontinuity theory. Any developmental theory that suggests development occurs through a series of qualitatively different stages or phases. Stages are usually described as having to occur in a specific order and as being universal across contexts and/or cultures.

Stranger anxiety—A negative emotional reaction to unfamiliar people that appears in normal development beginning around the age of six months and lasts through the second year.

Sucking reflex—One of the neonatal reflexes present at birth. If you stimulate the lips of a newborn, he or she will begin to suck.

Sudden Infant Death Syndrome (SIDS)—The death of an infant during the first year from respiratory failure that has no identifiable cause and usually occurs when the infant is sleeping. Research has identified a correlation with maternal smoking.

Superego—The part of the personality structure in Freud's psychoanalytic theory that develops in middle childhood. It is the part of the psyche that contains moral standards of behavior. These moral standards are internalized during the resolution of the Oedipal and Electra complexes of the phallic stage of development. The superego is the source of moral anxiety and guilt.

Survey research—A method used in descriptive research to collect a lot of information from a large sample of participants.

Symbolic representation—The cognitive ability to use one thing to stand for or mean something other than itself. A word is an example of a symbol. This ability comes in at the end of sensorimotor intelligence.

Syntax—The grammatical rules of a language.

Syphilis—A sexually transmitted disease that is easily treatable with penicillin. Syphilis organisms can pass through the placenta of an infected pregnant woman after 18 weeks gestation and cause the fetus to be infected, miscarried, or stillborn.

T

Tabula rasa—The term used by the ancient Greek philosopher Aristotle and the British philosopher John Locke to describe the mind as being blank at birth. This is an extreme nurture view in the nature versus nurture controversy.

Tay-Sachs disease—A fatal genetic disease caused by a pair of recessive genes which cause nervous system degeneration. Children with this disease normally do not live beyond childhood and typically can trace their ancestry to Jewish relatives from Eastern Europe or French Canadians.

Telegraphic speech—The term for the abbreviated speech of young children in which two or three word combinations stand in place of complex sentences. In this way the speech is economical.

Temperament—The term used for the characteristic way an infant responds to people and the environment. It is viewed as an early form of personality. The three infant temperaments are slow-to-warm-up, easy, and difficult.

Teratogen—A substance that can pass from a pregnant mother to the fetus and cause harmful effects.

Terminal drop—A term for the precipitous drop in cognitive functioning occurring just prior to death.

Test bias—Traditional intelligence tests have been shown to be biased against those from the lower socioeconomic class. It is theorized that this is because test items are drawn from the experience of members of the middle and upper classes.

Testosterone—The male sex hormone that is secreted by the testes and that directs the development of the male reproductive system during prenatal development and puberty. It, along with other androgens, stimulates the growth of secondary sex characteristics during puberty and stimulates the secretion of growth hormone (GH) which triggers the adolescent growth spurt.

Thalidomide—A prescription drug used by many women in the 1950s to control nausea during pregnancy. The drug caused birth defects in limbs, feet, hands, or ears depending on when the drug was used during pregnancy.

Theory of mind—The understanding that people have states of mind and what takes place in the mind of others is responsible for guiding their reactions.

Third trimester—The name for the phase of prenatal development from the ninth week through birth. The fetus is less susceptible to the effects of teratogens at this time.

Time out—A method of discipline that is based on the operant conditioning model. Children given time out are removed from the situation in which undesirable behavior is occurring in order to remove what is reinforcing the behavior.

Tracking—A perceptual ability to follow a moving stimulus.

Transductive reasoning—A characteristic of the illogical reasoning of the preoperational child. This is inaccurate thinking about cause and effect in which the child believes that events that have simply occurred together are causally related.

Triarchic theory of intelligence—A theory of intelligence proposed by Robert Sternberg that argues there are three types of intelligence: analytic intelligence, creative intelligence, and practical intelligence.

Trust versus mistrust—The first stage in Erik Erikson's psychosocial model of personality development that lasts from birth until age one. The positive resolution of this psychosocial crisis is when a child develops a sense of basic trust in people and in the world. The negative resolution is a sense of mistrust in oneself and other people.

Turner syndrome—A sex chromosome abnormality in which females inherit only one X chromosome (XO). These females do not develop secondary sex characteristics, cannot reproduce, and often have specific cognitive deficiencies or some degree of intellectual disability.

Twin studies—A research technique originated by Frances Galton to investigate the nature versus nurture controversy. Concordance rates for traits in monozygotic and dizygotic twins are assessed. If a trait is controlled by heredity, there should be greater concordance for the trait among monozygotic twins than dizygotic twins, biological siblings, and unrelated people. Examining concordance rates between monozygotic twins separated at birth and raised apart represents the best test of the nature versus nurture question.

U

Umbilical cord—The structure that connects the embryo with the placenta during prenatal development.

Unconditioned response (UCR)—This is the term in Pavlov's classical conditioning theory for the motor response part of a reflex.

Unconditioned stimulus (UCS)—This is the stimulus that elicits a reflexive response in Pavlov's classical conditioning theory.

Unconscious—The part of the psyche that Freud suggested contained innate drives and impulses. These instincts are described as animalistic and irrational. One instinct Freud underscored in his system was the libido or sexual instinct. The unconscious also is a receptacle for repressed thoughts. Thoughts that are unacceptable to the ego and superego are pushed into the unconscious to reduce anxiety. It is these repressed thoughts, however, that can lead to neuroses.

Uninvolved parenting style—One of the parenting styles studied by Diana Baumrind. Parents who adopt this style do not pay attention to the child or care for the child's needs. There are no rules of the household and no discipline. These parents are low in control/demandingness and low in acceptance/responsiveness. Children raised with this parenting style tend to engage in antisocial behavior.

Universality—The principle that developmental changes occur the same in all people across all cultures.

Unoccupied play (Functional play)—An early form of play in which the child repeats movements like rolling a car back and forth, but the activity does not appear to be directed toward any particular goal.

V

Vicarious reinforcement—The term for the control over an individual's behavior that is a consequence of observing a model being reinforced. Social learning theorists argue an individual is more likely to imitate a model's behavior if he or she observes that behavior being rewarded.

Visual acuity—The degree to which an observer can perceive details in a stimulus.

Visual cliff experiment—Eleanor Gibson's classic experiment done to test whether depth perception is learned or innate. She created a visual cliff using a box with a checkerboard pattern on the floor with a clear Plexiglas top. Half of the box had a raised checkerboard piece and the other half had the checkerboard pattern on the floor. There appeared to be a drop off at the halfway point of the Plexiglas top. She tested seven month olds and found the majority would not crawl across the visual cliff.

Vygotsky—The Russian theorist who created the sociocultural theory of development.

W

Wechsler Adult Intelligence Scale (WAIS)—A popular measure of intelligence in adults that measures verbal and non-verbal intelligence.

Whole language approach—An approach to reading instruction that de-emphasizes phonics and keeps reading instruction similar to the natural process of language learning.

Wisdom—A term that means a wealth of practical knowledge and insight into life's challenges that is a result of lived experience. While wisdom normally correlates with age, it is not only found in the elderly.

Working memory (Primary memory; Short-term memory)—The second memory storage system in the Information processing approach. Memories are stored here for a brief period of time, up to a few minutes, unless one uses rehearsal. Information is worked on and encoded in this system in order to be transferred from short-term to long-term memory.

Z

Zone of proximal development—Vygotsky's term for the range of a child's competence from what she can do working alone at a task, to what she can do working with someone who is cognitively advanced.

Zygote—Name used for the fertilized ovum when it is still only one cell.

Index